All Drinking Aside

THE DESTRUCTION, DECONSTRUCTION AND RECONSTRUCTION
OF AN ALCOHOLIC ANIMAL

Jim Anders

AN AUTOBIOGRAPHICAL FICTION

ISBN: 149239730X
ISBN-13: 978-1492397304

INTRODUCTION

In this 90-piece orchestration of autobiographical flashbacks, the author describes his descent into alcoholism while three fictional alter egos (unnoticed by him) discuss his prospects for recovery. This intense, introspective and illuminating fiction looks at alcoholism and addiction from the inside out and back again. In three parts, the Destruction, the Deconstruction and the Reconstruction, the alcoholic beast is revealed.

GRATITUDE LIST

Over the course of five years writing this book, many mistakes were made, lessons learned, catastrophes averted and wounds healed. The intelligent suggestions and emotional support of my sister, Tina, head this list where gratitude lives, in my heart.

The alphabet soup known as anonymity makes for an eclectic stew to which I also give my hearty thanks. Jose C., Eric M., Rob M., Rob P., Matt F., Carol S. and a host of others help make A.C.Y.P. the best little home group this side of Alpha Centauri! Big Dave, Mac and Marlene and Sheila, Cindy and Brittany are also bright stars in my sobriety constellation. And I simply must also add Mario C., Edie L., Nancy O. and Sandee H. Finally, and very importantly, I am also grateful for Doreen E. and Kathy M., my editors, who endlessly encouraged me to continue down this path. For each and all, named and unnamed, I wish to here express my gratitude, forever and always.

– Jim Anders

PART I
THE DESTRUCTION

1. ALCOHOL *IS* POWER

"I envy people who drink – at least they know what to blame everything on."
– Oscar Levant

MORNING MEDITATION

If the label on the bottle of pharmaceuticals (prescription or over the counter) read, "Don't take with alcohol," you'd better believe that I couldn't wait to see what kind of idle threat that was, hoping, of course, that the effect would make me glad I didn't listen. The hope was always there for a new and better high.

The telephone rang in Brigantine, the barrier island north of Atlantic City. The construction company owner's wife, Janine, answered the phone, hesitantly, on the fourth ring, as she did not recognize the phone number on her caller I.D. "Hello?"

"I got some good rock, if you want some. Are ya interested?"

"What? Who is this?"

"This is Aaron's friend. He told me you might be lookin' for some good rock."

"I don't know who this is, or what you're talking about," she said, with considerable fright in her voice, "but don't call here again," she continued, and then hung up.

Aaron had related all of this to me, and I knew that he was probably telling the truth, because I had received the same phone call from 'Aaron's friend.' It took me awhile to figure out that good rock meant crack cocaine. I also figured out that Aaron had sold his cell phone to a drug dealer so that he could buy more crack for himself. Aaron continued, explaining to me that it had been Janine, his boss's suburban housewife, who had answered his drug dealer's phone calls and that he ended up getting fired when his boss found out that it was on his phone that the call to his boss's wife had been made. The drug dealer had simply looked at the last calls dialed and the last calls received on the cell phone I had purchased for Aaron just the day before. He then proceeded to call each and every phone number, trying to score more crack sales. What an industrious and resourceful dealer he was, striving to expand his sales and sales territory.

I had bought Aaron that cell phone so that he would have a way to reach me if he had the desire to pick up and smoke more crack, his drug of choice. At 12-step recovery meetings one sometimes hears the suggestion, "Pick up the phone, instead of a drink." Not this. Definitely, not this. I had been Aaron's "Sponsor" as we are called in A.A. (someone with enough sobriety under his own belt to be able to help another recovering alcoholic with their struggles).

Frustrated, I asked myself just one question: "Now, who will help me stay sober?" You see, it was stress like this and disappointment like this that had often been a trigger in my own past periods of sobriety. One addict failing to help another almost upset my apple cart. In theory, my trying to help someone else stay clean would help me get another day sober.

Aaron's Anecdote (A. A. - ha ha!) is just one of the many examples I could cite about my many failed attempts at helping other people stay clean and sober. They are the corpses littering my sober past.

Is Aaron really dead? I don't know. In A.A., they just say that so-and-so "went back out there." "Back out there" is A.A. lingo for picking up a drink. For the alcoholic, the result is usually "jails, institutions or death."

And that does seem to be the plain, unvarnished truth. I no longer think of myself as a lousy Sponsor. Rather, alcoholism is just a lousy disease, with an incredibly high relapse rate. I should know. I am the Relapse King and the Self-Justification King. And the King of Blackouts. Check. And Check-Mate.

(**Sotto**): *Vatchi, this one incident alone, Jim buying Aaron the cell phone, and the serious consequences and their ripple effects. Kind of proves that old maxim, "The road to Hell is paved with good intentions."*

(**Vatchi**): *Yes, good intentions and unintended consequences.*

I thought I would die before I reached age fifty. Yet here I am, much worse for wear (worse and better, actually). John Lennon died in 1980. I was in a recording studio on that day. Thirty years old. The words I would have used then to describe my future death by drugs and alcohol would have been filled with Romance: The Death of a Tragic Hero – something like that. I did not know then that the Alcoholic Pain, my future pain, would hurt, be real and have no semblance of Romance.

I did not know that I was in a battle. I was in a battle with alcohol that would rage for decades. It is no wonder that I could never win because I didn't even know I was in a battle and that, submerged at first, it seemed like such an easy addiction. My drinking was one step behind or one step ahead of 'it's not so bad.' I could and would continue drinking for decades.

The not-so-sweet irony is that from the outside, I looked like the drug abuser, but from the inside, I felt abused by alcohol, when I would and could let myself feel that. Just so long as I felt some sense of control over something, my life with alcohol would seem livable. There was comfort in finding some idea of order in my life. Some parts of my life had to feel that they were staying together as the other parts fell apart.

I was making trade-offs for my drinking. "I want the drink now. I'll deal with the consequences later" was my conscious or nearly conscious thought. But now was always here and consequences would always be later. Consequences can wait. I want the drink now. I was resigned to the fact that I would eventually go down the drain with a drink in my hand. Alcoholism seemed to be my form of martyrdom, my crown.

Alcohol taught me how to stuff and a lot of other stuff. Emotions, guilt, conscience, anything, everything, be damned. I want a drink and I want it now. After my third relapse, getting thrown out of two liquor stores in one day did not seem particularly abnormal. It went with the territory. This is where my life was and I would just have to accept it.

(**Sotto**): *"My name is Jim and I don't know who I am." That's what he should say, Vatchi.*

(**Vatchi**): *Your name is Sotto, and you cannot speak for him. Give your interpretation, perhaps, your voice, but that is all, Sotto, please.*

(**Surimi**): *Jim is clever, deceptive, annoying, disturbed. Sotto, Vatchi, be careful with what you think you see and hear. Jim has constructed and destructed mirrors everywhere and they may not be mirrors of himself. And should he hold up a mirror to show you your reflection, he may deceive you. He may wish to make his thoughts seem that they are yours. You are both rubbernecking the train wreck of Jim's life, rubbernecking. He will survive this or he will die from this. Here his story ends and here, too, his story begins.*

I have to start somewhere. Alcohol was killing me and now I have stopped drinking. I have almost died directly and indirectly from drinking and there is dying all around me. I'm surrounded by dying. Death is easy. It's the suffering that rattles me so, rattles my bones.

Drinking changed over time from a gentle rain to an electrical storm in my brain. It seemed as if alcohol somehow cut off the flow of electricity in my brain and memories temporarily could not be formed. Blackouts were the thunder I could not hear because I was not there, at least not there in the sense of being able to form memories. Flip the switch and all capacity to form memories seemed gone. The icing on the cake was the next next drink.

Right now, this very instant, I'm in a dream in a library where bottles without labels line the shelves instead of books. These bottles are illuminated from within, each a different color, a different shape. Flip the switch and now I am awake.

Perpetual preoccupation with alcohol, amplified and I can't wake up from my waking dream.

And now I am awake. And now I am. New game. New life. Sober.

EVENING MEDITATION
Drinking used to be one of my three most favorite things to do. Eventually I forgot the other two.

> *"Because you are alive, everything is possible."*
> – Thich Nhat Hanh

QUESTION FOR TODAY
How far back do I have to reach to see that there is no future?

2. **PSYCHO ANALYSIS**

*"And those who were seen dancing were thought to be insane
by those who could not hear the music."*
– Frederick Nietzsche

MORNING MEDITATION
Dinner Party: An extravagant excuse to get plastered, like the time I roasted the
turkey upside down and couldn't understand why it was so difficult to carve the
breast, when in fact, I was cutting into the carcass.

I suspect that had I gone into psychoanalysis when I turned twenty, that
terrible moment when a child no longer thinks of himself as immortal
would have been pulled out of me like an abscessed tooth. No longer
immortal, this would have been my moment of clarity. Somewhere in my
early twenties, however, I knew that I could not possibly live to be older
than fifty (forty, really). I didn't think of myself as an alcoholic whose drug
was killing him, but rather, I was just a hard partier who would not live
long. Vague and dreadful fear hung over me like a dark cloud, more alcohol
induced than I would care to admit because alcohol was my friend or so I
thought at that time.

(**Sotto**): *He's trying to make us like him, Vatchi, and I don't like that,
already. What's he doing, playing the pity card, the sympathy card? What is
so adorable about portraying yourself as a victim? Pity the victim? Pity this
victim? "Pity me." No, Vatchi. No. I'm not going to listen to his crap.*

There was a time when I would have wanted to be glorified. I thought
of myself as the tragic hero who would triumph. The plain facts, the slow

descent downward, like a frog in a pot of cold water who sits silently, slowly boiling to death once the heat has been turned on, no garnishes, no savory adjectives, and no multi-media extravaganzas. Simple, with holes, loopholes, room for interpretation, desperation, emotionless. Empty. And then, nothing. Christ, sieve me. Save me. Just don't grave me. Frog in a pot of water, slowly boiling to death. That was me. That was my alcoholism.

I used to sweat so much that the alcohol poured out of every pore of my body. My armpits dripped like a leaky faucet. I would wear an undershirt, shirt and sweater and often (not always) the sweat would soak through all those layers and through my suit coat, leaving body-salt stains on the outside of my jacket when that sweat would finally dry.

But did I drink too much? Obviously not, because I wanted one now. Soon. Give me one soon so that I can stop sweating. Don't sweat the small stuff. Stuff the big stuff. Six or seven single olive martinis should fill me up, dam up my sweat.

My breath stank of alcohol and tobacco. Call the Federal Bureau of Alcohol, Tobacco and Firearms. Call somebody.

One drink will fix everything. One drink would fix everything. One drink did fix everything. Times fifty-thousand. One drink would, will, could, might. Gimme a drink 'til my uptight's tight.

Let me move this emotion here and that emotion there. Stuff and more stuff. The ordinary was extraordinary when I was high. When I'm not there, I'm ego-free. Diet soda doesn't fool this brain. But somehow, alcohol always did fool me. When alcohol began pummeling me, knocked me down, I would just get back on my feet somehow, wipe my brow, then proudly bow.

(**Vatchi**): *Sotto, Jim is President, Secretary and Treasurer of Self-Pity Incorporated. But the pity card is but one card in his not full deck. Maybe we can listen past him, through him. It's the goddamn game of "Listen to what I don't say." But I don't think he can know that, Sotto.*

"Diet Soda doesn't fool this brain." Did you catch him saying that, Sotto? He's saying that sobriety cannot be a substitute for alcohol. At least, that's how I hear it. Maybe I'm jumping ahead of myself. Now I need to slow down. Let's hear him out. I'm not sure of much, but I am sure of this: He needs a whole, new fucking life, Sotto. His life is broken and has been broken for decades. Decades.

Waking up, coming to, really, not knowing where I was or how I got there was not unusual. Usually alone, I would wake up in my own bed, at home, with the alarm clock I somehow had drunkenly set in a blackout, my bed covers in disarray.

I was a blackout drinker and eventually blacked out almost every night, far more often than not. This is not normal, but it became normal for me, gradually, over the course of over a decade, I guess. I accepted blackouts as a given. Each small change brought on by my increasing dependence on alcohol became part of the new and accepted fabric of my life.

One time, I woke up in the shadow of Independence Hall, the Philadelphia landmark, not remembering who I had been with or how I got there. Another total blackout yet not a wakeup call? How could that have been?

But it was alright. Somehow I would be alright. It'll be alright. I lied to myself, to others. I bent the truth. I somehow got to work in Atlantic City only (only, what a dangerous word) three hours late. Somehow it would work out. Somehow I would be alright. Somehow, a drink would make all this bearable again. Plow through the consequences of the night before, plow through eight hours of tunnel vision that others call the reality of a working day, plow through to that drink at the end of the tunnel. Plow.

"It's alright, Ma, I'm only dying," some song sings. Dying from and dying for another drink. Dying from, dying for, ringing in my head. I was Pavlov's dog in a thirty year alcohol experiment.

(**Surimi**): *Escape of self, escape from self, the illusion of self. Under the illusion of transcending reality, Jim's disease has taken him full circle. Trying to break his delusional alcoholic cycles, Jim now seeks a more humane, human journey.*

Romeo and Juliet. Jim and Alcohol. His sense of self, seemingly diminished without the drink, is still attracted to alcohol. Wings broken by alcohol still crave flight. He cannot be free when alcohol is within him. The allure of destruction and hope for recovery, like the Phoenix. Spread wings tempt flight. Sotto, Vatchi. Hear Jim out. Sober.

No need to make decisions. Alcoholic bells, alcoholic whistles. No pain can remain. I will drink when I want to and when I don't want to. Alcohol will replace want to, need to and must. I will hate you on sight. Don't intrude on my drink. TV's flying, no visitors wanted. Door closed. Passing out. Another suffocating absence of memory. Not moving. Where has my life gone? What is a decision? Shut up. My glass is broken, broken, broken.

EVENING MEDITATION

When I can remember that most of my anxiety is about an unknown future and my depression comes from reliving my past, I can then be happier living in the present moment, so long as a tiger doesn't leap upon me unexpectedly like that goddamned last one did!

"...closer to us than breathing, and nearer than hands and feet."
– Alfred Lord Tennyson

QUESTION FOR TODAY

How many bubbles are in my glass of champagne? How much of me can remain? If there is no future, then why don't I just drink right now? Why don't I think the drink or let the drink think me? Why don't who or you or me?

3. **COLOR ME EMPTY**

*"People have a hard time letting go of their suffering. Out of a fear
of the unknown, they prefer suffering that is familiar."*
– Thich Nhat Hanh

MORNING MEDITATION

For 25 years, I never failed to bring several bottles of wine or assorted liquors and liqueurs with me whenever I was a dinner guest. For 25 years, those bottles would end up empty. The hosts would say, "What a generous gift. You shouldn't have," but the truth was, I did have to. There was an elephant in those dining rooms. I ate the quail, the buffalo, the snake, but never the elephant.

Fortunately, I only ever once had an auditory hallucination. I was living in a room at the Brunswick Rooming House on Saint James Place, next door to Atlantic City's famous Irish Pub. My fifth floor window looked down on their outdoor backyard patio bar and I was drunk and could drink no more. I literally heard a voice, not a mere thought, which said, "Jump." That's all. Just one word: "JUMP!" I knew the voice was in my head and was not real, but it was not a simple thought. I heard it and it scared the shit out of me. I could not even look out the window. Sitting on the edge of my bed (there was no other furniture in the room, except for a small wooden bureau), I slid onto the floor, dizzy, but not dizzy from alcohol, dizzy from the distance between my head and my feet.

"If you want to be treated like an adult, then you have to start acting like one." I heard this from my parents many times as I was growing up. To me, and I'm quite serious here, the two main things that distinguished adulthood from childhood were drinking alcohol and smoking cigarettes.

My brilliant deduction as a child was that if I wanted to be treated as an adult, I had better start drinking and smoking, sooner and not later. That kind of flew in the face of their rhetoric which usually boiled down to "Do as we say and not as we do." That didn't work during my childhood and I doubt that it works any better today.

(**Sotto**): *He is an eternal distraction. He's not fooling me for a second, Vatchi. Behind what he is saying, I think he's still reaching for a drink. The way he hesitates. Between sentences. Between words. Maybe he doesn't know what else to reach for, Vatchi. I could be wrong, but I think he wants a drink right now. But I'm not wrong about this, Vatchi. Jim irritates me, with a capital I.*

There was nothing, it seemed, that a drink couldn't fix. The alcohol numbed other options. Options became secondary to the clink of ice in a glass. Life was a pain I could not feel. My denial was a pain that was not felt. Alcohol numbed that, too.

People wanted what I had, because, from the outside, I guess I looked slightly spectacular, a wunderkind. I felt like a boxer in the ring getting nearly knocked out yet somehow always being able to get back on my feet again. What doesn't kill me makes me stronger. Or so I thought, until alcohol knocked me down, slowly killing me. To a certain few and for a few years, I was a kind of hero for the amount of alcohol whose abuse I was somehow able to survive. Knocked down again. The crowd would cheer, "He did it again! Knocked down and back on his feet!" Alcohol incited the crowded crowd in my crowded head. And outside of me, I did not notice people as adeptly as I had fooled them into believing that I had noticed them. Not so much self-obsessed as alcohol-obsessed, or so I like to think.

Putting up the good fight became a lie, an illusion. Slowly losing ground. Putting on a good face. Slowly being torn down, eroded by alcohol.

(**Vatchi**): *Sotto, you are not Jim. Perhaps he distracts you because of walls you have put up. Consider yourself lucky that you are not him. I don't know if you know this, Sotto, but that auditory hallucination, that simple "Jump!" that Jim heard, that's late-stage chronic alcoholism. If he had gotten worse, he might have jumped out that window and people would have quickly written it off as suicide. Some suicides are not suicides at all, Sotto. They are addiction having the last word. Some suicides are not suicide at all.*

This memory is trivial. This message is sidetracked. This memory is traumatic. This memory is morphing. This memory is morphine. This memory is Librium. This memory is liberation. This memory is prison. This memory is prism. This memory is schism.

Ego is a place from which to dive. Ego is a place in which to hide.

This memory is morphing. This memory is morphine. This memory is more, fiend. More.

Shallow, hollow, yellow, dying, dead.

(**Surimi**): *The Mona Lisa, except this time, not the painting. The Mona Lisa, except this time, not a photograph. This time the Mona Lisa, a three-second motion picture of Alcoholism's promises to Jim. Promises, expectations, and then the abortion. Mona Lisa's abortion: Alcoholism's smile.*
Jim could not become father to himself.
Mona Lisa. Three seconds. Abort.

Acting up. Acting out.

I want to write an ode to Cheerios. I want to loop my Fruit Loops. I worship, kneeling, the Aztec God of Coffee.

A degenerate zone. Alternatives gone. Emotional bottlenecks. Discordance. Smoke-filled rooms. Traumatic memories and the trauma of no memories. The trauma of no memories. Empty me into the nearest trash receptacle. Empty me. Empty. Me. Emptied.

EVENING MEDITATION

I've heard from staunch Creationists that God buried dinosaur bones the world over as a test of our faith in Him. My theory is that Demon Alcohol forced me to dig my own grave with every intention of throwing me into it. Dem bones, dem bones, dem crazy bones.

> *"I believe in looking reality straight in the eye and denying it."*
> – Garrison Keillor

QUESTION FOR TODAY

How empty is that glass you think you do not want?

4. **DISEASE MANAGEMENT**

"You are permitted in time of great danger to walk with the devil
until you have crossed the bridge."
– Bulgarian proverb

MORNING MEDITATION
When I'm drinking, "Get help!" means, "Have another drink."

My first drunk driving experience was on New Year's Eve when I was a junior in High School. I wouldn't have been able to guess then, that a few years later I would lose my license and a few years after that, after moving to Ventnor, New Jersey, license regained, that I would voluntarily rip up my license after not being able to find my car the day after another blackout episode. It strikes me oddly that I should have been concerned that I could have killed someone else when driving in a blackout and yet, at the same time I did not know that alcohol was already slowly killing me.

That New Year's Eve in High School, I drove with the windows fully opened, driving through the snow with one eye closed because with both eyes open, I had double vision. I thought that the cold would keep me awake, which it did. Yet I felt absolutely no sense of danger, except for the possibility of getting caught. The snow silenced the car tires. The snow silenced my fears.

I'm sitting here now, at my computer and have decided, now that I think about it, I had many more driving mishaps than the ones that ultimately got me points on my license. I must have had five to six times as many accidents and near accidents as points on my license would have indicated. Alcoholics minimize negative effects. It's only this. It could have been that. It could always have been worse. It really wasn't all that bad.

(**Sotto**): *Great! He was a teenager. Shit happened. Yada, yada, yada. Memory dominoes…. All fall down. Tell me the truth, Vatchi. Do you think he can stay sober or will he stagger through his life only to trip and fall again? Will he be able to save what little life he has left? Will he fall again, whether he wants to or not?*

My college life was punctuated by four completely different living situations which should have catapulted me into adulthood at an even earlier age than those I grew up with. My freshman year, I commuted to school, a "Townie," which means I was typecast by the rest of the campus as "less than." Obviously, my family was from a lower income bracket than most other students who came from further away and further up the socio-economic ladder. I couldn't afford a school further from home and really hadn't even considered investigating other possibilities, unthinking child that I was. Sophomore year I lived on campus. Junior year I lived in an off-campus apartment by myself and by my senior year, I shared a house with three other people. These four distinct world views did not enhance my maturing process. Instead of maturing, I was busy getting stoned and pickled, much like the rest of the students I hung out with. My generation professed free love, free sex and equality and at the same time, in my college, at least, there was sexism, racism and an unconscious class-consciousness. Our ideals and our realities were worlds apart.

My dreams were just dreams, never all that far reaching, but alcohol and LSD would propel me past my merely stoned and pickled self, to become lost in a lost world.

(**Vatchi**): *Sotto, I'm only guessing, but could Jim's past have been actually far worse than he is sharing in his sobriety? I think he stretches the truth but also may be ignoring or lying or burying memories from his early childhood. What is the truth here? Where is the truth? Must it not always be more than it appears?*

Sometimes, a baby is scared by his own crying, unable, it seems, to recognize the source of the noise as his own. This can make him cry even louder and more fearfully and worse. Until a mother's arms and gentle whispers change the tide. Then sleep.

Was my life, and my relationship to my alcohol really that much different? Crying out, the bottle would comfort me, protect me. "It's the bottle talking" was the truth and an excuse and a lie.

How I fought near death for the bottle that would betray me, continuously and progressively. Now, today, sober, I know that I must manage this disease. And this I cannot do alone. And this I must not do alone. And this I will not do alone.

The bottle could still comfort me. Smother me. Comfort me to death. Manage my disease. Or die.

(**Surimi**): *A baby does not know to stop crying. Jim does not know to stop drinking. He is quite ill. What looks like acting out is still the drink talking. Sober, yet the ghost of a drink still speaks. The blood has dried. His bruises gone. This ghost has bones, Sotto. His disease is alive, Vatchi. He is quite ill. He has poor judgment or no judgment at all.*

Alcohol is unjust, self-justifying. Finding harmony after so many years of addictive discord makes me think his chances are slim. 'Bleak' and 'Optimistic' seek some common ground. The road ahead seems incongruous, an impossible nightmare to the alternate universe of his addictions.

I did not choose to be an alcoholic, nor was I chosen. What I once thought was a curse has turned out to be a blessing (so long as I don't pick up). I am discovering unblazed trails of sanity in my recovery (sounds nuts, doesn't it?). Unblazed trails of sanity? No wonder I can't drink. I can laugh at myself a little now, sober now, a little sober now.

Slow and easy, Jim. Breathe in. Breathe out. This is Disease Management 101, Disease Management 101 (I am nuts and I admit it). A little laugh. Now. And again.

Through college and beyond, everyone I hung with drank and drugged, back when straight had nothing to do with sexual orientation, but rather whether you were a pothead and acidhead or not. A jock or a druggie. A jock was straight and a druggie laced experience with drugs.

I did not choose to be an alcoholic, but today, I choose to remain sober. Or did sobriety choose me?

EVENING MEDITATION

An empty glass told me that I had been drinking.

> *"I would only believe in a god who knew how to dance."*
> – Friedrich Nietzsche

QUESTION FOR TODAY

Which of tomorrow's tears belong to yesterday?

5. **MAINTENANCE DRINKING**

*"You can come aboard the lifeboat, but I'm not jumping in after you,
because there are sharks out there."*
– Dallas Taylor

MORNING MEDITATION
I used to get dope sick, you know, sick of being a dope.

Atlantic City's transportation, besides the usual inner city buses, also relies heavily on Jitneys, which are thirteen seat vehicles zipping along like above ground unattached subway cars. The Jitneys are about the size and shape of a bread truck. So much so, in fact, that one morning at first daybreak, thinking it was a Jitney, I mistakenly boarded a bread truck. I scared the driver half to death, having taken him totally by surprise. I don't know how I finally got home after that experience either. I think I hit a MAC machine somewhere so I could have another drink or three before mustering up the courage to try to board a real jitney. I'll never know.

About this same time in my downward slide, fairly new to Atlantic City, Keith, a co-worker from Le Grand Fromage restaurant in what was then the hot part of town called Gordon's Alley, and I went out for a few after work one day. I don't know if it was after the tenth or more that Keith and I began heating our brandy snifters and started snorting the fumes. We seemed to be getting higher and higher, the alcohol vapors sailing into our brains in this new form, or so it seemed. Eventually we were both flagged for boisterously and shamelessly snorting (not cocaine, but) alcohol fumes. It may as well have been Sterno or gasoline. This all took place at a bar called Camillo's, which was located in the beach block of South Carolina Avenue. Most of the bars I used to drink in are no longer in business, the buildings boarded up or razed. I was still relatively new to Atlantic City and my drinking was still mostly outrageously fun. This was during the time when it seemed that opportunities were just falling into my lap. I didn't have to look for jobs. They came my way. Resorts International was the only Casino in town and the advent of casino gambling seemed to hold nothing but the promise of golden opportunities.

It was also the time when how drunk I got each night depended on how much money in tips I had made at work earlier that same evening. Whatever I made in tips immediately became the drinking fund for that night's escapades. I had no long term goals back then. My goals were short and immediate. Get fucked up now, worry about the consequences later.

My sister, Betty, six years younger than I, committed suicide thirty years after our last real conversation. She blew her brains out with a shotgun. No viewing. I don't think she had yet been cremated. Not even ashes at her funeral, except from my still smoking cigarettes. Sometimes death makes me edgy.

(**Sotto**): *Yo. Yo. Yo. Yo. Yo. His Sister uses her toes to trigger the shotgun that blows out her brains, and he mentions it in passing, as if....*

(**Vatchi**): *Shh! Listen...*

Death makes me edgy, brown wafer edgy, vanilla wafer edgy. Sometimes, just taking a ride in a car for an hour would make me edgy, too. Without a drink. The thought of no drink is edginess. Not just the subtle trembles before the onset of the D.T.'s. The thought edge, that brown edge on a Vanilla Wafer, or an old rusted razor blade. That dull/sharp edge I know so well. A thick, rough edge that many an alcoholic knows well or will never know.

When I knew the payoff would be big enough, a total wipe-out, one for the record books, I could savor that edge. My next drink would be spectacular, back then, when I could look forward to my next drink with joyful anticipation. Blow your brains out spectacular. That dark tunnel of blackout drunkenness, familiar, comfortable, yet strangely unknown.

The sweating would stop soon. I wondered if my friends, John and Charlie, sensed my fear, my eagerness, my edginess and the complexity of my emotions as we neared Fort Dix . Charlie's house, a dilapidated mansion in the country. Soon. Not yet. Calm down.

We turned right into Charlie's driveway and for once, it seems that the blackout preceded that first drink.

John and Charlie called that weekend the Daffodil Festival and I only know that because that is what I was told. So much of my life was what others later told me it was. It was this and it was that and it was the other thing. My life was as I was told it was. What is a life when the blackout precedes the first drink? Blow your brains out spectacular blackout drunkenness. What is life when a Big Bang blackout precedes the first drink?

(**Vatchi**): *Sotto, I don't think Jim realizes that he was still drunk before his first drink that day. He was already delirious, fading in and out of his blackout like house lights flickering in a thunderstorm. The delirium tremens would come later. Years later. The level of alcohol in his bloodstream never got low enough for serious shakes to start. He maintained. Maintenance drinking. For years, apparently. "What is a life when the blackout precedes the first drink?"*

Sotto, to this day, I don't think Jim knows that he was plummeting towards his bottom for years before hitting it.

How many bubbles are in a bar of soap?

I've got a little sippy cup with a flippy little lid. I'll fill it to the brimmy brim, not half empty, not half full. Hopscotch. Butterscotch. All scotch, scotch. Down the drain, scotch is rain. Sippy cup, flippy cup, bar of soap, dope.

How many bubbles in a bar of soap?

(**Surimi**): *Each drink an unknown neural suicide. Ask his sister, Betty. Oh, that's right. She's dead.*
Vitality murdered.
Depression assured.
Too many bubbles in a bar of soap.

No sippy cup today. No brimmy brim. Restful sleep, no passing out now.

EVENING MEDITATION

My problem was not that I had been rejected, as each of us is rejected in this life on one level or another. Dealing with the emotion of rejection or another emotion or any emotion, for that matter, was the problem. I drank emotions and my medication became my poison. I was the problem and there seemed to be no antidote.

> *"The chains of habit are too weak to be felt until they are too strong to be broken."*
> – Samuel Johnson

QUESTION FOR TODAY
Where is the fifteenth stone?

6. **THIS DISCONNECT**

"If I try to be like him, who will be like me?"
– Yiddish proverb

MORNING MEDITATION
I did used to get "dope sick" on alcohol, for real, for real. Alcohol made me vomit and alcohol stopped the vomiting. The curse (if you want to call alcoholism a curse) was the cure.

Not too long ago I was quite moved by an article I read in the Atlantic City Press. It was about a man from Japan who had actually survived the atomic bombs of both Hiroshima and Nagasaki. He was a traveling salesman who, having survived the first bomb, returned home to be nearly decimated by the second bomb.

Does that seem possible? Does reality seem possible?

My first relapse and the second time I hit bottom seemed equally impossible, as well, except, of course, in retrospect.

Bill Wilson, the co-founder of Alcoholics Anonymous, wrote a book called *The Language of the Heart*. I love that title and its deeper meanings. The human attempts to express the inexpressible. My love of language and the intrigue of the inexpressible drew me to the fringes of the human experience.

My last roommate before I left Bethlehem, Pennsylvania for Atlantic City, New Jersey was Dan, who was legally blind. And then, in Atlantic City, I had become friends with Jeffrey, Jean-Paul's nephew, who, being totally deaf, communicated in sign language. What other people may have seen as handicaps, I saw as fertile soil for exploration of life experiences and their means of expression.

Handicapped by alcohol, I seemed to seek out others challenged to negotiate their ways through this difficult world. The common sufferings as underdogs, suited my own perception of self. In denial about how much help I needed, I reached outward as a substitute for dealing with my own inward sense of emptiness. Out there stood the Platonic drink and subsequently my un-Platonic nightmare.

(**Sotto**): *Actually, he's quite charming here, Vatchi, struggling for words to describe struggling for words. He seems to have buried his sister and the memory of his sister at the same time. Am I connecting dots better left unconnected, Vatchi? Is that his possible reality? Displaced, misplaced, just slightly off to the side? No center.*

My Grandfather is dying. I never met my Grandfather. I am not dying. My Father is dead. He died before I was born. My Grandfather. He died after I was born. My Father. I am not dying. I am not dying. Open the window.

Open the window to the Daffodil Festival. Fort Dix. Roll down the window, John. I cannot put quote marks here because I am not saying this. My Father is not dead. My Grandfather is dying.

Roll down the window. The window is the dying. Open the window that is not dying. The window is glass. I need the glass. The glass that is not dying. I need a drink. The drink that is not dying. The glass is what is in the glass and the glass is not dying. The glass is what is in the glass and the glass is not dying.

I need a Daffodil Festival.

Not dying.

(**Vatchi**): *No, Sotto, you are not connecting dots better left unconnected. If I may extrapolate your thoughts, I'm getting a picture of the method to Jim's madness, a madness he does not fully know and a method he is still discovering. Your thoughts leave me with an impression, an analogy of sorts. The facts of Jim's life are like a bag of bones, disconnected. Some facts, naturally, are more important than others. His emotions seem to be almost like the muscles by which he's trying to pull this skeleton back together. What a scattered mess when the centrifuge stops spinning.*

Sotto, I really don't know. He seems to be trying and rambles haltingly. Give him a chance. Let us give him a chance. Let's just step back and listen, for now.

Where can I find gratitude? I will have to create it, invent it. Please help me to not pick up this drink. This drink that is not here. This drink that is in my head. An empty glass before me. Not drinking is dying and drinking is death.

Where can I find gratitude? Help me invent it, create it, discover it. I do not want this drink. If you help me not find this drink that is not here, I will be grateful. Thank you for helping me not find this drink.

That is not here.

I want.

(**Surimi**): *Life moves towards warmth and away from pain. Until the Medicine Man comes a knockin'. High on attention. High on medication. Pain aversion. Spiritual disconnect. No exit.*

My image is decaying from this disconnect. Blackouts are not memory lapses. Memories are formed, human clay transformed, some sense of permanence. With blackouts, there is nothing left, held, remembered. No leaves pressed in shale. The debris of "I did what?" Nothing to connect. Rats.

My image is decaying.

EVENING MEDITATION

Worthless, feeling worthless, alcoholism tears you down, like spousal abuse, until eventually you feel that you deserve no better. Emotions eroded by the flood of alcohol and in its wake, emptiness.

> *"And whether or not it is clear to you, no doubt the universe is unfolding as it should."*
> – Max Ehrmann

QUESTION FOR TODAY

Does one need a reason to survive?

7. **THE BOTTLENECK**

"The deepest definition of youth is life as yet untouched by tragedy."
– Alfred North Whitehead

MORNING MEDITATION
I wanted alcohol and serenity. What I got was blackout and pass out.

At first, the idea of being sober seemed to be an idea of light at the end of the tunnel, not the light itself. In a sober tunnel, the possibility of change seemed possible in theory only. My emotions were in denial about possibilities, closed to all except their own broken state. Nothing seemed possible on the emotional level, drained as I was. I don't know when it happened, so it must have been gradual, but I slowly became aware that I was no longer in a tunnel and that the hope was not out there, but inside me. I stood in a clearing of sorts, unconfined, unimprisoned. Free, hope recaptured, redefined, possible. Sobriety became possible. I became possible.

Curious thing about blackout drinking: how is it I never smoked crack or shot up heroin when in a blackout? The opportunities were there before I went into blackout mode and yet I am sure I never did.

(**Sotto**): *I don't know why, but this is the first time that Jim has motivated me in any real way. Why do you think that is, Vatchi? Why should I care?*

The glass is too full. I cannot pick it up. The glass is too full to pick up. The glass is half empty, too full to pick up. A half empty glass is too full to pick up. Drink it down. Fill it up. The glass is half empty.

I am a cup.

(**Vatchi**): *Sotto, you say that you are beginning to care for Jim, thinking about it. I hope you're not motivated by his self-pity, puddled around him. Trust me on something here. We all absorb and reflect each other's lives, Sotto. This day is young. This earth is not some burnt out cinder. Not yet. Are you almost ready to trust Jim, Sotto? He's been sober for awhile now. Are you ready to trust him?*

Oh, Alfred North W., my life has been touched by tragedy again and again and the youth escaped, evaporated in an alcoholic haze, broken down and wrinkled, and still a child.

How is it that I feel like an innocent bystander of my own train wreck? Now, when I cry for others, why do they feel like the tears that I should have had, but never did, never did shed for myself? Is empathy a rear view mirror? A way to not cry out alone? A backlog, a log jam of tears. Why am I now bleeding where once I should have scarred? Why are the tremors I am now feeling the sober echoes of my unfelt drunken and painful past?

Emotions in the bottleneck, first drink to last. Thirty year bottleneck, rubberneck, train wreck.

I am bleeding now where I didn't bleed then. What goes around comes around again within my brain. The grooves go around in a loop. Empathy teaches me now what was always around me then.

(**Surimi**): *Impatient for pain to kill more pain. Learning to lose. The figure eight of infinity as zero. Sotto, Vatchi. Jim is bleeding as he heals. His new pain, the new pain formed from this cleansing of the old.*

Where did responsible and irresponsible intersect? How am I not so innocent a bystander of this train wreck?

(**Sotto**): *Surimi, I am caught up in this.*

Padded rooms, padded lies.

(**Vatchi**): *Sotto, sympathy can become empathy.*

God damned frog on this pad, pad, padded lily pad.

(**Surimi**): *"More will be revealed." How much must be revealed? How much will be ignored?*

EVENING MEDITATION

I felt as though I never had the choice to stop before I got sober that very first time. There was fun yet to be had, jobs to be lost, love to be shattered and smashed. Denial ruled until I crashed, until my bubble burst. Until I finally had no choice but... STOP!

> *"In order to gain anything, we must first lose everything."*
> — Buddhist saying

QUESTION FOR TODAY

What is the cost when you have profited from what you have lost?

8. **AN ALCOHOLIC IS.**

"We learn as much from sorrow as from joy, as much from illness as from health, from handicap as from advantage - and indeed perhaps more."
– Pearl S. Buck

MORNING MEDITATION
I had difficulty accepting rejection. Is it any wonder that I should turn around and reject acceptance?

Shortly after graduating from college, my housemate, Gene, and I would catalog our discussions on the relative merits of various wines, domestic vs. imported, Spain vs. Chile, the similarities and differences between Cabernet Sauvignon and Sauvignon Blanc, all this and more, until we would have the inevitable after-dinner drinks and discussion of this type of glassware and that type of glassware and this corkscrew type vs. that corkscrew type, until in an eventual drunken stupor, I would blackout, pass out and suffer through my next day hangover. Hangover preventions. Hangover cures. The ins and outs of drinking. How to become a really, really, really good drinker.

Alcohol was taking over my life in each and every form and I didn't even know it. I had learned more and more about scotch and wine and beer and cocktail recipes and this glass and that glass, boiler-makers and hot toddies and which garnish goes with which drink and on and on. More and more knowledge about alcohol and no real knowledge of alcoholism. Generally speaking, as I got more and more entrenched in alcoholic behavior, the more I felt sophisticated, the less sophisticated I must have appeared. Who could see the forest? All I saw were trees.

24

I do not know when I wrote this next poem. Chronology was superfluous when I was under the influence. "Some one time, a woman is" is about the search for freedom, I guess. It belongs right here and right now only because I think it does:

"Some One Time, A Woman Is"

Some one time, a woman is
Sleeping and blankets are upon her
And some one time, the blankets are
Heavy and burden her
And some one time, a woman is
Black or Hispanic or Gay or
Simply,
A Woman.
And some one time, she awakens
And she feels the burden,
The burden of many blankets
And some one time, she awakens
And peels the blankets off of herself,
Peels them off of herself and then,
Some one time, a woman is.

(**Sotto**): *Vatchi, do you see the irony here? The contrast between the supposed increasing sophistication that he feels as his lifestyle of drinking increases, as the freedom of the woman in his poem increases? I'm not sure if he sees or knows why he puts next what he puts next. It's almost like he's asking himself, "I wonder what's under this next rock?" Can't he see the connection? Is he oblivious? Isn't it obvious, or is it just me?*

One elephant, many elephants, herds of elephants. This world I lived in, this world within my head, slowly, was being covered, layer upon layer, by alcohol and drugs. Drugs and alcohol and lies, learned lies, lies taught, layers of silt, of sediment covering all, covered, buried, this buried life, dinosaurs and minotaur buried by the weight of generations, buried by their own weight, buried by addiction.

Fossils. Fossils. Fucked and fuck. My elephant was alcohol. And alcohol was me. In a bottle. In a jar. In a bar.

(**Vatchi**): *Sotto, you just reminded me here of something I thought long forgotten. It's called "The Fifteenth Stone" and I can't recall if it's a true story or an allegory, or what. But let me explain of stones and elephants. Somewhere, Japan or China, who knows? San Francisco? A garden exists somewhere, a rock garden; let's say the size of a tennis court. You can walk* *completely around it, but you are not allowed to cross its borders. This rock garden contains fifteen large stones of varying sizes, say, knee high to chest high. And this rock garden is so constructed that no matter where you stand on the garden's perimeter, only fourteen of the stones are ever visible. One stone, forever changing, is always hidden from view. Fifteen stones in the garden, and no matter where you stand, only fourteen are visible.*

Which stone is Jim, Sotto? Which stone are you, Surimi?

Why do I stand in my own way? Unlearning seems so much more difficult than learning. Unlearning the drink. Staying sober is such hard work. "Sobriety must be earned," I've heard someone in the rooms say. No wonder I need help. The grain of this grain of alcohol is ingrained in my brain. Fuck "the rain in Spain." Ingrained.

(**Surimi**): *Which stone is not you, Vatchi? A stone is not an elephant. An elephant is not you. Recuperation is not recovery. The thing before is not the thing after. This is not that. That is not something else.*

Sotto. Vatchi. Jim does not yet know that he is working on becoming the eighty-five year old man he may live to be, should he live that long. Truly, now, he is beside himself. He is his own Fifteenth Stone.

Alcohol always stood in my way, blocked my path, whatever my path might have been. Alcohol always won out and became my path. My path became a maze leading through alcohol to more alcohol. I would not be led to think that ever I could live without it. Always back to square one, subtly changed, rudely reliving it again and again. My Crutch. Crunch. Crunch. My elephant was alcohol and alcohol was me. Crunch. Crutch. Such. Much. In a jar. In a bar. Too far. Too far.

EVENING MEDITATION

The now near empty bottle of vodka did not merely evaporate. The blackout drinker who had become my life consumed more alcohol than time itself could ever remember. The full ashtray told me that I had smoked cigarettes all night long. The empty life had finally stopped talking to me. The empty me had finally stopped listening. Nothing, then less than nothing.

> "Nothing happens unless first we dream."
> – Carl Sandburg

QUESTION FOR TODAY

Which seeds, when lost, may still bear fruit?

9. PACKING PEANUTS

"Everything you own, owns a part of you."
    – Gracie Allen

MORNING MEDITATION
When I hit bottom, I accepted the pain of loss, but not the loss itself. My beautiful, beautiful Alcohol had died.

Goodness gracious. How far I have traveled from my humble, drunken, drug-infused youth. From fifteen cent soda fountain cherry cokes after school at Prospect Drug Store, a block from my high school in a bedroom community predominated by Bethlehem Steel Corporation employee families, I moved on to the college life expected of me. I can remember the first few bars which I entered, easily served, yet underage, in Bethlehem, Pennsylvania, home to my college and several others. The Last Call Tavern was a college bar and underage drinking was far from uncommon. Back then, in the late 1960's, through the '70's and presumably still today.

(**Sotto**): *Oh, god, save me from this! What's next? About his B.A. in English? Hey, Vatchi, know what the B.A. stands for? Boring Asshole. Christ, I hope this is just some cul-de-sac that he has entered and not another endless "Jim" story.*

My Father died last week, again. In my memory, he just died again. Death reoccurs in a landscape of dreams.

My Uncle Dave golfed at the Country Club when I was ten. That was in 1960. In February of 1961 my Uncle golfed with red golf balls so that they would not so easily be lost in the patches of melting snow. Sand traps and

27

snow drifts mistook each other. My Uncle used red golf balls in 1961 and in 2010 my Father died. Red golf balls. That is all. Really. Red golf balls. Dead. Death reoccurs in a landscape of dreams, sand traps and snowdrifts.

(**Vatchi**): *Christ, Sotto, quit complaining about another endless Jim story. Your ears prick up like a German Shepherd's. You can't deny that you're listening. Complaining is contagious, but whatever you're selling, I ain't buying. Jim's not buying or selling anything here, Sotto. He's moved to sobriety and he's still unpacking. Cardboard boxes filled with consolidated memories. And his blackouts, you might ask? They're his packing peanuts. Packing peanuts!*

I've survived protesting the Vietnam War in the late 60's while my stepbrother, a marine, was in Vietnam. He came home strung out from the War to find me strung out on drugs and alcohol. I don't think either of us knew how badly off the other was.

One of my few reported auto accidents was several blocks from my stepmother's house in Quakertown, Pennsylvania. I sideswiped a carload of Spanish speaking people, three generations of one family or so it appeared. I was tripping on LSD (acid) at the time. My parents couldn't even tell that I was having a bad trip and a bad day. Emotion was to have a place just out of reach for them, conveniently never lost, just misplaced. Their depth of reflection excluded others as well as themselves.

My flirtation with Buddhism, the Beatles and the Maharishi was over by then. I thought drugs and alcohol were the road to my redemption, never knowing that that road would become littered with bottles, broken glass and deception.

My memories cannot fill this empty box. I am rebuilding my life. I could not drink today.

(**Surimi**): *Oh, Vatchi, please. Jim must let go. I know the past still has him in its grip and he must not allow himself to forget it. But he cannot let it haunt him. His blackouts. And Sotto, my message to Jim is silence. A kind silence, Vatchi. Let go and let reality fill the crevasses left behind by blackouts. The teeth chatter, the mind chatter: Let it go. Let silence enter. A resilient silence.*

It's my ego that clings to my past, I guess. Even the bad stuff. Can I cobble together some kind of self-image? My Scrapbook is a Crap Book. Like two hundred and fifty TV channels and nothing worth watching. That's my past: No news is my news. Ego. And nowhere to go. Too much self and not enough help. Chaos.

EVENING MEDITATION

When I first got out of Lakewood Hospital's rehab wing, I wore the plastic patient's I.D. bracelet for three months. That bracelet was my Scarlet Letter and my Red Badge of Courage, ever reminding me that I have a sickness, an illness, an identity that I could not change, that I am an Alcoholic Forever. One of my forever's would have to be that I would have to change if I were to remain sober. I did not know it then, couldn't have known it, but that plastic I.D. bracelet was like my own personal "Serenity Prayer" incarnate, unspoken, felt, neither consciously known nor understood.

"It is difficult for one person to act a play."
– Chinese Proverb

QUESTION FOR TODAY

"Where are the bullets?"

10. **THE LANGUAGE OF ADDICTION**

"It's not the mistake that matters but what you do about it."
– Jeff Jarvis

MORNING MEDITATION
My "First Step" (Step One of the 12-Step Recovery process: an admission of powerlessness over alcohol and an unmanageable lifestyle), first time, was a surface surrender, like Moby Dick coming up for air....

The irony of a poem I wrote called "The Pub" is that I was tripping on LSD when I wrote it during my junior year of college. I swallowed quite a bit of acid and other pills in the late 60's and early 70's, but it was eventually alcohol that swallowed me. I include just one small segment here:

"The Pub"

In its tables waxed and burnt with cigarette marks, in its peanut shells and its glasses, endless piles of glasses, in its cold-eyed stares and the smell of stale beer, in its wine, in its whisky and in its smell of people cramped into a crowd of loneliness, I see life struggling to come to terms with itself.

In the laughter and the sadness of the pub and in the people's faces I see a dizzy happiness reeling away and toppling over in the morning and I see the hope that morning will not come and I see the fear that each man's suffering will be felt and I see that the suffering is felt but cannot be reckoned with...

... And I see that I drink my beer in silence and however occasional smiles.

(**Sotto**): *Christ, Vatchi! The beast is inside Jim. The beast surrounds him. Alcoholism: his elephant, within and without. An insect trapped in amber, Vatchi. Jim's entire life has been the train wreck of alcoholism. Was his crash inevitable, unstoppable? Pardon me for being a prophet of doom, but damn, the signs must have been there for a long, long time.*

I salivated like Pavlov's dogs all the way to Mexico because I knew I could purchase over the counter drugs there that could only be obtained through a prescription in the States. I broke as few laws as possible, thereby increasing my chances of not getting arrested. That was part of the original lure of alcohol for me. When I turned twenty-one, alcohol became my legal drug, nearly state-sanctioned.

Call me Dr. Jim. I knew what I wanted and where to get it on either side of the border. It's just that sometimes I was so high that I couldn't read my own prescription. Misdiagnosed. Misdosed.

Snort laughter. Snort cocaine. In short - snort, snort!

It's 1975 and there's a burn victim in Guatemala. Gene is in the hospital. The radiator cap on our Ford Econoline van exploded from the built up steam pressure. I can't deal with this now. I can't express this now. I was so needy and I thought the need was alcohol. Drunk and not caring that I could not care. Alcohol for me was like the gauze and salve on Gene's arms from that explosion of steam.

Walking through the marketplace on Easter Sunday with Gene's hands bandaged somehow reminded the local Guatemalans that this was a sign. Gene's hands in bandages from the radiator burn were a sign of Jesus Christ on the cross to them.

Some moved further away in fear. Some moved closer in awe. I walked in a stupor like a character in *The Birds*, trying to cautiously find my way back to the van.

I once cared. I no longer cared. The alcohol was slowly robbing me of my emotions. I was pathetic then. I can admit that now. No empathy. No sympathy. Just pathetic. A pathetic, hopeless drunk.

I did not drink today. It was a very good day today. I did not drink. Very good.

(**Vatchi**): *Not only do I think that alcohol robbed him of his adulthood (some say, and, of course, it's an exaggeration, that an alcoholic stops maturing at the beginning of his drinking career and remains stagnant, never reaching adulthood, until after he drinks his last drink), but in some sense, Jim was robbed of his childhood, too.*

His childhood memories seem memories of memories of memories. A life not lived, and what was lived, barely remembered, and what was remembered, distorted.

Mirrors in a Funhouse, Sotto. Probably nothing could have stopped him. I don't know. But I do think that nothing could have stopped his alcoholism. What has not yet been destroyed could yet be saved. His history cannot be rewritten. With any luck and a lot of hard work, he can save what he has left. Who, alcoholic or not, can do more than that Sotto?

Learning Spanish over the course of a few months was no big deal back in 1975. Six courses in French helped, but I just picked up language quickly, too.

I learned the language of addiction quickly, too, that internal, silent language of "More." I sold .the bundles, bags and bits of pot I bought. Divided. Sold at cost. No profit. Just a little set aside so my pot smoking would be free, cost me nothing. Not really a dealer. Same deal with alcohol when I bartended, to be honest. Whatever I made in tips bartending was immediately consumed in alcohol when my shift ended. For me, living hand to mouth was always about alcohol and never about food. I was never really starving to death until two or three relapses ago. Living hand to mouth over alcohol. Alcohol. Borrowing money for alcohol. Living on borrowed time. For alcohol. I would seemingly never grow up. For alcohol. Psychotherapy, as the joke goes, works so well for many alcoholics because delving back into early childhood is such a short trip. That's not funny. For alcohol. I'll gladly pay you sometime for the next drink now. The language of addiction. To alcohol. For alcohol.

(**Surimi**): *Learning Spanish easily. Learning the Language of Denial, easily. Denial sells its wares to each alcoholic at the cellular level and at the level of the intelligence of its victim, a chess match. "Know your consumer" is the hallmark of any good salesman, and Denial is the King of Consumer Knowledge. The alcoholic brain barely stands a chance. Terminal disease. Train wreck ahead. All aboard who's coming aboard. The drinks are free.*

I have survived addiction, but do not know if I can survive freedom and the responsibilities of freedom and my fears. This is not easy, has not been easy, will not be easy. I really, really, really need help.

Fuck you, Alcohol. Fuck you.

EVENING MEDITATION

I chose to tear up my driver's license when I moved to Atlantic City out of fear that I might strike someone when driving in a blackout. Another small example of always choosing alcohol over any alternative. Alcohol shaped all my decisions for almost thirty years.

"I hid in bars, because I didn't want to hide in factories. That's all."
– Charles Bukowski

QUESTION FOR TODAY

Does every act have unintended consequences? Did alcohol kill you from behind? Does something really have to be behind the drink? Does sobriety mean you really have to think?

11. **BIRTH. INSANITY.**
RECOVERY OR DEATH.

"Strange as it seems, no amount of learning can cure stupidity,
and higher education positively fortifies it."
— Stephen Vizinczey

MORNING MEDITATION

I used to think of alcohol as a coping mechanism. Coping, doping: Not the same thing. Hoping, hoping, hoping. Change.

Somehow it seems that every generation is a "Lost Generation" when I think about it. Not just F. Scott Fitzgerald and the rest of that generation. On a personal level, my generation's feelings of being lost resulted in finding hope in drugs and a bottle (at least the kids I hung out with). But, boy, for an alcoholic like me, there was no putting the genie back in the bottle.

(**Sotto**): *Get ready, Vatchi, here it comes. He's cast out the fishing line. He's trying to reel us in, slowly, slowly. Come on, Jim (he's almost got us now). Slowly.... Vatchi, have you got your hip boots on?*

When I was maybe ten years old, I can remember overhearing my father discussing a possible career move to South America, or California, or somewhere else, anywhere else. I fantasized about living somewhere else, with maps of the world whirling around in my head, images from National Geographic fueling the fire. I can only guess at my father's motives. Chasing after a better career? I don't really know. But I do know that my young dreams were not to escape reality, but to capture fantasy. I could not even yet imagine that what I had been living was a cookie cutter life. House after house, block after block nearly identical in Waspishness.

Cookie cutter lives. As a ten year old, the big, big moves, the giant moves, were in my mind. The snow fort we built in the back yard during the blizzard of 1960 was a fantasy captured. My imagination had me being an Eskimo living on whale blubber. Oh, how I resented being asked to take out the garbage, reality, a youthful intrusion. The giant moves were in my mind. Are in my mind. In my mind. In my mind and under the influence. Fantasy not captured.

(**Vatchi**): *"Cookie cutter lives," Jim says. Sotto, listen to him. He casts his net wide. By land, by sea, by air. He casts his net wide to catch whatever attention he can. He seems desperate to fit in, the part of the cookie dough the cookie cutter couldn't cut. He thinks of himself as substandard somehow. Thirty years in the meat grinder called alcoholism didn't change that. He's still a misfit. To us and to himself. Only from a distance could one be amused, Sotto. Even when he sometimes comes off as attempting humor, he struggles with his needs. Sotto, Jim is needy.*

Now sober, I can't blame my alcoholism on any particular set of events or circumstances. Events fueled the quantity and frequency of my alcohol intake, but were not the cause. Fuck the cause. Alcohol was in my head regardless. In a perfect world, I am still an alcoholic. What is the cause of my alcoholism (like that could make a fucking difference)?

The more I drank, the more I drank. And so I am, I am, I am an alcoholic.

(**Surimi**): *An alcoholic's life story is in three parts: The childhood before the first drink, the time from the first drink until hitting bottom, and thirdly, recovery or death. As usual, this and all other cookie cutter oversimplifications require hip boots, Gentlemen. It is only in individual examples that these waters get muddied. Birth. Insanity. Recovery or death.*

Every example breaks every rule, including this rule.

I am alcoholic.
We are alcoholics.
I did not drink today.

EVENING MEDITATION
I did not really know how much help I needed until I felt well enough to reach out and help someone else.

"The real voyage of discovery consists not in seeking new landscapes but in having new eyes."
– Marcel Proust

QUESTION FOR TODAY

If you are hiding because you don't know what you seek, then who is the winner and who is the freak?

12. CLICK ME SOBER, CLICK ME DRUNK.

"Worry is like a rocking chair. It gives you something to do,
but it doesn't get you anywhere."
– Anonymous

MORNING MEDITATION

The further alcohol took me away from myself, the less I understood that I was losing my foothold. From the outside, I am sure it looked like I was becoming more and more selfish, but increasingly, I was not feeding myself, I was feeding my disease. The more selfish I may have appeared, the more my disease had dissolved my 'self' away.

I've been ticketed by the police while walking twice in my life, once plastered (disorderly conduct, public intoxication) and once sober (jaywalking). The jaywalking ticket hurt more because I didn't have the alcohol to soothe the pain before, during and after. And I didn't have the alcohol to blame. My sentence for public intoxication included shoveling snow away from storm drains and then clearing out the debris. The forgetful snow and debris from the past once sober were considerably more difficult to clear away.

Jane is now dead. She was once the best of drinking buddies. She became my landlady. The entire year I lived in a bedroom of her home in Mays Landing, half an hour car ride from Atlantic City, I did not know that she had become a heroin addict. I was too into my disease at the time, unable to cross the parking lot from the Mays Landing Diner where I worked as a food server without cracking open a bottle of vodka. I had learned to control my shakes until after I had punched out. I would keep my eye on the prize. Don't shake. A drink is waiting, I would think to myself. The prize.

Jane died of an overdose of heroin. I wasn't there at the time. Not in Mays Landing, not actively in my addiction. I didn't see it happen. In the rooms of recovery, death from addiction becomes almost commonplace. Numbed by alcohol in my addiction. Numb to the death of others, a different numbness, in my recovery. I've learned to lower my head and say to myself, "Oh, I see."

Jane left three children behind her overdosed corpse. To fend for themselves, I suppose. They were her collateral damage. This is the war on drugs. This is part of the war I see, the damage that addictions cause, many generations at a time overlapping.

Click back two relapses. Exhume Jane's corpse. Breathe life back into her. Put Bob's knife at my throat. Leave Jane in Atlantic City with her new boyfriend. Leave Bob, the father of two of her three children at home. Click me there. Go ahead. Put Bob's hand on Bob's knife. Put my throat on Bob's knife. Put my neck on Bob's lips. Click me to that moment which I knew must be the kiss of death. Click Paula, Bob and Jane's oldest daughter, in the next room. Click open a pill bottle. Don't let me know that Paula is stuffing pills down her throat to kill herself. Click me not hearing Bob screaming at me. Click an ambulance on the way to answer Paula's cell phone call for help. Click the police arriving at the same time as the ambulance. Click the neighbors on their front porch. Click just, just, just, just drunk enough to not forget. Click me drunk enough to barely remember. Click soldiers. Click Vietnam. Click Post Traumatic Stress. Click. Click. Click. Click. Click all you want to click you fucking bastards. Click me sober. Click me drunk.

"Where are the bullets," Bob screamed at me, stumbling toward me with a knife in his hand. Why in the world would I go back into Jane's house before the police arrived? It was stupid of me to go back in, but I was drunk and out of alcohol and would need money from my bedroom stash to take the bus to Atlantic City after the police arrived and this all got sorted out. The only reason to go back into that house was alcohol and alcohol is beyond reason. "Where are the bullets," screamed, not even a question.

Click. I'm done. Not the click of a gun. Click. I'm done. Click in my brain. My brain can't go through this right now. Not again. Over and over, but not now. Click. My brain is done right now. Click me done.

(**Sotto**): *This may have really happened. I'm almost sure that it did. But, "the kiss of death"? Isn't he being overly theatrical, melodramatic? Is he trying to entertain? Inform? Thinking of the movie rights? And Vatchi, is this about alcoholism, or is it really about him, Jim, trying to garner* *attention? Jim saying "Look at me. Look at me"?*

Click me done. How do I confront my life? How do I pass through it? How do I move on? Click me through. Click me over. Click this whole damned thing. Over.

The different deaths that I have survived, including my own near deaths, are like those dark brown pleated papers in this near empty box of chocolates, crumpled and empty. Most of the few remaining pieces seem to have been picked through. Pinched. Examined. Rejected. Don't drink. Save whatever is left in you. I'm trying to listen to myself, over the din of "drink me, drink me."

Here I sit, seemingly headed nowhere. I don't even know who the hell I am anymore. As if I ever did.

(**Vatchi**): *Seriously, Sotto. I don't think he's trying to garner anyone's attention, particularly. He seems to be sifting through his experiences and finding lumps of emotion he needs to pick up, examine and resift. Like chocolates. Bitter chocolates. Brown, pleated wrappers, crumpled, drunken notes to self – stained and illegible.*

I'm visiting too many places in my mind, in my memory, too fast. Emotions and memories crowd in around me and I can't breathe. Slow down, Jim. I'm telling myself to slow down. When I was drinking, it was always more and faster. This is something new. Slow down, Jim. "Don't get too well too fast." Raw nerve endings – stories left unfinished, rushing in on me. And then the next unfinishable story. Click. I'm done. Slow down, Jim. Slow the fuck down.

(**Surimi**): *These are nerve endings. Jim's nerve endings. Short-circuited synapses in his brain. And now, in sobriety, years of his stuffed emotions are surely and slowly unraveling, unraveling.*

He can survive this. He must survive this. Or? Or he will pick up a drink. Adapt or die.

Dysfunctional life, malfunctioning brain. Dismal and dying. Ten thousand days of dying. People, places and things. Fifty thousand drinks are gone and today is today is today.

He seems to know that he cannot do this alone. Not this time. Not ever.

After eight years, Jane had seen my slow descent from the outside. She'd seen me as her sober bartender at Seven South Bar. She'd seen me relapse. It was Jane who'd helped me go to the Mainland Hospital when I'd crashed to another bottom during my second stay at the Brunswick Hotel. It was Jane who'd offered me a place to live in after Seven South unexpectedly closed and I was fired from Dunkin' Donuts for showing up drunk at the end of a binge, still disturbingly drunk after being passed out for twelve solid hours.

"Where are the bullets?" Bob keeps asking me again and again. He only ever really asked me once. Maybe twice. But in my mind, my memory I hear "Where are the bullets?" over and over and over again with a knife at my throat. I don't know where he got them, three days out of jail after a multiple year stint. He was drunk. I was drunk. He passed out. I took the box of bullets to the next door neighbors at two or three in the morning and had the neighbors call the police.

Cop-killer bullets, next door. Suicide attempt, next room. Ambulance on the way, cops on their way.

"Where are the bullets?" Click. Make me three days drunk in Atlantic City after all this. After all this. Click me sober, click me drunk. Bob plea-bargained himself into Ancorra Mental Hospital. Two months later, for whatever reason, he sought me out at the Mays Landing Diner upon his release from the hospital. He said he was there to ask my forgiveness and to take me out for a drink after work. I told him to come back in two hours when my shift ended. Scared, I ran to Atlantic City for another three day drunk.

I will leave that behind me now. My sobriety is not bullet-proof. Sobriety is not the Pope-Mobile.

EVENING MEDITATION

Loose ends with no center made for a very loopy life. The only thing that connected anything was alcohol. Every day I woke up to a pile of questions that had no answers. In the mental hospital called addiction, alcohol never once gave me hope of release from alcohol. Never.

> *"Nothing is more difficult than competing with a myth."*
> – Francoise Giroud

QUESTION FOR TODAY

What questions do your memories ask and what answers do they seek? Which promises did you ever keep?

13. **THE HALLUCINATED SELF**

"The worst loneliness is to not be comfortable with yourself."
– Mark Twain

MORNING MEDITATION

"Drink like a man!" God knows I tried. And as my tolerance for alcohol increased, my disease progressed. I wonder how many men think they're drinking like a man, when in fact, they're drinking like an alcoholic?

I've got to watch out. Minimizing my own sobriety can be disastrous. I know from past experience that when I start lessening my sobriety's importance, my attendance at group recovery meetings begins to diminish and I know that I am on my way to a relapse. The leash I keep myself on must be kept short. And I know that's true. My past informs my present, continues to teach me lessons. My life unraveled then. I'm still unraveling my past now. Twisted? Very. Life with Jane and Bob, the incidences of which I've barely scratched the surface, happened more recently than life with Ted. I'd have to go back quite a few years further to begin to capture the beginning of the end between Ted and me. The end, in reality. Not the end in my mind. Ted is still in my mind.

When I got home from work that night I expected to find Ted waiting for me. Instead, I found that the door had been left opened. I should have known then that something was wrong, but somehow my response was positive, almost as if it had been my birthday and I would open the door further and a room full of people would yell out, "Surprise!" But, no. I was confronted by near total silence. Just some faint, distant white noise. To the left, inside the entranceway, I saw the kitchen with the refrigerator and sink, and to the far right, the open bedroom door. Between where I stood and the bedroom was the door to the bathroom.

Two steps inside the apartment door allowed me to hear the water from the bathroom sink run down the drain from the cold-water faucet, barely more than a drip. It ran over the broken green bottle of Aqua di Silva cologne. The broken green glass made me think that Ted had cut himself, but there was no sign of blood anywhere. I heard what I at first thought was a distant voice shout, "Ted" and I turned around to discover that that had been my voice. Part of me stood separated from that moment. My own voice had startled me. I know now what must have been deeply buried beneath bottle after bottle of alcohol. Without his psychiatric medication Ted had been getting sicker and sicker and I should have known and I guess I did know, but by then, denial had become a part of my way of life. "Ted." I heard my feet racing down the steps to the street. My right hand had automatically turned off the cold-water faucet. My voice trailed behind me. Fear separated, fear dissected. "Ted" was now an echo in my head. Fear controlled.

(**Sotto**): *Jim talks about diminishing the importance of his sobriety, then ricochets headfirst into whatever this incident is about. This sense I feel of impending doom: Is it him? Or is it me, Vatchi? His life upon the very precipice of doom.*

I ran across the street to the Rendezvous Bar. Frank was bartending. The Rendezvous was a true watering hole for me, a buffalo alcoholic with a buffalo thirst. "Hold the ice. Make it a double" was my thought. Where is pain located? In the brain, right next to fear? Or in an empty glass not refilled quickly enough?

Frank knew to pour me a drink, even though he knew I should not find the time to drink it.

"Jim," Frank said, with a forceful concentration above the din of a handful of customers, "Ted's in the hospital. An ambulance picked him up an hour ago." Here it was, the long and short of it, unvarnished as Frank had to tell it and tell it quickly.

I'd known Ted for almost a year, understanding fully that he was on psychiatric medication and had been on "scripts" (prescriptions) for years. Ted functioned completely within the bounds of "normal" for our entire first year as roommates. Then he decided, after years of being on psychiatric medication and being perfectly fine, that he was fine and consequently, obvious to him, he no longer needed, wanted or required medication. Or so he must have thought. Thus began his slow descent into a psychiatric hell. No one would know that he had stopped taking his medication. Not me, not his family, not his doctors. His changes occurred slowly but were only seen by me in retrospect. His balance and stability depended on his prescriptions. Without them, his house of cards slowly collapsed.

His suicide attempt seemed sudden and unexpected. If I had been sober, I'm sure I would have seen his slow descent into madness. It was unbelievable to me that he had stolen my personal I.D. and entered the hospital's emergency room using my name. Ted actually believed that he was me. He hallucinated that he was me, as nearly as I can tell.

Remember now, that I was drunk throughout all this. I lived, by that time, in the world of what is so lovingly and mistakenly called the "functioning alcoholic." It was my actual degree of dysfunction that was made apparent here. Here was Ted, attempting to kill himself thinking he was me. Here was me, thinking I was a "functioning alcoholic." In some wild hallucination of otherness, I knew neither his insanity nor mine.

And here am I now, in the present, stuck in this past like an insect suspended in amber.

(**Vatchi**): *I'll tell you what I think, Sotto. I think he's seeing his own life in the life of others. The empathy he is now beginning to feel rewinding and reviewing Ted's train wreck in a way he could not have, at the time. His own train wreck, anesthetized in the past, he is reliving in the unanesthetized present. He has to relive his past sober to forgive his past drunk.*

There would be a knife here soon. In months, three months, there would be a knife, intended for my throat. Or my back. Or heart. Everything could have been different, could have turned out differently. Within three days, Ted was shipped by ambulance from Atlantic City Medical Center to Ancorra State Mental Hospital. He would be there for three months.

In those three months, my drinking would be propelled to new heights of drunkenness, new lows of drunkenness and wide-eyed, wild drunkenness. Each night was my unknown, unfeeling escape to unreality. Those shot glasses would glide unmercifully downward for years before crashing and bouncing off the floor of the chasm which my life had become.

(**Surimi**): *A knife, intended for his throat: The unintended consequences of alcoholism, far beyond the destruction caused by alcohol alone. The effects with no provable cause and effect. The insanity of alcoholism does not operate under the rules of logic, of this cause or that. Unknowable, unexpected heartbreaks and disaster. Collateral damage. Damaged souls drawn to one another. Alcohol consumed. Sanity consumed. Catastrophic consequences inevitable. This cannot be good. Ever....*

How often must I visit the past before it becomes a repetitive obsession, a nightmare in its own right? Clearly, I do not know. And equally clearly, I am sure, that at some point I must just let go. There are lessons to be learned and behaviors to be unlearned. I paddle my canoe into my past, explore that land of half-memories, collecting and recollecting. Surely, quietly, I take this oar and push off that shore and paddle, presently, into the unknown future.

I am so glad that I did not even think to drink today.

Ted. Neither of us knew then how we each were engulfed in our separate insanities, schizophrenia and alcoholism. Not so separate. Not so separate at all.

EVENING MEDITATION

I could not suspect or know that I would diverge from all the social drinkers in the world about me in my early years of drinking. By the time my Kryptonite, Alcohol, had taken hold, my long, slow death spiral had already begun. Suspicion, divergence, insanity, brick wall. "Pride goeth before the fall." This I did not know. I drank that knowledge away.

> *"To be yourself in a world that is constantly trying to make*
> *you something else is the greatest accomplishment."*
> – Ralph Waldo Emerson

QUESTION FOR TODAY

How wide is your memory of now? How wide is now? How wide are you now? How wide now?

14. **THE UNSEEN BAR SCENE SEEN**

"A man who suffers before it is necessary suffers more than is necessary."
– Seneca

MORNING MEDITATION

I have made up a million excuses to drink, but have needed only one reason to quit: I am powerless over alcohol.

No one could believe that I had stopped drinking when I did finally stop. Of course, I couldn't have known this, because for the first few months I had severed all connections with the "Bar Scene." In retrospect, they must have guessed that something catastrophic had happened to me. This was borne out much later when after a sustained period of sobriety I entered a bar just off the Boardwalk on South Carolina Avenue called Reflections, one block from Resorts International, Atlantic City's first casino.

An old drinking buddy and pool player, Donald, came up to me there and asked me how my "prescription regimen" was going. I must have had a fairly perplexed look on my face, because, to tell the truth, I had not an idea in the world what he was talking about. It turned out that since I had suddenly stopped showing up to take part in the local bar scene, the rumor mill wrongly deduced that since I had been such a hard partier (and ever other euphemism for drinking that ever existed), and that I had quit drinking, I must have AIDS.

I guess when you are confronted by a bar crowd whose regulars are fully in denial of their own alcoholism, it shouldn't be surprising that they would have to concoct some outside reason for anyone quitting drinking. After all, who in their right mind would quit drinking for drinking's sake? Wouldn't that be insane? "Cunning, baffling and powerful" is how the rooms of recovery describe the insanity of alcohol. How odd that the reason for picking up the next drink is rarely for the simple "I am an alcoholic." There are always reasons, people, places, things.

(**Sotto**): *I get this, Vatchi. A bar full of regulars, not particularly caring, or even thinking about Jim. But slowly, a story evolves, the contagion spreads. I don't know if this little episode is more about a bunch of drunks, or human nature in general. The children's game of "Whisper Down the Alley" starts with "Jim stopped drinking" and by the time it gets passed on to the last person it has mutated into "Jim must have AIDS."*

And here's another little irony of the people, places and things of my disease: Tyrone, my second to last roommate, before my own eventual descent to my first bottom, contracted AIDS from needles he shared with other heroin addicts. He may well have started shooting up while we were still roommates, although he swore to me later, that he never had even tried heroin until after he had moved out. I couldn't really tell you if he was lying because, at the time, I was drunk enough most of the time that I wouldn't have noticed unless I had stumbled upon one of his needles or other paraphernalia. Which I hadn't.

Curiously, alcohol was his gateway drug to heroin. Now, in recovery, I fear not becoming addicted to another drug, but of any other drug taking me back to my (and I hate this phrase) "drug of choice," alcohol. "Nothing short of AIDS could have stopped him from drinking," is how Donald had explained the origin of that false rumor about me. I guess all those alcoholic bar patrons did not see the possibility that I stopped drinking because alcohol was killing me. Like mass hysteria, there exists a certain kind of mass denial, I suppose, cultural denial. A "Ship of Fools."

(**Vatchi**): *It's interesting that you bring up human nature, Sotto. "Curiosity killed the cat." Is that human nature? And here, he mentions "gateway drug". Another drug to trip you up and drop you back into the same bucket of crap and worse, excuse my French. Is that human nature, Sotto? That must have been some really rough going for him back then. A lonely bottom, realizing the drunken bar crowd's drunken thinking. Lonely at the top. Lonely at the bottom. Is that human nature, Sotto? What is Jim left with, Sotto? What is anyone left with?*

Twenty millions suns (I stole that from somewhere?) couldn't have convinced me before I quit drinking that I would ever quit. I sort of imagined myself as some ancient, noble Eskimo, wandering off into the northern lights with bottle in hand to die some unknown, tragic, heroic, and drunken death. I romanticized my disease when I was drinking until the reality got so bad that the romance had to die, with me following on its coattails. At each step in my slow, downward progression I would tell myself that it couldn't get any worse and that however bad I was, it wasn't anything that another drink couldn't fix. But it did and could and would always get worse. Never would I think to stop drinking. Attempts to modify my drinking to a more reasonable amount of consumption failed on a nightly basis. My resolve dissolved. My *Drinking Man's Guide to Bar Exercise* lost all momentum on the stillness of my barstool.

(**Surimi**): *Gentlemen, we are pack animals, like wolves. Separated from the pack, the chances of survival diminish. Alcoholism is this disease of separation. The alcoholic needs alcohol to the exclusion of all else. Recovery is largely about rejoining the human race. Connecting with self, reconnecting with self. Connecting with others, reconnecting. Overcoming alcoholism, the Great Excluder. The irony and paradox of Happy Hour can silence even me.*

The loneliness of an alcoholic death. That's what many of my recollections boil down to. Is it too early to be this honest? Reciprocity is keeping me sober. Sharing with another alcoholic. It really is that simple. I used to drown the loneliness caused by alcohol with (what else?) more alcohol. Solitude seemed an impossibility when a bottle of booze sat next to me. Alcohol lorded over me and made solitude an impossibility. Loneliness, inescapable. Solitude, unattainable. Sobriety, unimaginable.

That was then, but now my life is changing.

EVENING MEDITATION

I never wanted to get sober. Getting sober sucks. Getting sober is worse than drinking. But when drinking is slowly killing you, it's the only option left. In war, captured enemies are water-boarded. I was liquor-boarded. Alcohol was my enemy. Alcohol was my friend. Alcohol was everything and I was nothing in the end. Chemical betrayal. I did not think that I could ever get sober. And stay sober. Ever. And a day. I did not drink today.

"Opportunity may knock only once, but temptation leans on the doorbell."
                                                            – Anonymous

QUESTION FOR TODAY

Who gave Alcoholism such a bad name? Anyone, everyone and no one?

15. EVERYTHING CHANGED EXCEPT ME

*"The real voyage of discovery consists not in seeking new landscapes
but in having new eyes."*
– Marcel Proust

MORNING MEDITATION
"Live Free or Die": State of New Hampshire or State of Recovery?

I must be getting pretty damned old. It occurred to me today that I could
GPS almost any intersection in Atlantic City, and like a Chinese menu (pick
one from column A, one from column B and one from Column C), I could
select from any of a variety of memories. Just one example: The
intersection of Indiana and Pacific Avenues. It was the site of the Midtown-
Bala Hotel's Chip's Restaurant and Bar where I worked for years, on and
off, as a waiter and a bartender. Sands Casino, which had been adjacent,
later bought the property and it became part of their then new front
entrance. The Sands Casino was then imploded to make way for a new
casino. That entire square block sat leveled and vacant for a few years and
now is the site of what appears to be a sunken ship.

Selective memories, indeed. For the longest time, everything changed
except me. Alcoholism is cruel.

(**Sotto**): *Geez. This reminds me of those time-lapse photography videos: see
the plant grow, bud, bloom and die in 30 seconds. Time compression. He's
giving me a headache.*

How strange life is. Like now. Bethlehem, Pennsylvania, my hometown,
once home of Bethlehem Steel Corporation, where I worked for two

summers while attending college, and from which my Father retired as a mechanical engineer, is now defunct and has been rebuilt as the Sands Bethlehem Casino.

Life goes on. Sing a song. Don't die yet. More change is surely coming (cue Bob Dylan).

(**Vatchi**): *He's talking about time here, Sotto. He seems almost to have a grasp of things and so do you. Just from a different vantage point. Jim seems to mentally leave the room and then come back again to solid ground.*

Other people's consciousness is such a strange thing to watch, Sotto. And here I am watching you watch him. My job's easier. Relax, I think we're nearly halfway through Act One.

And now, change has surely come again as I have moved to another Atlantic City location down the street from another vacant tract of land (no, not my mind!), a site formerly Playboy Casino, then Trump's World Fair Casino and now a rectangular goose egg. Looking out over this empty tract of land, I see the emptiness that was me, drunk but empty, when I did advertising work for Playboy. I vividly remember the alcoholic haze which prevented me from meeting with Joanne, the director of advertising, except in the late afternoon. The bigger the account, the later in the day I would schedule that appointment, because I knew I reeked less of alcohol as the day progressed.

Bad breath and alcohol-infused body fumes were just the tip of my morning iceberg. One morning with a prospective client, a waterbed store owner, I reached into my breast pocket to hand him my business card and a pack of rolling papers flew out of my pocket and onto his desk. My morning shakes, I'm sure, had something to do with that bad move. Playboy's Joanne would not have liked to have seen that move. I always could have been worse. As could anyone. Alcohol told me that drunk and sobriety tells me that sober.

(**Surimi**): *Sotto, Vatchi, we all see and hear Jim from different vantage points. We three were strangers. Now illusion is our common bond. Or nothing is. Now Jim has my attention, our attention. It is better that he did not drink today. This I do know.*

Growing older as the world changed all around me. (Oh, I was changing, alright, entrenched in my disease beyond knowledge of time's passage.) I woke up sober one day only to discover that the world had changed and grown but that I had not. My disease had progressed but I had not. A snail's pace twenty-seven year rollercoaster headed for sea level and below. I could not have guessed that my three-martini lunches would turn into what felt like this faceless chemical betrayal and assault.

Live and don't learn. Live and don't learn. Then, live and learn.

EVENING MEDITATION

Diplomatically searching for others equally high, we (my disease and I) would manufacture memories out of blackouts like free-range intoxicated chickens.

> *"A man who has committed a mistake and doesn't correct it*
> *is committing another mistake."*
> – Confucius

QUESTION FOR TODAY

Which mask do you drop first when, at last, you have reached your turning point?

16. YOU ARE EVE BEFORE THE APPLE AND I AM ADAM AFTER THE FALL

"To live is to suffer. To survive is to find meaning in suffering."
– Viktor Frankl

MORNING MEDITATION
So, I asked myself, "What is larger than me that I might want to be a part of?"
Hmmm.... The human race might be a nice start.

What is hollow? A hollow heart? A chocolate Easter bunny? A hollow point bullet? A hollow point bullet. Let's start there. No. Let's stop there.

Barbara Borden lived across the street from me from the sixth to the twelfth grade. Her brother, Jim, was my best high school buddy. Barbara had physical and mental impairments. I don't know what words to use because every word is politically incorrect. Let's just say that as a very young child I sensed her entrapment in her inability to express herself. And yet somehow, without words, she was able to express some sense of loss at being different. A psychiatrist might diagnose this as projection on my part, but nonetheless, it felt real.

Words fall short of expressing the inexpressible, but sometimes the look on one's face or a posture capture that moment, Barbara Borden.

(**Sotto**): *"Words fall short," he says. "Give it a break, Shakespeare." That's what I say, Vatchi.*

My heart is sometimes so full of passion and sometimes totally dispassionate, like a brain surgeon. No. Brain surgeons have passion for their work. Stop here. No. Do not stop here.

Oh, Barbara Borden, Barbara Borden. If only we were just a little bit more different from each other or are our lives not so very different as the whole world would have us seem? Are they so different, Barbara Borden? No, Jim, no. They are not.

This earth whirling around the sun at times it seems to have made misfits of us all. Barbara Borden, Barbara Borden, in our element, perhaps we're not so different after all. You are Eve before the apple and I am Adam after the fall. That is all.

(**Vatchi**): *You're not hearing what I'm hearing, Sotto. I'm hearing the voice, no, the heart of a murderer expressed through Jim's voice, his response to fear expressed as an emotional vacuum. Jim was left to feel alone in himself. Hollow point bullets? He has survived this, but he must still face this. That strange survivor's guilt, that knowledge, barely felt, that he could have held that knife or gun. Hollow. Part of him is empathetic victim. But when he turns his back on empathy, he turns his back upon himself. Man's inhumanity to man looked squarely in the eyes and immediately ignored. The hollowness that survival bestowed upon him. What about that state of mind, Sotto? Denial of his alcoholism is not even part of that. What of the glint in those murderous eyes? The glint of the knife? The denial that is both empathy and emptiness? He stared at the knife and the knife stared back at him. He shut himself off as a way to survive.*

Sotto, Jim is really fucked up. The mere thought of hollow point bullets. Memory. Fear. Diversion... Barbara Borden. Confusion as a survival strategy. He has the will to get better, to work through things, to survive. Confusion as survival. Confusion survived.

Déjà vu: The most regret I have for my past is the past which did not continue once I picked up my first drink, my first drug. My regrets for my drinking past are few because in retrospect, I can see where it was going, where it did go, where it went. And where it went is here and now. And where I am now is not at all where I would have landed except through this circuitous course to Now.

The Funhouse Horror Mirror of my past led, finally, to this: Déjà vu, through my distorted past to a comfortable Here and Now.

(**Surimi**): *Jim's thoughts about Barbara Borden are part of his defense and his denial, a diversionary tactic of his disease. He must now face the memory of his fears. Bullets. Knives. A deadly bottle of booze. They all sit upon the mantelpiece of his memory and must be faced. This is the nature of recovery, of inspiration, coincidence and very good unintended consequences. The good, unintended consequences of sobriety.*

Are you listening now, Sotto? He shut himself off and now sober he is slowly opening himself up. There is insanity in recovery, too. At least in Jim's recovery there is. Walk through the fire of your memories, Jim. This is possible. Recovery is possible.

Some old-time drinking thoughts creep back into my head sometimes saying, "You deserve a drink." I have to pull the reins back on my wild horse impulses. If I lose these inhibitions, I will lose myself again. Death by reflex. Death by habit. Death by alcoholism. Not death by a hollow point bullet. Not this time. There.

I need not drink today, Barbara Borden.

EVENING MEDITATION

Who I aspired to be, what I aspired to do, did not, could not fit into the hand I was playing when I drank. That hand was always reaching for the next next drink.

"The men who really believe in themselves are all in lunatic asylums."
– G. K. Chesterton

QUESTION FOR TODAY

Which uncertainty is the best tool for my recovery? How might uncertainty give me hope? Has not doubt opened doors?

17. **FOSSILIZED**

"The louder he talked of his honor, the faster we counted our spoons."
– Ralph Waldo Emerson

MORNING MEDITATION

I fooled myself. Why could I not fool you (all this time, my disease was laughing, laughing like a fool)?

Twice in my life I remember friends making predictions about what my future would hold. The first prediction was by my boss, friend and eventual five-year housemate, Gene, just prior to our three-month road trip to Mexico and Guatemala. He said to me, "Jim, if we don't go on this trip now, I know you. You'll never travel anywhere." Did Gene know that I was already trapped in my disease or trapped in myself, or both? Now, that could be a coincidence and selective memory on my part, but shortly thereafter I moved to Atlantic City and for the next thirty years (from blackout to blackout) I did travel nowhere.

The second prediction was a warning from Ted, my Atlantic City roommate who would eventually plot my undoing. After observing my continual string of drunken days he quite seriously (and correctly) predicted my future one time saying "you keep drinking like that and one day you'll be puking you're guts out and still you won't be able to stop drinking." I hear the water dripping from the bathroom faucet. I see my footprints on the stairs trailing to the street. I smell the Agua di Silva through the broken glass in the bathroom sink. I did end up puking my guts out, unable to stop drinking not right then, not right there but later, years of blackouts later.

(**Sotto**): *Yeah, yeah, yeah. And the gypsy couldn't have any children because*

54

her husband had crystal balls! Out of a million things heard in anyone's past, at least two or three are going to appear to come magically true. This is coincidence. Big deal. Who is he kidding? What's the big deal?

As if it could be otherwise.

"You'll never go anywhere," Gene said.

I'll never be anything except a fall down, can't stop drunk. I felt that, believed that, accepted that, lived that. And now I must claim ownership of my realities, predicted easily though the observations of Gene and Ted at that time, yet rejected adamantly by me then. Resentment and denial, my real best friends. Puking my guts out in a toilet, then. Now, pouring my guts out? Weird world, wired weird. Pouring my guts out thusly.

(**Vatchi**): *Jim's memory of his past is so fragmented, distorted. Underneath it all he knew that he was alcoholic, but just didn't know, couldn't know, how bad it would really get. Until his roller coaster crashed.*

How can I be emotionally explicit now, when most of my emotional life was muddled, like the fruit in my Brandy Old-Fashioneds? And not be bitter now, unlike the Angostura bitters in that same drink? You are what you eat, but what are you when you are only what you drink?

I replaced my 'self' with alcohol. The sediments of my life fossilized by alcohol.

ATTENTION: Jim Anders will not be able to perform tonight. He's drunk. His role will be performed by his understudy, Alcohol.

Fuck. Fuck. Fuck. Fuck. Fuck. Fossil-fucked by alcohol.

(**Surimi**): *Jim's body built up a tolerance for alcohol (not to mention his mind, his heart, his soul). It would take more and more alcohol to achieve the same effect. Except it never really was the same effect as his tolerance increased. It had "cunning, baffling and powerful" similarities to the same effect, but the cumulative effect was another story. Only slowly did he learn that as he began to look more and more like an alcoholic to observers he did not feel the difference he wanted on the inside. "More" trumped "effect" and in a very long blink, he was consumed by his disease.*

Now, Sotto, Vatchi, your understanding of him will change as he changes. The metamorphosis of change and the metamorphosis of the understanding of change. That is "the play within the play." His sobriety, at first, was like a bad translation. Time takes time (and understanding).

The illusion of escape. The biggest magic trick of all. Ossified, fossilized. Rational eyes, rational lies. Crumbs of whimsy, crumbs of whimsy. I'm done.

Fossil-fucked by alcohol.

EVENING MEDITATION

Only twice did I ever stand outside a liquor store waiting for it to open, literally sweating those last few minutes before the doors finally opened. "Open, damn it!" I measured my life in pints instead of hours. Only twice I stood outside waiting. But it could have been (and really was) 10,000 days.

> *"Life is too important to be taken seriously."*
> – Oscar Wilde

QUESTION FOR TODAY

How many keys did I have to lose before I would learn that alcohol no longer opened doors?

18. **THE DISTANCE OF DISEASE**

"There is no way to happiness. Happiness is the way."
– The Tao

MORNING MEDITATION

Tell me that hope can be enough. Teach me how to listen. Whisper something true. Cleanse me. Purify me. Please listen to my disease, to me. Please.

If I had to pick the year that was the turning point in my addiction, it would have to be in 1979. It seems like that was the year wherein every job and professional or artistic commitment or opportunity came my way. Damn, but this is difficult. But it was then that my alcoholism really started to spiral downward. It was then that my opportunities for achievement were just starting to present themselves to me. I really did hide my doubts and fears about my future possibilities within the bottle. Smirky, smirk-smirk: fuck.

There was my New Jersey State Education Grant with Ventnor Middle School. I had been hand-picked to teach several elementary art classes on the topic of artists and writers working together. The assignment I gave them was to illustrate my poem, "Thirteen Ways of Looking at an Aardvark," which, coincidentally, had won me lifetime honorary membership in the American Association of Aardvark Aficionados. For that entire semester I showed up at the school first thing in the morning severely hung over (eventually hangovers would be a thing of the past as I would eventually have more alcohol in my system than would allow for a hangover, or so it seemed). I was embarrassed that I couldn't show up in better shape and wondered, but was afraid to ask, if my breath smelled (of course, it must have smelled, as I know alcohol would be pouring out of every cell in my body, not just my breath). It wasn't alright, but somehow it would have to do. I couldn't be embarrassed twenty-four/seven, but I could be legally intoxicated twenty-four/seven, so embarrassment gradually phased out of my vocabulary and thoughts.

1979 was also the year that I wrote "Storm Warning" for Joe Frazier, the World Heavyweight Champion, turned singer. Not particularly a boxing fan, I did indeed appreciate how adored he was by his fans, no matter how underappreciated he may have been as a singer. I must say that I was always just plastered enough when working with his musical director, Jon, to not have even the most remote idea if he was more, less or equally high as I was. If at all. If I wondered about it, it was a passing thought, at best. I would have always been drinking for several hours before working with Jon as it would always be very late at night and I would have already had my buzz on by then. Maybe I was a storm warning to Jon, as in "here comes trouble."

How the hell would I know?

To tell you the truth, a lot of times, what may have appeared to be fishing for compliments, was actually fishing for facts. Where was I? What did I say? Did I act alright? Did I borrow money? How did I get home? All this crap while trying to appear self-assured and having my act together. What may have been obvious to others was not obvious to this drunk. Not at that time. Not then. What else is not so obvious to me now, but someday might? I'll have to get back to you on that.

(**Sotto**): *He doth boast too much in his self-deprecating manner. Actually, I do feel a little sorry for him. Damn it…. He has me playing into his hand, now!*

Self-assurance was my mask. Still is my mask? I could be drunk and still perform. Or so I thought. I'll be all right. I can do this. Being drunk allowed me to deal with the drunk in me. Blame the drunk in me. I can accept that you blame the drunk in me.

(**Vatchi**): *You're playing into his hand, Sotto. Sympathy can help or hurt, Sotto. Check your motives.*

My younger sister's addictions came on harder, faster, and stronger than mine. A certain frailty, susceptibility, took over Betty sooner than it took over me. Our common genetic predisposition could have led to my death instead of her suicide, but that's not the way the addiction balls bounced. We had become too distant, detached. Our addictions kept us apart. I dissolved into mine. She dissolved into hers. There was no "We" as "She" and "I" dissolved into our addictions. It was distance that kept us apart.

Not the distance between Pennsylvania and New Jersey. The distance of disease, if you please.

The distance of disease if you don't please.

(**Surimi**): *Cognitive dissonance. The life lived and the life one could have lived. Jim's emotional brick walls are the walls to a maze, a diseased rat's race. The walls of that maze may lead him to a better understanding of self. Or not. He's so unpolished. It will take some time to discover what is beneath all his alcohol-induced isolation.*

Trying to live sober? Quit trying.

The distances between planets seem so far until I consider the distances between stars. The distances between people, then, really aren't all that far at all. The distance of disease, if you please. The distance of disease if you don't please.

EVENING MEDITATION

An accumulating mountain of evidence did not slow my descent. There were no intersections, no neural connections, no one plus one equals two. Ever-increasing orders of magnitude: Crash, then burn.

> *"Anticipate the good so that you may enjoy it."*
> – Ethiopian Proverb

QUESTION FOR TODAY

What did addiction borrow? What did addiction steal? What did you give so freely? What does the truth reveal?

19. **TRANSFORMERS**

"One faces the future with one's past."
– Pearl S. Buck

MORNING MEDITATION

When I thought I could stay sober alone, I wound up drinking alone.

Ted is too easy, his name is too easy, for how unbelievably convoluted things became. Ted was sent to Ancorra Mental Hospital after attempting suicide. His transformation after he stopped taking his psychiatric medication was insane. When he stopped taking his pills, his schizophrenia was no longer in remission. It progressed to the point of his attempting suicide. No one could believe that he had taken over my identity in his mind. Like psychiatric wards with patients thinking they are Jesus, Ted's disease took ownership of his mind. Ted thought that he was me and then attempted suicide. That was his alternate reality and that is the reality that I would have to live through. And I did live through it: drunk, drunker, drunkest.

Three months later, apparently stabilized on medication for his schizophrenia, Ted returned to the old apartment we had shared. I had already moved out, renting a bedroom apartment two blocks away on Ocean Avenue.

This will be short. It has to be. I can't deal with this now. I am not Ted, but Ted oh-so-too-clearly thought that he was really me.

(**Sotto**): *"Hell is other people." That's what Sartre and some of his existentialist buddies have proclaimed. But Jesus, when the other person thinks that they are you? Vatchi, do you think Jim is making this shit up?*

Who's running this asylum? Maybe I'm crazy. Can one identify so closely to another that all self is lost? Couldn't Ted have chosen Jesus? Why in God's name would he choose Jim, to think that he was actually him?

I must deal with this. Let it be now. Let me deal with this now.

The truth is that I think I couldn't deal with anyone whose problems were as large or larger than mine. Ted's slow psychiatric decline after he stopped taking his medication mirrored the progressive nature of my disease, but I can guarantee I wasn't clear headed enough to know that at that time.

By the time he had been sent from Atlantic City Medical Center to Ancorra Psychiatric Hospital, I had already decided to move out. I could no longer deal with him. I could only talk at him, not with him. Is this how I distanced myself from myself in my disease? Face this squarely, Jim. Don't let yourself get sidetracked. Okay. All I knew was that I couldn't deal with anything like this ever happening again in Ted's life. Or to my life. When Ted got out of the psychiatric hospital three months later and I had moved and essentially walled him out of my life, he could not deal with all of those repercussions and planned, planned, planned to really kill me this time. Me as Jim, not Ted as Jim. Ted would kill me, Jim.

A knife, witnesses, police. Ted knew that I would walk by him on the street. I was drunk. He was steeped in his illness. Knife, witnesses, police. I survived. He was arrested. Too shook up (and plastered), a written testimonial was all the prosecuting attorney determined I would be able to give. Ted lost the case. I wasn't in the courtroom. He went back to Ancorra. I went back to the bar.

Let it go. Let it go. Let it go.

For now. For today. Don't drink today. Let it go for now. Sometimes the details really matter. They do not matter here. What's done is done. Move on.

(**Vatchi**): *There are probably hundreds of people in mental hospitals who think they're Jesus or Napoleon Bonaparte. Why anyone, including Ted, would believe that they were Jim, Sotto, is beyond my comprehension, but insanity has a way of doing that. I can't say that I blame you for doubting some of what Jim says, Sotto. He was a blackout drinker. Sometimes I think you have to give people the benefit of the doubt. But I believe that belief can never be complete, that there will always be some shred of doubt. Mother Teresa, speaking in religious terms, struggled with doubt of her faith in God for years.*

Suicide Bombers - there's beyond the shadow of a doubt for you, Sotto. Sometimes, even lies are the truth.

Move on to the anonymous second attempt at my life. Forget one by remembering another. Whack a mole. I was fucked up when I was followed home from the bar drunk. I guess I spent so much money over the bar and was so drunk that the stranger who followed me, apparently just a few feet behind, must have figured that I had plenty more money where that came from and I would be an easy target to roll.

I found out later, having survived a broken nose, jaw, cheek bone, broken ribs puncturing my lungs, busted teeth, etc. The security cameras in that last bar apparently could offer no useable clues as to the suspect's identity. He was never caught, an anonymous stranger. So I'll never really know if it was a hate crime or a robbery turned violent by someone whom I suspect was probably a drug addict. Crack head was the best guess of one of the nurses who attended my physical recovery.

This anonymous assault on me was my second near death experience. First was Ted and all the drama that came with that experience. And then this. Ted's near assault was merely witnessed as fully intended (I think), knife in hand on the street where we had lived.

Nothing would stop my drinking. Nothing. It had not ever occurred to me that alcohol could be to blame because alcohol was involved in every aspect of my life, good and bad. Alcohol was a given. Alcohol could not be the cause of everything now, could it?

After both of these attempts at nearly taking my life, I just continued drinking. This, that and a third couldn't stop a thing. Powerless.

(**Surimi**): *Like Jim says, "Alcohol was a given." Immersed in alcohol, the only world he knew. What is not a given? Everything is a gift. Everything.*
Jim's not done telling his story here. Guaranteed. That's a given, too.

I could work around my drinking problem. I tried to, up to a point. Just a few minor hospitalizations, a few lost jobs and apartments, just a few demolished relationships, just a few detoxes. It could only get better, right?

You want an example? Alright, I'll give you an example. I was out one night with Jeff, the future Mayor's son. Playing blackjack at the Taj Mahal, I was drinking and winning and winning more and drinking more. At one point I had said to Jeff, "Here's seven-hundred and fifty dollars. Hold it for me. Don't give it back no matter what I say." I played with the other five-hundred I still had hidden in my pocket and when that ran out after playing and drinking and losing and drinking and winning and drinking and drinking and drinking, I said, "Jeff, give me back my money."

"You made me promise not to," he said.

"That was then, this is now," I said. I forget how, but somehow, security got involved, my money was returned to me and eventually lost, after yet again more drinking and gambling. As usual, I didn't know how I got home.

Jeff refreshed my memory the next day. Who wouldn't resent him for returning the money to me that I'd made him promise not to? Not me. Not drunken, skunk drunk me. Alcohol could not be the cause of everything, could it? Could it?

I would walk past Kornblau's Delicatessen one way, not drunk enough to eat and later, return the other way, hours later, too drunk to eat. Did alcohol have something to do with that? Is that what you're telling me?

Alcohol was part of every plan. Does that mean that alcohol was the plan? A bar tan replaced my beach tan. Whose fault was that? You're trying to blame me? I brushed my teeth every day. Maybe toothpaste was my problem. I took a shower every day. Maybe showering was my problem.

When had alcohol suddenly seemed so demanding? Fuck you. Gimme a drink. Gimme a drink. Now.

EVENING MEDITATION

Once upon a time there was work and there was play and they seemed opposite. But as my alcoholism progressed, playing wasn't fun anymore as drinking became my necessity. Alcohol turned all my would-be fun into clinical depression. Synonym and antonym became the same insane, like loosen and unloosen. Who knew fun could be so wearisome? The meanings of words changed meanings until nothing meant anything. Quote? "The opposite of fun, for me, is alcohol."

> *"It's not trespassing when you cross your own boundaries.*
> – Anonymous

QUESTION FOR TODAY

Where do trees go to school? The school of hard knocks? Where is your sense of humor? Did you lose it? Will you or it ever return? Can I get a refund on fun unfound? Can I have roots and still not touch the sky? When will I inherit the intelligence of trees?

20. **MEDITATE OR MEDICATE?**

"If the brain were so simple that we could understand it,
we would be so simple that we could not."
– Emerson Pugh

MORNING MEDITATION

Not being able to drink is not so bad. Not being able to not drink is devastating.

This is very interesting. The very process of writing this piece has increased my self-discovery. In my notes, typed in without asterisks, italics or exclamation points, I found this simple entry, a note to myself: "Alcohol replaced self-discovery." Like that was an insignificant afterthought, interesting, but of no real importance. And yet, there it was, brushed over, cast aside, almost ignored.

Let me add here that from about the age of 16 to 20, I sincerely believed that the answer to the problems of ego and self existed outside myself and that the controlled use of substances like LSD, marijuana and (minimally) alcohol, would lead to the discovery I would need to untangle, unlock and open the doors to self-understanding. I still, as a matter of fact, have lingering doubts of this improbable possibility. Some inner voice, even today, tells me, "Well, if you weren't an alcoholic these keys could unlock those doors."

Controlled use of substances. There was the illusion. A thirty year illusion may not keep an audience on the edge of their seats, but it certainly kept me on the edge of reality (and beyond).

Now I'm beginning to understand why I put this poem here. No asterisk, italics or exclamation points necessary.

"Needing Nothing"

Needing nothing
Used to fill a certain need in me.
But now the flowers in the field have gone to seed
And loneliness seems destiny.
Was I ever really free?

(**Sotto**): *I've got to admit, Vatchi that once you've gotten to know someone a little better, your preconceptions tend to melt away. Or, at least, thaw a little. I do, at times, allow Jim to amuse me.*

"Alcohol replaced self-discovery." Was I obsessing then? Am I obsessing now? Somehow, beginning to feel good about myself sober brings me to the edge of a drink. Newly sober, feeling good made me want to drink. Refraining from a drink meant that I had to remember the many pains that alcohol had caused me. There can be no good reason for me to drink. "My name is Jim and I am an alcoholic." That sounds so simple, but it was not so easy to say, at first. And then, after saying it a thousand times it can become too easy to forget just what that means.

(**Vatchi**): *I agree with you up to a point, Sotto. It seems that every time he starts to make a little sense, he just seems to slide back into emotional chaos. I don't know if it's some defense mechanism of his, a flashback, or what? Maybe his alcoholism is still replacing self-discovery.*

EPIPHANY: I didn't realize it until now, but I was a dry drunk during the period I didn't drink, smoke pot or take sedatives or speed in the 1970's. I had very half-heartedly learned and practiced Transcendental Meditation, but that was before my alcoholism had really started to kick in. My disease was pretty much asymptomatic back then, but it was still there, semi-dormant, a tiger preparing to leap and devour me.

I was in the drink without the drink, a dry drunk. Two months physically drug-free did not make me mentally free. Unknown to me, I was already a prisoner of alcohol, with or without the drink. I was lost at sea sober with no guidelines and no quick reinforcement. Two months sober with a little meditation under my belt could not possibly be instantly great. There is no 'instant' sober and I was used to instant relief and escape through drugs and alcohol. Transcendental Meditation was not fast enough for me; I thought it could never work for me. Impatient? Undoubtedly. Impetuous youth? Hardly. Hardcore Alkie, Baby. Hardcore.

Drunk without the drink. Meditate on that.

(**Surimi**): *Jim's sobriety, anyone's sobriety, is fragile, Vatchi. Almost* *everyone goes through phases of trying different methods of self-discovery. Alcoholism chose Jim before Jim was able to choose something else. When the door to Jim's alcoholism swung open, "all bets were off." Now that the doors to his recovery have swung open, new paths will open. Every day is an opportunity for self-discovery, if Jim can remain responsible.*

It has taken time to still my mind instead of passing out as I used to do. To glide seamlessly from waking consciousness into a blissful night's sleep, waking up refreshed, alert and drug-free. This did not happen overnight and thankfully, I have enjoyed this slow transition. Two months of Transcendental Meditation could not have done this for me. Impetuous youth and alcohol had not run their courses.

The subtlety of simple wakefulness, the nuanced ebb and flow of my gentle breathing. This is not "addicted to chaos." This simple act of merely letting go took time after being wound up like a toy soldier, alcohol as fuel. Toy soldier, letting loose. Sober someone, letting go. This gift of 'nothing' is hard to hold, shouldn't be held and can't be held. This is not 'one day at a time.' This is one joyful moment at a time. This is now.

EVENING MEDITATION

I have proven to myself again and again that 'addicted to chaos' is another form of denial. Sobriety was such a rude, uncomfortable and painful awakening. My addiction wants me to continue down the familiar path of more: a rock, a hard place, trapped. Addicted to chaos? Hardly. Addicted to alcohol? Most assuredly.

> *"Man's main task in life is to give birth to himself, to become what he potentially is."*
> – Erich Fromm

QUESTION FOR TODAY

Which emotions get left out in the crowd and which get crowded out? Which crowd? Why?

21. **MY POWER GRID**

"Never confuse movement with action."
– Ernest Hemingway

MORNING MEDITATION

New shoes: reality doesn't seem to fit. Maybe I can grow into it. My reality hurts. Can't I have just one drink?

Right after my note to myself, "Alcohol replaced self-discovery" in the last chapter, I ran across my next blasé-blasé note to myself: "Addiction steals power," of no more apparent critical importance at the time than "pick up laundry after work" or "buy postage stamps."

Sometimes I must not listen to my own inner voice. "Addiction steals power." I find myself standing outside the house I spent my childhood in, watching that aluminum disc circling around inside its glass protective globe, clicking off the electric use for the meter reader's next visit. It was like a watch, but instead of measuring time, it was measuring power. Well, whatever power is, that's what addiction steals.

Growing up, watching "Wide World of Sports" included this phrase each and every week: "The Thrill of Victory and the Agony of Defeat." How I loved that phrase. That's how I had imagined my life would be when I was a thirteen year old, except it wouldn't be limited to sports: I wanted it all.

(**Sotto**): *You know, Jim's got a point here. The future you saw for yourself as a child looks nothing like what it turned out to be twenty or forty years later. And you can't project what you've learned since then back into the eyes and mind of the child you actually were.*

Whatever power is, that's what addiction steals. I need to repeat that to myself again. The dreams I had are gone. The dreams I have left are held closer to my chest. My old dreams eventually dissolved into the next drink, and the one after that, after that, after that.

Cold beer in a hot shower. "Time to go to work." That's what I'd say to myself, blasé-blasé.

(**Vatchi**): *"Addiction steals power." That's a good one. And power is time. Addiction. Benediction. The party's over. But Jim never, ever goes home. He'd rather black out. He'd rather pass out. "I think I died last night." That's what coming to is.*

Addiction steals power. Why my blackouts weren't more frightening is beyond me. Repeatedly drink, drunk, blackout, drink, drunk, blackout. And more drinking. Blackout. Power out. Blackouts make me sad.

I look at my watch. Time for a drink. Cold Beer. Hot Showers. Close Shaves, blasé-blasé.

(**Surimi**): *Films. Lectures. Discussions. Recovery classes. All these things have a subtle and cumulative effect. An addict and alcoholic knows his disease from the inside, but even fear of repeated negative consequences alone couldn't keep Jim sober.*

Breathe in. Breathe out. All I know is that he cannot do this alone. He never could. He never did. He never will. Breathe, Jim. Just breathe.

Suit up. Show up. Pursue this, pursue that, but finish this drink first. Kill this thirst first. Drink first, last, only and always.

If only I didn't drink last night.... I'll never drink again.... Just one.... To take the edge off.... Let me just finish this one, then we'll go.

What time is it? Where did the time go? What didn't I do? What did I say?

My Power Grid is Broken. There is no meter reader. I'm done but just keep drinking, drinking (extreme insanity). Self-discovery replaced, power stolen. Lost.

EVENING MEDITATION

Emotions induced by alcohol, unbridled emotions. Emotions twisted. Unforeseeable results. Lashing out with nerves exposed. Harmful emotions, hurt emotions. All this life perverted by alcoholism's insanity. Immediate gratification (not gratified), prolonged pain (immediate, delayed, prolonged). This is a shopping list of things I did not want or need yet could not know because all I knew was being in the throes of my disease.

Let this be my last good-bye to my last last drink. That last one was, finally, enough.

> *"The heart cannot worship what the mind rejects."*
> – Bishop John Shelby Spong

QUESTION FOR TODAY

How can I best bring balance to my life?

22. THE INTELLIGENCE OF TREES

"Hard work is a prison sentence only if it does not have meaning."
– Malcolm Gladwell

The part I have played in history is very small; close to zero shall we say. I was not a leader and I did not know that I was a follower. Out of touch with myself and definitely out of touch with any sense of "History in the Making," I received ample evidence of this recently watching a PBS special on the year 1969 as pivotal in their production called "History of Sex." I have memory of neither "The Women's Movement" boycotting the 1969 Miss America Pageant in Atlantic City (nearly a decade before I moved there), nor of the start of "The Gay Rights Movement" in the Stonewall Riots in New York's Greenwich Village. In point of fact, it wasn't until two years later, when I had turned twenty-one, that I even realized that such a thing as a gay bar even existed, small town chump change, an historical nobody, as I was.

"The Intelligence of Trees"

It took me half a century to learn of
The intelligence of trees,
Why and how their leaves know how

To lift their underbellies to the rain.
How many centuries did it take
For the trees to learn this?
How grateful should I be
For the power of observation?
When will I inherit the intelligence of trees?

How could I learn of trees, from trees, when I was becoming more and more unteachable, unreachable? The old sense that children come into this world as blank slates upon which the world will write their story and, in fact, how they will see the world, for me, an alcoholic, became seeing the world not through rose-colored glasses, but through booze-colored bar glasses.

From utopia to myopia. Adulthood, stunted. Thirty years passed. When will I inherit the healer within? Here, finally, traumatic stress and traumatic growth unite. This is my sobriety.

The daily effects of alcohol, always taking me on such an artificial high with those first few drinks, and then slowly, thereafter, down I flowed. The little kiddy-car ride of my early years of alcoholism's ups and downs, escalated slowly into an amusement ride gone haywire on the tracks of time.

I learned to medicate my alcohol with speed and valium to extend or cut short the inherent highs and lows which alcohol naturally produce. Other drugs were like the fine tuner knobs on my alcoholic TV set. Other drugs actually enabled me to imagine that I was in control, that alcohol would not control me.

Sometimes I just have to stop. Like now, right this instant. I stop dead in my tracks and simply follow my breath and any thought that enters my mind, I gently release and place any thought on a leaf to float away on my stream of mind, a cool, dark stream. Sometimes I just have to breathe and sigh, relieved just to still be alive. Right now.

(**Sotto**): *Unteachable self-medicator? I don't think he would listen to anyone when he picked up his first drink, perhaps before. And all these other drugs he's admittedly taken, Vatchi? They, too, might have been a phase, but I guess it's at least partly true, what I've heard, that the normal physical, mental and social maturity that comes with growing up stops, or at least severely slows down, once the alcohol hits the brain of an alcoholic mind.*
Christ, now he has me making excuses for him in my head.

I was the Ringmaster of a Three-Ring Circus! The Circus was my life! Escape into alcohol and drugs. I had sold myself on "For Entertainment Purposes Only." Sure. Sure. Sure. I didn't like my reality or any reality. Aldous Huxley's 'doors of perception' were safe, available and easy. I'd have been a fool not to, right? Right? I used other drugs to control (who the fuck was I kidding?) my alcohol high. I took uppers and downers only when I had gone too far sideways. I was in control. Until I wasn't.

(**Vatchi**): *In control. Out of control. The illusion of control. Only an alcoholic has this perpetually deepening illusion of control despite continually worsening negative consequences. The disease is hard at work. Social drinkers do not drink like this. "Why doesn't he just stop?" The social drinker does not understand the alcoholic insanity.*

The die may have been cast through heredity at Jim's birth, but each drink slowly soldered shut some door. Slowly. Soldered. Shut.

I falter, stumble and fall like a baby learning to walk. Walking sober, waking sober, being sober, living sober. Rivers of air flow through my nostrils. Rivers of thoughts flow through my brain. I am a living fossil of alcohol becoming more.

(**Surimi**): *Learning to unlearn his alphabet of insanity. The hieroglyphs of shot glasses. The balloons of nitrous oxide thoughts. Jim's head rises from a string held in his hand. Dreams of predators real and imaginary. Dreams that only alcoholics and rats in mazes can conjure up.*

His haze is lifting. Looking down, he sees his feet upon the ground. Except for others like himself reminding him, his disease will help him forget its own insanity. On one very serious and stable level, he can only live 'one day at a time' no matter how many of his dreams he yet may capture.

The History of Man is the power of man and I shall not live to see that next potential evolution. I am on this wheel-go-round and as my cycle reaches its completion, I hope to turn out sober.

A sober dream awake is not a drunk dream asleep. The chemical assault is over. Not today. No. Not today. No.

EVENING MEDITATION

Who do I aspire to be, what do I aspire to do? Nothing fit into the hand I was playing when I drank. That hand was always reaching for the next next drink. Now. What next? A clean and sober hand. Start there.

> *"A man is his own easiest dupe, for what he wishes to be true*
> *he generally believes to be true."*
> – Demosthenes

QUESTION FOR TODAY

Where is my eight foot tall ball of rubber bands? I know I left it somewhere, but where? Do you have it? Didn't I lend it to you? Didn't I?

23. **FIREWORKS OF DARKNESS**
WITHIN DARKNESS

"It's not denial. I'm just selective about the reality I accept."
– Bill Watterson

MORNING MEDITATION

When we stood in a circle at an A.A. meeting last night, the guy to my right was shaking like a leaf - the D.T.'s. For 30 years when asked why my hands were always shaking I had always explained that my nerves were bad. The nerve of me. What nerve!?!

It is endlessly fascinating how memory works. I can remember very clearly the fear I felt when I got off the bus from Lakewood, after leaving my very first Rehab Hospital. Just short of kicking and screaming, I literally begged to not leave the Rehab after the mandatory maximum fourteen day stay. I knew what had always happened to me in the past. I would leave a detox and despite myself, a drink would find its way into my hands that very day. That is all I knew to do when I got out. I knew how to drink, but I did not know how to not drink. All kidding aside, how could I put all drinking aside?

I was sick and tired of relapse after relapse yet, despite my best intentions, I knew I could not do it alone. My downward slide continued for years and only occasionally would I ever ask myself, "How did I get this low?" I never thought it could get worse. It was always, "this is as bad as it could get," as far as I was concerned. Then it would get worse and the refrain would repeat itself: "This is as bad as it will ever get."

Let's see now.... Which attempt at my life do I wish to rehash today? Crack-crazed crazy # 2, schizophrenic Ted, knife-wielding cop-killer alkie or.... blackout Jim? I can't let myself forget that killer, Alcohol. Or how about being the suspected murder accomplice? That was a cute, drunken police detective episode if ever there was one.

(**Sotto**): *He's lying. I don't know why, but I think he's lying. Vatchi, are you picking up on this? Why would he lie? What is he trying to hide? Is he leaving something out besides what he has forgotten? My suspicious nature is once again taking over here, Vatchi. What is he hiding? What is he holding back?*

I can't even write my own autobiography because I was hardly ever there. Rarely present in my own adult life. That old joke about not finding your obituary in the newspaper? I could hardly write my own fucking obituary, although my list of accomplishments would be short compared with what my drunken ass was unable to accomplish. I could not find myself on any given day. Obituary omissions. Swiss cheese.

And all the people who were hurt by my drinking. And all the people I do not know my drinking hurt. And all the life I could have lived to fill the empty spaces blackouts once inhabited. And all the and and and and ands....

Fireworks of darkness within darkness, implosions. The ultimate conclusion to the Big Bang Theory. The explosive fact, black on black on black, imploded.

Jeff Black... forty years retired from the military, well into his seventies, wearing a bad rug. Drunken New Year's Eve. He tells me he just came out of the closet and has not, had not, ever, ever kissed a man. His whole life a denial of desire. Desire unfulfilled.

(**Vatchi**): *I'll tell you what he's trying to hide, Sotto. He's trying to hide from himself that for him, his desire for alcohol, his addiction to alcohol, replaced all other desires, finally, and nearly, the desire to live. More of addiction is less of everything else. The denial continues. The denial changes hands. Sobriety continues. Life goes on. Time takes time. The punishment for addiction is time served. A daily reprieve.*

Enough is enough. Move on, Jim. Whatever the lie, whatever he's hiding, Sotto, forgive him.

All our lives are filled with unfulfilled potentials, not just we who are alcoholics and addicts. That's life on life's terms. We would all, each and all, splinter into fragments trying to achieve mutually exclusive potentialities.

When I reached a fork in my road, the knife of addiction chose for me. I know that must sound like an excuse to a non-addict 'normie' but initially, eventually, the power of choice is removed and responsibility for my sobriety wasn't learned until after several relapses. The stigma and shame of admitting my alcoholism kept me out there before I got sober and the shame of relapse keeps many (but didn't keep me) from returning to the rooms of recovery. The rooms of recovery give many the strength they need to regain a stronger foothold in sobriety. Relapse for me was a baby learning to walk. Falling was learning to walk. Relapse was part of learning to live sober. Not easy. Never easy. Not like taking candy from a baby.

Sometimes my sobriety is as simple as a sigh of relief and sometimes that is enough, more than enough. So much of the debris of my past is littering the wayside, never formed memories, blackouts stacked upon blackouts in a pyramid of days.

I am not drowning in self-pity. I'm not looking for pity from others. This is how it worked out and today is about not repeating the same insanities again. There's plenty of room for new mistakes.

I need help to remind me that I am entitled to just this one thing: another day sober. And entitlement is not exactly the exact word because I must work for this. Getting and staying drunk became hard work for me. So too, getting and staying sober is work. My daily reprieve is worked for, sought after, earned.

(**Surimi**): *Jim must join the Witness Protection Program, change his identity. "The person he was will drink again." That's how they say it in the rooms of recovery. His "fireworks of darkness within darkness" wait only for its fuse to be relit for another implosion to begin.*

Although unthinkable, a relapse is not impossible, as his experience has shown. Yes, Vatchi, as you've already said, "the punishment for addiction is time served."

Addiction is its own punishment. Judge and Jury are now dismissed. Our culture itself must need be changed, Vatchi, Sotto. But that, my friends, is for some other book.

I can remember very clearly the fear I felt when I got off the bus from Lakewood after leaving my very first rehab hospital. I'm learning that delicate balance of remembering my past so that I neither repeat it, nor get trapped in my memory of it. I need to spend a little time in Now. The harmony of Now. Now, that soothing balm I forget I always carry with me.

Oh, wait. Here it is. Now.

EVENING MEDITATION

Keeping it simple: Alcohol is a depressant. Sobriety is an anti-depressant. Alcoholism is insanity. Recovery is reality. In addiction, the doors of perception become the doors of deception. All, over-simplifications. All, simply true, mostly true, sometimes true.

"Sometimes a majority simply means that all the fools
are on the same side."
– Claude McDonald

QUESTION FOR TODAY

What is the radioactive half-life of addiction?

24. **TRIPLE-DIGIT DRUNK**

"A mind stretched by a new idea never shrinks back to
its original dimensions."
– Oliver Wendell Holmes

MORNING MEDITATION
At some point, I reached the point where using only served the purpose of postponing withdrawal. Is that what pointless means?

Breathing with my head turned sideways on the exhale, only breathing inward when I faced someone directly. I had to try different kinds of breathing exercises after my usual heavy nights of drinking. I no longer got hangovers, but hoped to be the Zen master of deceit, bad breath-wise. Turn head. Exhale. Face person again, inhaling only. Speak. Get a concerned look on my face, as if I was listening. No morning meetings. Do not schedule any morning meetings, if possible. Turn head away. Exhale.

Who did I think I was kidding? For nearly a year, I lived in daily fear of anyone smelling alcohol on my breath, especially first thing in the morning, when I would reek of alcohol most strongly. This was during the time I worked at Resorts International Casino Hotel as an Advertising Coordinator. Merv Griffin owned Resorts at that time and I occasionally worked with Merv filming television commercials. I even got Merv to autograph one of the books he'd written at an Employee Pep Rally, of sorts, when he first took over the property.

One of my major resentments while working there was coming up with the idea of presenting Merv with 'the World's Largest Birthday Card' signed by over a thousand of Resorts' employees and presented to him at a private party to which I was not invited. Not enough to piss off the Pope perhaps, but enough to piss me off completely. Only the next higher tier of employees were invited to that party despite it having been my idea in the first place. Is that the fur on my neck I just felt stand straight up?

I'm over it now, all these many years later, obviously, but I use it to illustrate how alcohol seemed capable of making me hold a resentment longer, harder, wider and deeper than ever would seem otherwise possible. I drank like a motherfucker over that one: alcoholic insanity.

Some (but not all) of my old resentments while drinking seem silly to me now. Believe that one and I'll tell you another one.

I could not let go of my emotions when I was in the drink. A selfish, drunken child in the drink. That was me. My resentments in the drink are a potent sober reminder of the importance of my remaining sober. I am not in the drink today, but in a curious way the drink is still in me (fur on my neck standing straight up). My mind was so alcohol addled by the end of my one year tenure at Resorts that I don't clearly remember the controlled crisis that the Human Resources Department was apparently trying to create by getting me to speak to a psychiatrist in Brigantine about my drinking problem. In retrospect, I suppose they were trying to save me from my disease by forcing me to confront it. My ego could beat my drinking problem. Or so I thought. They probably imagined that I would fall on my knees in gratitude as they whisked me off to a rehab somewhere. The best I could do was promise her, the dear Psychiatrist, that I would try to control my drinking by limiting myself to only six drinks a day, that being only beer.

The "Beer Experiment" did not last even one night. Beer was far too weak for me. I couldn't drink it fast enough. So, after the sixth beer, I decided that drinking beer was like drinking nothing, but certainly, I could limit myself to six scotch on the rocks. The beer simply wouldn't count. And, as the story goes, after the sixth scotch, I said "To hell with this beer experiment." So I then went on to get fucked up royally, my routine at that time, that night, or any night. This King deserved another Crown Royal (or something equally potent).

At that time, my attitude was "Screw Resorts!" Rather than confronting my disease, my part-time employer at that time, Pal's & the Other Room, immediately put me on a full-time schedule, and I was off to the races. Yes, I was off to the races and I drank like a horse. My Triple Crown might be another three day drinking binge. Might be? Was.

(**Sotto**): *Christmas City, Batman! He must have just taken two breaths to write all this. Clearly clever. Clearly deluded. He thinks he's so much better now. But is he really, all drinking aside?*

This is pissing me off. My mind is wandering. Talking about myself seems fruitful at times, but it can piss me off, too. What can it prove? How might it help? Self-doubt, then. Self-doubt, now. The emotions undistorted by alcohol. Rubber-necking my own train-wrecked, derailed life. Oh, what's the use. I may as well drink.

Derailed, directionless and drunk. What the fuck.

I examine the tarot card carefully, placing it squarely on the tabletop and instantly forget it. The past does not read my future, but if I don't forget it, hopefully I won't repeat it. I will be okay now. And the tarot card reads...

(**Vatchi**): *You spoke too quickly, Sotto, baby. Moments of clarity and then... kaboom! He's holding his sobriety close to his chest. He's clenching. A subtle, sober panic. Then nothing. This is the establishment of a new rhythm in Jim's life.*

The end of the beginning.

And the tarot card reads....

Holy Cow! "Time to Dine," the name of my weekly news segment on local Channel 53-TV every Friday. Like an advertisement for my former self, popping up out of nowhere. Before Merv. Forget chronological order. Without order, how could I possibly have chronological order?

Holy Wow! "Time to Dine," thirty years later I finally see the irony. By the time I had that TV show, my days of dining were clearly already over. This raging alcoholic did not dine anymore at all by that time. I only ate after I was already fucked up (except for taping the show days before). Food screwed with my alcohol delivery system. Most of the time I did not eat a single bite until I was already plastered. That was normal. On an empty stomach I could more easily control my intake of alcohol. I required the proper dosage, properly administered (guzzled), uninterrupted by food. I had power over my alcohol and it was manageable. That, of course, was one of alcohol's biggest lies, the illusion of control. Eating first was like taking a commuter train when I clearly wanted only the Express Train. This illusion of control will probably only be understood by another alcoholic.

"Time to Dine?" No! Time to get fucked up, then gorge, sometimes in a blackout, sometimes not. "Time to Dine?" Never. Time to drink? Always, and, what seemed forever.

(**Surimi**): *Rhythm of the Dance, Gentlemen. That's what early sobriety is like. Almost everyone has two left feet when they first get sober. A life lived under the influence isn't going to be easy to change. Biorhythms, brain rhythms, Rhythm of the Dance, gentlemen. Learning to live sober is a whole new dance. Everything is changing, and at different rates of progression. There will be setbacks and missteps. Rhythm of the Dance.*

One hundred percent drunk, one hundred percent of the time. That is the goal of my disease. A tsunami of alcohol. A volcano, tornado, hurricane, avalanche, flood. Every and all disasters, natural and unnatural. Not one percent alcoholic. Not ten percent. Triple-digit, one hundred percent alcoholic. Triple-digit. Nothing less than nothingness.

"Hello, Police? I'd like to report a theft. My identity has been stolen... No not my I.D. Not my Social Security card. Not my credit cards. My identity has been stolen... When? I don't know. If I knew, maybe I could have stopped it...."

Okay, Jim, stop this insanity. This tarot card reading is over. The gypsy has gone home. Reshuffle.

EVENING MEDITATION

I never wanted to get sober. Getting sober sucks. Getting sober is worse than drinking in certain respects. (Why did I relapse? Why didn't I listen?) But when drinking is slowly killing you, it's the only option left. And liquor is not quicker when it's you hanging on for dear life and always wanting, needing more. Alcohol was my enemy. Alcohol was my friend. Alcohol was everything and I was nothing in the end. I did not think that I could ever get sober. And stay sober.

"Every recovery meeting is an intervention between me and the first drink."
– Anonymous

QUESTION FOR TODAY

What will stop a Swedish horse?

25. **OBVIOUSLY OBLITERATED**

"Sometimes the truth of a thing is not so much in the think of it,
as in the feel of it."
— Stanley Kubrick

MORNING MEDITATION

The door to the prison of addiction opened and I was afraid to leave. Fear of leaving was fear of living, because I had not lived beyond that door for decades.

My living in Atlantic City began as a vacation. I came to get away from a failed relationship back home. I'd never really been away by myself before and twenty-four hour open bars helped me drown my then recent past in liquor. The collateral damage from drowning my past was destroying what was then my present. "Prone to occasional blackouts" would come to be a gross understatement, as I eventually would blackout nearly every night, never knowing if I got home by Jitney, bus or cab.

Some people drink and become like Jekyll or Hyde. I was Jim and Jim drunk. Jim was separated from his self (Is that what he wanted?). Separated from self. Me and my bottle were inseparable (but I was "separable?" WTF?) Nothing ventured, nothing gained (everything squandered). What's your name again? What's your name again (nothing will stick)? No memory could form. Nothing to stick (what's your name? what's your name? what's your name?).

(**Sotto**): *Jumbled lies. He's incoherent, not making sense. Give him a drink, buy him a drink, shove him a drink, lie him a drink, give him a drink on me, Vatchi. Give Jim a drink on me. There's an undercurrent here. Drunk chic. Drunk sheep. Drunk cool. Drunk fool. His Crazytown is getting home.*

Somehow, pathetic is a little too pathetic to feel sorry for. Vatchi? I think I'm through with Jim. Now, I'm ready to move on.

I really have close to nothing left from my drunken past. No addresses, no phone numbers. Most copyright forms and advertising samples from my advertising career are fairly obliterated. Close to nothing left from my alcoholic ruins, my Pompeii. No bodies preserved in lava. No artifacts. Or facts.

(**Vatchi**): *Your feelings for Jim's alcoholic destruction must be tempered somehow, Sotto. Addiction is a disease, Sotto. It changes the riverbeds of the alcoholic's brain, of the alcoholic's life. It dredges out new gorges and leaves gaping holes in peoples' lives, Sotto. Forget Jim altogether, Sotto. Let Jim live as an example. Part of him is forever dead. Part of him will never live. There is no whole Jim left. A hole is in him that only his new, sober life can fill. He is but an example. Too pathetic to feel sorry for? Perhaps, Sotto. But he can still feel pathetic and I think he does. Crazytown is in his head. It need not be in yours.*

What with all my blackouts and years of slowly going down the tube, my geographical self truly is an archeological dig. It's like, "we know that dinosaurs nested their young..." with much of my past. Occasionally I'll say to myself things like, "I know I was in a recording studio the night John Lennon was shot" and then run across a date somewhere to sort of figure things out. Which radio or television jingle was I producing that night? I have no idea.

See what I mean, jelly bean? I'm still digging up clues from thirty, twenty, even fifteen years ago. Excavator alligator.

(**Surimi**): *"Dinosaur Bore." Drunk as a Whore. So much of Jim: Drowning, sinking, floating, dying. I don't even know if I'm making this up, but Jim is like that guy in India with the eight-foot tall ball of rubber bands. Interesting, but useless. Trivia. Each day's drunk beating some previous record. Predictable, yet beyond understanding.*

Turning around an ocean liner. This is Jim's life. It will take this: Improvisation, Strict Rules and Crossed Fingers.

That just popped up out of nowhere. Digging for clues from my past. "Excavator Alligator" was part of the children's book I wrote called *Animal Zoop*. Like alphabet soup, but it was an animal dictionary in rhyming couplets. Seventy two different animals like "Billy Goat Afloat" and "Dalmatian Flirtation" right up through "Newsreel Seal" and "Underground Basset Hound". "Mc Graw-Hill Alcohol Swill" should have been one, too, because I was that animal. An Alcoholic Animal. An animal destroyed, defeated. An Alcoholic Animal. That's me.

Christ, I worked so hard and played too hard. But alcohol was harder, so, so much harder than my work or play. Hard Liquor was so, so, so very much harder. Animal Zoop took place in my life in 1984, for real, George Orwell. This was Gulliver's Travels. This was my Electric Kool-Aid Acid Test and I failed and I passed out and I woke up again to drink-drink-drink again and again. My own drunken past helps float my sobriety boat today.

Hot damn. What're ya gonna do?

X-ray Stingray

Yackety-Yak Yak

Zestful Nest Full

Alcohol became my life, took over my life. It is not fear of my past or fears from my past that have slowed the pace of my recovery here. This is a quiet pace. My past unravels as my future unfurls. That's about as well as I can express it. I am at a time of patience, a rest stop. Neural connections reorganizing. Irrational desires supplanted by rational hopes.

I cannot rush past my recovery. My recovery is today.

EVENING MEDITATION

Loose ends with no center made for a very loopy life. The only thing that connected anything was alcohol. Every day I woke up to a pile of questions that had no answers.

> *"We learn something every day, and lots of times it's that what we learned the day before was wrong."*
> – Bill Vaughn

QUESTION FOR TODAY

Didn't you used to be somebody?

26. POMPEII IN MOTION

"The world breaks us all. Afterward, some are stronger
at the broken places."
– Ernest Hemmingway

MORNING MEDITATION
Faith without works is... a relapse?

The train station in Philadelphia is quite beautiful, despite being radioactive from all the granite from which it is composed. Somehow it reminds me of a mausoleum, just peopled by the living rather than the dead. Pompeii in motion.

My memory is so faded, so distorted, by alcohol, by the crush of life. Even where the facts may seem to lack a certain accuracy, the feelings often times are intact, if distorted. Distorted by alcohol, then. Distorted by my memory, now. Losing things because of my drinking and then drinking more to get over the loss. Then drinking to forget drinking over those losses. I wallowed in the pain, then. Am I wallowing in the memory of the pain, now?

The last time I was in Philadelphia's train station I was plastered almost beyond recognition. But then, unexpectedly, I was recognized by Trent, who spotted me in my complete and utter drunken state and instantly fled as if leaving the scene of an accident. When I'm drinking I seem to only know how low I've sunk through the observations of others' words or looks. My disease blinds me to the progression of my own disease. The drunken language of my disease constructs a progressively inelegant Tower of Babel. Even a rat would tire of the alcoholic maze and haze in which I lived.

Trent, his name is Trent. I was the alcoholic debris he wisely chose to leave behind. Drunk and disorderly as a public offense is one thing. But drunk and disorderly is more often a private affair, the emotional hurricane passing through the lives of those around an alcoholic. Now seeing him several years after he wrote me out of his life, I saw by one quick look in his eyes before he fled the scene that I had far exceeded his expectations of how low my alcoholism would eventually take me.

I am the unchangeable history in the lives of many other people's past. Fact, pure and simple. I can almost hear an announcement over the train station public address system. "The train to Reality has been cancelled." Losing things because of my drinking and then drinking more to get over the loss. Or did I say that already? Doing the same things, saying the same things, again and again with the same results which a drink won't quite fix. Repeat. Repeat. Repeat. "For whom the bell tolls...."

(**Sotto**): *"Wallowing," he says. For some reason, Vatchi, I'm getting the picture of a hippopotamus in a pool of mud. Sad when the irreconcilable difference is alcoholism untreated. Jim seems stuck in looking at this and I feel stuck in wanting to look away. Give me the picture of a hippo in a pool of mud instead. Not Rodin's "The Thinker" and certainly not Jim's insanity.*

Trapped in my drunkenness, waiting for a train. Going from point A to point B was measured in drinks. New York to Philadelphia: five drinks. Philadelphia to Atlantic City: three drinks. Life measured in Alcohol: the "X" Factor. Factor the "X" into everything. How many drunken call outs equal one getting fired? How many drunken lies, promises and broken promises, excuses and inexcusable actions until a relationship unravels? This is life measured in a retrospective I could not measure then. Alcohol measured me in a row, one drink following the others, ducks in a row on an amusement pier, shot down by a water pistol, no prize every time. People rush to catch a train in getting somewhere else. Once they arrive at their destination, they most often do not move as quickly. They slow down. They have arrived.

Drunk in the train station this one time was like being awake in a drunk dream: Trent ran because he could not scream.

Granite. Alcohol. Pompeii in motion.

(**Vatchi**): *He's not wallowing, just slightly submerged, the hippo's eyes just above the waterline, Sotto. This hippo's feet (in my underwater camera) are not quite touching the bottom.*

That famous painting, "The Scream"? That was Trent's face when he saw me in the train station a few years after extricating me from his life.

Yes, his was a silent scream.

Approximations of reality. That's what getting sober is. It's like coming to and mumbling, "Where the fuck am I?" Slowly, slowly coming to. That's early sobriety. Trying to approximate a reality called sobriety, this new subject which I knew nothing about. Not quite at the intersection of time and place. A bad 3-D movie, red and blue plastic lenses, scratched from wear. Scratched from "Where?" Black and white, a discolored color. Black and white rehashed. Something, everything, slightly askew. Mismatched. Reality uncoordinated in this new state.

Sobriety. Time takes fucking time and if reality is only finding your centered self, so be it. Nearly Forty Years of Drunken Wandering. Surely, Enough.

(**Surimi**): *An inexcusable paraphrase, but here it is: A fish does not know water, a bird does not know air and Jim will never, ever know himself.*

And you, Sotto. And you, Vatchi. You and You and you are my hippopotami.

All I have is now. All I need is now. All I am is now. And that's okay. And that is good. It's understood: The world is still and I am moved. Now is a food and I am full.

Trent ran from me, his face a silent scream, and me, too drunk to follow him, as he would have expected. I could not ask for forgiveness drunk. Drunken promises. Broken dreams. Friendships ruined. Broken bottles, lies, hearts. A silent scream. This must have happened to a stranger because it could not have happened to me. On a run. On the run. When would I trip and fall? Or had I already fallen, running with a tray full of drinks, a lifetime full of drinks?

EVENING MEDITATION

Denial was my Tootsie-Pop, the caramel of addiction within this hardball sugar coating. Gumballs, lollipops and cocaine. Wrapped too tight, too loose to explain. Blackouts rolled in coconut. Or cocaine. How did I survive this? How will I survive this? I cannot, should not, must not do this alone.

> *"The ego is not master of its own house."*
> – Sigmund Freud

QUESTION FOR TODAY

Where do you turn when you are your own "people, places and things"?
Why does that have such a familiar ring?

27. FUCK YOU, GENTLE READER

"Whoa" means nothing to a Swedish horse.
– Stacy at onesentence.org

MORNING MEDITATION
Now that I know that I need help, I don't feel so helpless.

Day 27. As good a time or place as any to hit bottom. There. I hit bottom. That's it. There's nothing here. There is no here. There is no nothing. There is no is. There it is. Done.

(**Sotto**): *I want to continue where Jim leaves off sometimes. There's more to come, I know, but why couldn't it just stop here?*

Pack up and go home, everybody. The show's over. The fat lady will not sing. Go home. Done.

Fuck you, Gentle Reader. Passive-Aggressive enough for you? Damn! When I hit bottom, what resentments I had. Not for people in my past. For the fucking therapists at Lakewood, my first real hospital-slash-rehab (I don't include regular drunken hospital stays and detox stopovers).

"Write a Gratitude List," they kept saying.

"Alright, Cocksuckers," I said to myself, "I'm grateful that you're a fucking asshole. I'm grateful that this fucking Gratitude List sucks." - That kind of thing.

Pumped up on Librium, I'm surprised I could react so strongly to anything. Resentment, outward. Feeling, inward. Mostly, I didn't. Couldn't, wouldn't react. Too much effort would have been required to give a shit about not giving a shit. But I was grateful for my resentments. They gave me something to feel.

Sobriety sucks. Fuck you. Thank you one passive-aggressive fucking ton. Am I nicer now? Or are my resentments more veiled? I resent my sober self, forced by my sobriety to raise myself, to grow up, to raise myself up. Hungry, Angry, Lonely, Tired. I resent that my triggers are triggers. Sometimes I really, really have to just let it go. But bad habits make letting go of no longer needed emotions difficult.

Letting go.

As a child, I saw a chicken get its head chopped off and its body slip out of my Uncle's hand. That chicken ran headless, down a deep slope and into the swimming pool. Blood everywhere. My Uncle's hand let go.

Letting go is hard to do.

A pool of liquor awaits me.

(**Vatchi**): *I really wish that Jim would not curse. In the end, it is really so inexpressive. Curse words are like hiccups. Unnecessary interruptions. Have you noticed, Sotto, that when Jim curses, it shows which emotions he does not yet have a handle on? He either curses, stops, or changes subjects when he hits an emotional roadblock. At least his sober insanity is a little more predictable than the insanity of his alcoholism. A dope with hope. That's Jim.*

A pool of liquor. Bigger than a vat of bathtub gin. This is Prohibition of the most difficult kind. Liquor, not illegal to me, just deadly. I must prohibit the onslaught of my disease. I must not lose my head or I will lose my body. The bloody, headless chicken headed into the swimming pool, senselessly twitching straight down. There is no shallow end. Just a deep end dead end. No exit. No light at the end of my tunnel.

I must learn to let go and to not let go, a balancing act of the sober kind. The voices of my disease call out for me to drink. Alcoholics Anonymous has become my lifeguard. Control and letting go in balance.

Christ, I really do need help. I really, really, really do. Anybody got a funnel to pour myself through?

(**Surimi**): *Emotions. This will not be an easy trip. This sober road is unfamiliar. To stumble and yet not fall. Regain your footing. Jim needs a strong foundation on which to build a sober life, starting from almost nothing. Yet, this can be done. He can do this.*

Getting sober is like getting out of prison, I suppose. Recidivism and relapse seem to be nearly the same thing. The support I needed early on I eventually renounced, refused, denied, ignored. I could not stay afloat alone. My vessel, solo, overturned. My sippy cup is collapsible and so was I.

Chronic, supersonic gin and tonic. This I could not do alone.
    All-consuming alcohol consumed me.
    Thirsty little fucker.

EVENING MEDITATION

Diplomatically searching for others equally high, we (my disease and I) would manufacture memories out of blackouts like free-range intoxicated chickens.

> *"Delusions of grandeur make me feel a lot better about myself."*
>   – Jane Wagner

QUESTION FOR TODAY

How is it that tomorrow never comes but that the next drink always did?

28. **DIDN'T YOU USED TO BE SOMEBODY?**

*"There are three mysteries in the world: the air to the bird,
the water to the fish, and man to himself."*
– Hindu expression

MORNING MEDITATION
Alcoholism is the disease of greed. Its progressive desire for more is its own punishment.

Just for fun, let's pretend that this is my first day sober.

There. Now, wasn't that fun?

(**Sotto**): *I knew there'd be some kind of twist here. Like, "here's a good spot to throw a monkey wrench into this whole barrel of monkeys." I'm starting to get to know this Anders guy. I didn't say like him. I said "know him."*

A good reputation is a burden. Achievement measured by other people's expectations. The existential nausea of seeking approval from others whom you condemn. Now, there's a reason to drink. And then there's that, that wanting and needing to drink with no reason at all except that the soul of alcohol is "more."

"Didn't you used to be somebody?" I still hear that occasionally (ringing in my ears if nowhere else). And the big, big irony in all of this, is that there's a very good chance that the gentleman that asked me that question initially, could be asked that very same question by the guy sitting on the bar stool next to him today.

I didn't know then that I was very near finding some bottom, one bottom, a bottom. But I know now that what I need to do is to move forward, and to build on whatever little life I have left. Shared courage is where I find the strength in my recovery. My alcoholic mind left alone is headed for relapse because it's crowded up here in what remains of my brain. There are a thousand forms of denial in recovery but the one denial that has always doomed me to failure and to relapse is trying to stay sober unaided and alone, not admitting my need for fellowship with others in recovery. I don't think I will ever be smart enough to go it alone because addiction has formed a partnership with my brain. It has been compromised. It seems that way because it is that way. Maybe not for others and for all, but for me that is the way it is. It is.

(**Vatchi**): *Like I said before, he likes changing it up. Changing subjects, emotions, perspectives. Sometimes a tool for hiding from himself, and, sometimes, a tool to allow his self-knowledge to be revealed. Sotto, time changes everything, sober or not, recovery or not, alcoholic or not. Flip-flop, whiz-bang, done. There's a certain rhythm to it, perhaps not obvious at first. There is a rhythm to all of this.*

NEWSFLASH: Cocaine sped me to my bottom. The more cocaine I took, the more alcohol I could drink. The two substances fed off each other, a feeding frenzy, my brain being the main course. Already plummeting well enough on my own, cocaine and other dry goods sped the process.

"Upside Down, Sideways, Here I Go Again" coulda, shoulda, woulda been a song to sing as I was doing my thing and my thing was doing it's thing to me. Easy, Peasy, Louisey!

For me, Alcohol, in combinations with any and many other drugs, was the Quicker Fucker-Upper (Sorry, Bounty Paper Towels). Cocaine sped me to my bottom. Hallelujah! "Do Not Take With Alcohol." Hallelujah! Today I am grateful for everything that sped me to hit bottom. Everything.

(**Surimi**): *These are the tremors after the earthquake, the unsure fear which asks "what next?" This is early sobriety. This is the drunken sailor on dry land, trying to walk after a thirty-year Big Gulp of alcohol. This is possibility. This is change. This is partnership with sobriety and with others in recovery. It will take whatever it takes for these tremors to subside.*

Uppers, downers, inside-outers: They turned me in, they turned me out; they turned me into sauerkraut. And when they stopped one feeling, they stopped all feelings. A numb beheading would not make me flinch. A yard of tears for me were one dry inch. Drugs of yellow, drugs of red. Black and white and candy-striped. The melting pot of drugs that my world dipped me in would be my gateway to a new reality, or so I thought. Instead, instead,

instead. I went from being intoxicated to being toxic. Hatred of that place in me stops me here. I believe I need to cry.

Now.

Stop.

EVENING MEDITATION

An accumulating mountain of evidence did not slow my descent. There were no intersections, no neural connections, no one plus one equals two. Ever-increasing orders of magnitude: Crash, then burn. Repeat. Repeated. Repeat.

> *"I find that the harder I work the more luck I seem to have."*
> – Thomas Jefferson

QUESTION FOR TODAY

Why are delusions so sadly less than infinite?

29. REUPTAKE ALCOHOL, DELUSIONAL EFFECTS

"When I do good, I feel good. And that is my religion."
– Abraham Lincoln

MORNING MEDITATION

A faith so strong that some must have only serves to alienate me. I go deaf ear. Don't preach at me, and stop me in my track if I do so. That's what I pray. My prayer, my shield, my silence, my division.

I will become power. The cocaine will keep me awake and enliven the best that is within me. And the drink, it will calm me. The cocaine will help me remember and these blackouts will end. I lived there somewhere, sometime. When?

I'm standing outside the Chez Paree Discotheque on New York Avenue. It is 1979. I took the Quaalude twenty minutes ago....

My dark tan and Summer Tourist clothes make me stand out in the crowd. I would ignore this person if I were to meet him today. I would think he was a pompous asshole. But if I waited thirty minutes, I would have pity on this pathetic gentleman. In thirty minutes he would be carried out by two bouncers, plastered, wasted, coked out, luded out....

I will be confronting him again and again as I look backward at my life, as disconnected from my past now as I was disconnected from the present, then.

I sigh, and plod forward in my sobriety....

(**Sotto**): *Vatchi, I get this. The spiritual disconnect, his floating adrift, lost. Just short of grief. I can almost hear his plaintive sigh. There is so much*

94

sadness here.

Getting clean and sober is probably the hardest thing I never chose to do. Getting better, at first, was sometimes as painful, and sometimes more painful than hitting bottom. At least when I hit bottom, I was anesthetized.

Chronic pain. Chronic relapse from pain. Nothing and the absence of nothing. How I got here took years of suffering, relapse after relapse, before feeling this unbelievably good. You will have to believe that I have to stop right here, right now, to give my thanks... for air.

(**Vatchi**): *"His plaintive sigh." Sotto, even you can be funny sometimes. Half of human bones are in the hands and feet. And in your case, Sotto, I think the other half are in your head. Your brain is sometimes nothing more than bubble-wrapped thought balloons. Jim, if he could hear you now, might actually be amused. Your opinion of him has changed a little over time, Sotto. I hope you're beginning to understand that.*

I'm not a Doctor. I can't talk "reuptake inhibitor." But "reuptake alcohol?" That I know. The boundaries of my early sobriety kept changing, like the undulating circumference of an amoeba under the microscope. "Reuptake alcohol." Inhibit nothing. Class dismissed. Life destroyed. Cause of relapse? The first 50,000 drinks. The illusion of cause. Delusional effect.

(**Surimi**): *The illusion of cause. The delusional self, haunted by possibilities, seeking escape. Addiction to alcohol has changed every boundary in Jim's life. Around eighteen years since he first got sober the first time. Invulnerable. Invincible. These lies have been exposed. Now Jim is mending fences, building bridges. He is blind. Alcohol has blinded him.*
    Illusion is cause.

All of this. All of this is the insanity of getting well. Getting well is insanity reversed (almost). Will the 12-steps of recovery reverse my insanity? Pull a rabbit out of my hat? Out of my brain? Out of my insane? Plod. Trudge. Plod. Trudge. Limping toward recovery. My bar tan is fading, fading. Pilot to co-pilot: "Assessing damage. Over and out."

EVENING MEDITATION

Oh, Alcohol, Alcohol, Alcohol. Can you not even be the anti-hero you fashioned me after? Must I have separate hatred for you; separate from this monster me you have created? Bartenders are the Priests and Goddesses of my god, Alcohol.
Drink, drank, drunk. Fill this vessel of me which can contain only all of you, my dear god, Alcohol. Cheers. Amen. Almost dead.

"It only takes one person to change your life – you."
– Ruth Casey

QUESTION FOR TODAY

Can an apple carry you?

30. **HAMMER AND CHISEL**

"Rich man down and poor man up - they are still not even."
– Yiddish proverb

MORNING MEDITATION
Back in the day, incurable meant hopeless. Today, there is hope in recovery.

The year is 1980. I need money. It is three o'clock in the morning. I'm staggering on the sidewalk by the ATM machine. I fake a $300.00 cash deposit into my personal checking account and am amazed that my account thirty seconds later allows me access to the money that never existed. I withdraw $200.00, stumble over to the intersection and flag a cab.

I did this. I remember doing this. I was not in the blackout mode I would eventually find myself in before the night would be over. This would be Saturday night and there would always be Sunday morning. My Sunday mornings, almost consistently for close to a decade, were pretty much the same: wake up with only four or five hours sleep (Sleep? If passing out is sleep, then yes, sleep). My resolve, after trying to slack my thirst, would be to pick up the New York Times and the Atlantic City Press and maybe Rolling Stone, Advertising Age, or Interview Magazines and proceed to any of a number of favorite watering holes and by ten o'clock Sunday morning, I'd be off to the races.

The best laid plan (of mice and me) was to get as drunk as possible as soon as possible so that I could go to bed as early as possible and get as much sleep as possible so that Monday morning would be possible. On this particular Monday, following what I knew would turn into a showdown with the bank, I was wringing with sweat even more profusely than usual.

(**Sotto**): *I don't like where this seems to be headed.*

I can't let my past, my memory of my active addiction, pull me into some kind of inescapable vortex, to relive it all, again, through another drink. The past itself, my mere memory of it, can turn into a drink if I am not careful. Or I can live forever in the memory of my past and find it impossible to move forward. It would be a mistake to ignore my past. I must look at it. Hold it up to the light. Examine it. Then, let it go.

"Don't worry, Jim. You can let it go," I say to myself.

"Don't worry. I'll be back to haunt you," my dear Alcohol replies.

(**Vatchi**): *Yes, Sotto, something bad has happened here. Jim can and can't face the music here. He can and can't go on here. He's in a cul-de-sac here and does not know it. There is no room in the present for this Jim. His past has succeeded in crowding him in. And out. There are no answers for him here. These are disconnected memories. This past, his past, is a secret society. "Can I become a member?" This is what he is thinking, I think. "Can I become a member of my past?" This is the question I hear Jim asking himself.*

Reeking of alcohol, first thing on Monday, I head for the bank, alcohol more on my head than the consequences of alcohol. I'm called up to a bank officer's office after two weeks earlier having conned him out of a substantial loan so that I could afford my employee payroll expenses and equipment payments and office rent and utilities and, and, and....

I can't remember his name, so let me just call him Fred. "Fred" informed me that they have me on videotape "visibly intoxicated" (as I remember him calling it). "Jim, what you did, making a false deposit, and having it be captured on camera is all the proof we would need to have you arrested...."

Blah. Blah. Blah. If it hadn't been that I had just talked the bank into a loan of several thousand dollars, which Fred knew could never be paid were I arrested... Blah. Blah. Blah. I'm thinking "what do I have to do or say to get out of this one." I'm thinking, "I'll never do this again." I'm thinking, "I need a drink."

I can't talk. I can't face this now. I've got to stop this. I can't face this now. I could drown out the pain caused by liquor with more liquor. Mask the pain with an alcohol-induced haze. I can deal with now, now. I just can't with then, now. Gotta stop then, now. Fuck this, then now. This is fucked up. Then. And now.

(**Surimi**): *Sometimes, I just don't know what to think. Jim is full of confusion and doubt. He's reliving much of his past. He needs to go there, to sort* *through this. But it will not be easy for him to do. Persistence. Alcoholism and addiction do not take breaks. "Keep it simple" sounds simple, but some problems are irreducibly complex.*

"You can't turn a pickle back into a cucumber." Many truisms, such as this, famous in the rooms of recovery, scratch the surface of truth. It's easy to scratch the surface. What Jim needs is a hammer and chisel!

My past can suck me back into the drink again as easily as my disease can. Guilt, remorse, fear. All kinds of emotions from my past can suck me back into the kneejerk responses of my past. Drink the emotions away rather than deal with them. In the past all my coping skills were wrapped up in alcohol, like chocolates wrapped in tinfoil. The only tool in my toolbox was alcohol. My old toolbox is 100% poison. I am 100% alcoholic. I can never drink again. And the anxiety of 'never' makes me want to pick up. The anxiety of 'always stay sober' makes me want to pick up. "Always" and "Never" are too absolute. The only absolute I ever knew was Absolut Vodka.

EVENING MEDITATION

Like certain herbs, rosemary enhancing the flavor of lamb, for example, I thought alcohol and drugs would enhance and enrich my life. I did not suspect that they would become the main course, and thus, malnourished, my life would go rancid, distorted, dying on the vine.

> *"The world is full of people looking for spectacular happiness while they snub contentment."*
> – Doug Larson

QUESTION FOR TODAY

Can anything be empty? Is emptiness a thing? Can carrying nothing be a full load?

PART II
THE DECONSTRUCTION

31. UNNATURAL DISASTER

"The unexamined life is not worth living."
– Socrates

MORNING MEDITATION
My last relapse taught me that my brain wants more alcohol than my body can endure. Ever.

When I was very young, say six or eight, I didn't know the difference between a toy soldier and a dead soldier. Cowboys and Indians was more what we played in my neighborhood. And no one volunteered to be an Indian.

And then the flood came. It changed my life. Not at the time. At the time, I just moved from the front porch of my Aunt and Uncle's house to inside the first floor as the waters rose. Then, up to the second floor, quickly, as told, when the waters escalated.

A life-changing event, that seemed to have changed nothing. Not at that time. Not at that age.

Up to the attic when the waters continued rising. Toy soldiers, dead soldiers, seemingly the same. Homes swept off their foundations and obliterated. Years later, the exposed basements became my eight foot deep sandboxes. Dead bodies hung from trees, dragged there by the raging flood waters, caught up in the branches as the waters receded.

Parts of human skeletons remained in some foundations of houses swept away among the silt and sand of the flood's residue. Toy soldiers. Dead soldiers: Same thing.

When I thought of myself as a "functional alcoholic" (and that was for years), I guess I thought that there were two different kinds of alcoholics, those who did function (have a job, a place to live, friends, relationships), like me, and a second kind of alcoholic, who was quite unlike me. I had not been exposed to the knowledge that is behind any 12-step program. I was unaware that there is only one kind of alcoholic and that they are all 100% alcoholic and that if they are functional at present, it is only a matter of time until that progressive, downward spiral jettisons them from whatever functional path that they may have thought that they were on. Toy soldiers. Dead soldiers. Same thing.

It was the eternal optimist in me that would consistently respond to 'bad breaks' as 'dumb luck' and never, ever attribute the consequences to alcoholism. "This is as bad as it can get." "It's got to get better." And then, with peaks and valleys, progressively, it would get worse.

"What will I become?" slowly turned into "What has become of me?" Once again, by the time I had a reason to stop drinking, reason no longer had anything to do with it.

(**Sotto**): *Vatchi?*

Drunk, starving to death, literally. Afraid. I'm sure I would have frozen to death had it been wintertime instead of summer.

Bob had plea-bargained himself out of doing more jail time for possession of the hollow-point, cop-killer bullets. The system sent him to Ancorra State Mental Hospital because, clearly, he was (shape-shifter, smoke and mirror making) insane.

But then, three months later, he acted himself sane (oh, how lovely and sometimes so, so simple to appear sane). And now. Now he stood before me while I worked as a food server at the Mays Landing Diner. I remember wondering if he got out of the mental hospital early, on good behavior, as he had gotten out of prison after a seven year stretch for the same ability to play the role expected that would best serve his needs. Bob did what he had to do to be free of the rule of law. Act like a good prisoner. Act like a sane person in the mental hospital long enough to be reprieved. Fool doctors, parole officers, whomever you have to. This was Bob's modus operandi. Get free to be free to return to insanity. Welcome to Bob's brain.

Why did I not know what he had been in prison for in the first place? Some sense of "too much information"? Fear? Just general drunkenness? I was in a fairly steep downward slide when he got out of jail in the first place. By that time, although I never did drink while working at the diner, I remember sweating profusely once I hit the door after punching out, and being too hurried for a drink to do anything but immediately crack open a bottle of vodka in the diner's parking lot and drink at least half a pint to calm my shakes on the half-mile trek home.

Bob said he had stopped by the diner to forgive me for calling the cops on him through the neighbor's phone, offering to buy me a drink after I finished work. I played along and told him to come back in two hours, when I would be done with my shift.

As soon as he disappeared from sight, I told one co-worker that I had to leave immediately, giving no excuse whatsoever, but, guaranteed, they knew what was up. I had shared with one or two co-workers the story of the bullets and my subsequent disappearance into my drunkenness in Atlantic City after leaving the police station to give my written testimony of Bob holding the knife to my throat. I couldn't call the cops to say I felt threatened, because there was no reasonable cause and I wasn't going to stay around to provide reasonable cause, because I might be dead in the meantime. I couldn't trust that he wouldn't slice my throat the moment he might stand near me with no witnesses in sight.

Besides, my only thought, my immediate thought, was alcohol. More alcohol. All alcohol. And nothing but alcohol. Like being sworn in to testify at a trial with the words, "the truth, the whole truth, and nothing but the truth," I stood in testimony that alcohol could and would somehow set me free.

For four days I lived in the woods between two liquor stores a mile from each other. When one liquor store refused to serve me, I would wander back to the other. I didn't call work to tell them I wouldn't be working, no call, no show, again. Back and forth between the two liquor stores until I sobered up enough to be served or through a shift change of cashiers. Vodka and cranberry juice. And nothing else. No one came looking for me. Jane, still early in her heroin addiction (unknown to me at that time, thanks to my alcoholic oblivion), still was able to somehow hold onto her blackjack dealer position at the Sands Casino. Yet she was unaware of my disappearance from her house for days at a time.

I would pass out and come to in a pile of leaves a few yards off the roadway. I counted sunrises and think I counted four. I was killing myself with alcohol because, at that point, it was all my disease would let me do. "Missing in action" falls short of where I really was at that time: Out of commission and completely unmissed. Finally, I stopped a cop at a convenience store and I demanded an ambulance. He offered me a sandwich. "Eat something. You'll feel better," he said.

I knew that if I ate anything I would throw up. I laid down in the parking lot, not passing out. I had just reached the end of the road. An ambulance finally took me to freedom.

(**Vatchi**): *Sotto, it's alright. You don't have to say anything now. Sometimes it is best to just listen. Let Jim talk on and on. It may help him. I guess it's helping him to let it out in whatever form or fashion he is able to.*

I don't remember which hospital I was taken to. I don't remember how long I was there. I don't remember how I got to Jane's house, what I used for money, where I went, how I got there, how much time had passed.

Nothing. Nothing. Nothing. Time passed, shit happened. Nothing happened. A jigsaw puzzle with half the pieces missing. I hid in my disease so Bob couldn't find me. This makes no sense, I know. I guess I was delusional. I hid in my disease, a fortress against the reality of my potential murderer. I hid in my disease because I felt safe there. The safety of insanity. I found myself in Atlantic City Hospital this time or another time, or somehow and sought refuge at the John Brooks Recovery Center for the second time. It was a Thursday or Friday and I couldn't be interviewed for their detox program until Monday. Ducks lining up. Ducks lining up in a row.

Homeless again.

Help me. Help me stop. Make it stop. Someone stop my insanity. Make it. Make it stop.

(**Surimi**): *Nothing could break his fall. Jim's fear of Bob's reprisal, real or imagined, served to speed his descent. Feeling safe in the House of Alcohol, consumed in flames, rafters falling all around. The insane fire for one more drink before closing time. Make it a double. Unnatural disaster. A flood of alcohol. This is insanity. Starving to death and self-deception. Self-deceived, the self as deception, illusion. Money for nothing and a disease that stops at nothing.*

Toy soldiers. Dead soldiers. Victims and unintended victims. One nightmare reminding me of another. One death not different from the next. An empty glass, a full glass, the same thing. I am only alcohol and alcohol is king. I am victim. I am cup. I am cut. I am bleeding. Toy soldiers. Dead soldiers. Same thing.

EVENING MEDITATION

I should hope that somehow this sorrow for myself will end. It never may. It exists within my current self, my sober self. It is a sorrow and a pity for my younger, drunken self, that self near dead, containing a dormant predator. This predator waits for me to let down my guard. Self-pity is one of many baits my predator disease lays out, a mouse trap in my recovery maze.

"There are two ways to slide easily through life – to believe everything or to doubt everything. Both ways save us from thinking."
– Alfred Korzybski

QUESTION FOR TODAY

What did you forget to buy on your shopping list of memories?

32. I KILLED REALITY, REALITY KILLED ME BACK

"In a full heart there is room for everything, and in an empty heart there is room for nothing."
– Antonio Porchia

MORNING MEDITATION

In my sobriety, I'm trying to gradually taper off my assholism, but this turkey can't go cold-turkey on that. Not yet. Not yet. Not yet. Turkey peckin' at a grain of truth.

I cannot deal with Bob right now. Switch to Ted? I'm a mess as I switch to Ted. Honestly, I need help. Can I, should I deal with Ted now? Attempting suicide while using my identity and then three months later attempting to murder me for real? Bob? Ted? I could not deal with either of them. I cannot deal with Bob. I cannot deal with Ted. It's me I cannot deal with. It's me. I cannot deal with me. There. I cannot deal with me. I've said it.

I couldn't testify against Ted, not because I was too emotionally fractured, as was determined by the prosecuting attorney appointed by the State. My emotions were the mere collateral damage of my severe alcoholic plummet. Plunging my head, like an ostrich in the sand, my emotions, my alcoholism and the insane facts around the entire Ted fiasco formed a vicious, vicious circle, vicious cycle. One insanity fed the other and I stood, then fell, then crawled, immobilized.

Ted is not Bob. Tom is not Dick or Harry. Bob is not Ted is not Dick or Harry. I am not, was not, all of the above.

I'm guessing that the prosecuting attorney did not know that it was the alcohol in me that made it so that I couldn't put two sentences together.

The twisted factual realities of those moments. There was the court case and there was the case that was in my head, intertwined, twisted, entwined. This is where the causes and effects of alcohol become more blurred than my vision was at that time. Problems propelled the drinking. The drinking caused more problems. What eased the pain of the moment caused more pain, immediate and eventual. Alcohol is as alcohol does.

Still, I couldn't believe that Ted was carrying my photo I.D. I couldn't believe that he actually believed that he was me. And then attempting suicide. Was he trying to kill himself or kill his memory of me? When the plot of a dime store novel becomes the realty of your life, you feel worse than any fiction could possibly capture.

At the same time I was asking questions about Ted, I was asking no questions of myself. Dead inside. I drank more and more and more, trying to figure this one out. And I found myself trying to kill this one emotion because it was too twisted for me to deal with. And in using alcohol to kill this one emotion, it was killing all emotions. And in killing all emotions, alcohol was killing me, just as Ted was trying to kill me by killing himself.

This is how my world went around. It was not some fucking plot twist in a dime store novel. This was happening to me and it was real. Kill the realness. Kill the reality. Fucking, give me a fucking drink!

Drinking to stop one feeling stops all feelings.

My former self fell off the shelf. Now I was broke in two. "Bartender, let me have one for the road." That still sounds so romantic to me. "One for the road." The way I wish it could be yet never was or will be.

.

(**Sotto**): *"Jim, don't include this." That's what I want to say. Vatchi, sometimes I wish Jim could hear us. Even so, he probably wouldn't listen to our advice or anyone else's.*

One of the saddest things of all to me about my alcoholism is that in using alcohol to squash, smash, subdue or stuff one emotion, all my emotions were equally squashed, smashed, subdued and stuffed. Involuntary collateral emotional damage.

Thrown out of bars. Thrown out of apartments. Thrown out of jobs. Thrown out of relationships. No list necessary. I was discarded. Human refuse. Garbage. Trash.

(**Vatchi**): *Sotto, you say, "Jim, don't include this." To you, Sotto, I have this to say: Don't exclude Jim. Don't exclude his experience. Don't exclude his fears. Don't exclude his realities. Don't exclude his pain. Sotto, even when he is meaningless. Even when he is trauma and drama without purpose, stand back, give him room, let him speak. Let him breathe. Sotto, even though he does not know we're listening, listen anyway.*

Listen. Any. Way.

Tomorrow is a storm coming over South Mountain. The lightning's light will quickly reach us. The thunder's rumble: an old man shuffling our way. I thirst for rain, the hope for change. I hold hope and turn it in my hand like a hand holding and turning an apple. Tomorrow is the apple seed of now. I do not know where their branches might spread or what bright wings of birds might land upon those branches or if I will live to witness this.

Crunch! The apple in my hand. Crunch! The memory of my footsteps in the snow. Crunch! Eternity condensed into this Now. Crunch! The illusion of my power. More important than "What do you carry?" is "What carries you?"

Crunch! Tomorrow is the apple seed of now and nothing more. Tomorrow is the apple seed of now and nothing less. Crunch! I carry an apple. An apple carries me.

Recovery is my apple seed of now, my apple seed of now.

Ted, court ordered, returns to the prison of the mental hospital.

Jim, quart ordered (pun intended), continues in the prison of his addiction.

This is how I would write it to fade into the present; that is how I did write it and this is how the present is: Recovery is my apple seed of now.

(**Surimi**): *Sotto, you say, "Jim, don't include this." Vatchi, you say.... Never mind. Both of you. Cut the crap. Neither one of you realize how close you are to the truth. I think Jim wants to exclude himself from his own story, in a way at least. He wants to write it down to expose it. He wants to speak it as a way of letting go. In a strange sort of way, letting go of himself, his story, is a way of letting go of his addiction.*

If he could know this, then he would learn that he is already on his way. His path is the path that he is on.

I do not know where Ted or Bob ended up or almost everyone from my most alcoholic path. My most vivid memories are no more accurate than my most twisted memories. Alcohol played tricks on me, twisted, vivid tricks. My alcoholic brain is all that could remain. Most of my drinking past consists of loose ends which will never be tied again or understood. My alcoholic loose ends will be forever loose ends. The only reality I have is to keep moving forward.

This is sobriety. This is now. Play it forward, pay it forward. No one knows where life will end. Perhaps it starts and ends with now.

EVENING MEDITATION

Emotions flowed through my veins like alcohol. Emotions caused by alcohol. Emotions distorted by alcohol. Emotions deadened by alcohol.
I did not flow through alcohol today.

> *"You can't separate peace from freedom because no one*
> *can be at peace unless he has his freedom."*
> – Malcolm X

QUESTION FOR TODAY

Will some shoes always fit? Can these feet change direction at will? Can a sideward glance caught in a plate-glass window forever change a life? How can you know that it is you staring back at you?

33. I'M SOBER. JEAN-PAUL IS DEAD.

"If you wish to make an apple pie truly from scratch,
you must first invent the universe."
– Carl Sagan

MORNING MEDITATION
I did not drink today. It was a good day.

Hitting bottom and not dying is my greatest achievement.
Jean-Paul dying and never finding even one day sober was his greatest loss.
(My loss is lost and wandering around inside me.)

(**Sotto**): *Now he's pissing me off. He ends yesterday with his "an apple carries me" and then segues into Carl Sagan's apple pie today. What's he trying to prove here, Vatchi?*

Jean-Paul. Jean-Paul. You could not call him Jean. You could not call him Paul. "My name is Jean-Paul," he would say. "Call me by my name." And only Jean-Paul could say that and not come off as a snob.

He was my best drinking buddy. Whatever lies I may be telling myself elsewhere in this extended monologue, here, I want most clearly to tell the simple, yet baffling truth. I already said he was my best drinking buddy. When he came from Rome in the springtime or from Australia in late summer to spend time with relatives in Atlantic City, he would know which bars to find me in. He never called. He never wrote. He just showed up and the party would begin where it had left off.

Only Jean-Paul could keep up with me on my all night sprees or my three-day binges. No need for speed. The alcohol was fuel enough for him and for me. Only Jean-Paul lived to drink as I drank. And only I was shielded from the knowledge of his dying, that he could not live for even one more year.

It was only after his funeral a few short months later that I found out the truth of his dying of AIDS and that he wanted to go out in a blaze of glory, partying his ass off with me, without me knowing that. "Because that would have changed everything, had you known," as his Nephew explained to me. He had wanted to protect the knowledge of his dying from me so that in his final days everything would be as they had always been with us: A giant party that could not, would not, did not stop.

(**Vatchi**): *Why is he romanticizing everything: living, drinking, death? All denial. Sotto, I think you're right about him. He just tries to prettify all. Going from one extreme to the other. No wonder he was misdiagnosed as bipolar when he first got sober. He seems to over-describe or under-describe everything. He doesn't seem capable of experiencing life's extremes with any kind of balance. He's not nearly packed so tight as he supposes.*

I'm sober. Jean-Paul is dead. And this is where I have to stop. To think, to feel, to figure this out. A forced epiphany. Brick wall, brick wall and then just one moment more....

Now I get it. Jean-Paul had never lived a sober day in his life. He wasn't trying to protect me from knowledge of his impending death by AIDS. He used that as an excuse to continue living in denial about his own alcoholism. Jean-Paul died of AIDS. But it was alcoholism that killed him. No epiphanies for Jean-Paul.

(**Surimi**): *That, my dears, Sotto and Vatchi, is one of the ironies of addiction. What you are dying from and what kills you need not be the same thing.*
Jim did not drink today. This is a good day for him.

"Jean-Paul died of AIDS, but it was alcohol that killed him." That's what his tombstone should read. Like Jean-Paul, I did not know then that life could be lived sober, that there could be life after alcohol, life after the party, life after alcohol killed the party. Addiction makes not using seem like a punishment. Jean-Paul did not live to know the many joys of sobriety. I must not drown in survivor's guilt. I must keep pushing forward.

EVENING MEDITATION

There was a time, living in Atlantic City, early on, when anytime I heard a gunshot, I would automatically assume that the sound was from a firecracker (remembering the experience of my youth in Bethlehem). Time taught me otherwise. Learning, learning what a gunshot is, what a gunshot sounds like, until one Fourth of July after years in Atlantic City. I mistook the sound of firecrackers for gunshot. Sometimes the only news from Now I have is what's inside me.

Bang. Bang.

"I am not afraid of storms, for I am learning how to sail my ship."
– Louisa May Alcott

QUESTION FOR TODAY

If you continue to carry it with you, why do you continue to call it your past? Is it the words that count or what they make you think? What is letting go?

34. SEEING EYEBALL TO EGG YOLK

*"You can avoid reality, but you cannot avoid the
consequences of avoiding reality."*
– Ayn Rand

MORNING MEDITATION

I did Step One of my 12-step recovery program (powerlessness over alcohol, life unmanageable) and moved on. Denial left me and came back again disguised as an old friend who could set me free.

Can you remember being seven years old and being told that your Aunt Alice was dying of consumption and you didn't know what dying was and you didn't know what consumption was? And do you remember being ten years old and finding out that Karen, the seven year old Gallo girl next door had died suddenly and you still didn't know what dying was? Or when you were thirty and Carl was forty and had a heart attack climbing a ladder and literally dropped dead?

(**Sotto**): *I can't listen to him anymore, Vatchi. I wish he would just stop.*

Ten years old: Walking around aisle after aisle of clocks and watches, antique timepieces everywhere. Shiny metal and glass cases. Grandfather clocks, Mantelpiece clocks. Ticking everywhere. Pendulums. Gears, interlocked and clicking.

(**Vatchi**): *Sotto, why do you stop listening to him? Are you that much better or different? God is dead, so you took over? You're no box of chocolates. Maybe the wrapper. Maybe wrapped too tight, Sotto. Have some patience.*

Go with his flow.

Do you remember the 1800's tile works site visited in 1973? Remember the fireplace, tall enough to stand in? And the tiles, glazed, faded blue and off-white? Anvils and tourist crap for a tourist trap gone bankrupt? Some kind of "Renaissance Fair" poorly publicized, if ever?

Falling asleep (passing out) into a plate of sunny side up eggs, eyeball to egg yolk in 1979? Disco cocaine and disco scotch? Orchids growing in a climate-controlled sun porch three flights up between the sea and the bay? Saltwater and freshwater tanks in the living room with thousands of dollars worth of exotic fish?

Thoughts like these would flash randomly through the mind of someone dying.

Talking to yourself, Jim? I ask myself that. I call myself by name. Dying like you have already died, Jim? My name is Jim and I'm an alcoholic, dying, Jim. I did not drink today and I am still alive, Jim. And yes, I will grow old, get sick and die, but still, and yet, I did not drink today.

(**Surimi**): Eyeball to Egg Yolk: *that should be Jim's next book. It makes sense and it doesn't make sense. Like the Cubist Art Movement in Paris. Except his Cubist Art is in ice cubes. Ice cubes and scotch. Delirium as toxin and anti-toxin. Conspicuous consumption and not-so-conspicuously consumed. Hopscotch, butterscotch, eyeball to egg yolk. Joke to no joke. Done.*

Time. Time. Time. Time. Time. Time waits for no one. Time marches on. Having hit a cascade of bottoms before finally gaining several years of continuous sobriety, I've learned this one thing, and I'm learning it now. I have survived the alcohol and now I must survive myself.

And now I must survive myself. My emotions, hollowed out by my addictions, have survived. I cannot now separate myself from living, from living sober, from moving forward, from learning how to feel again, this time, this time, not under the influence. My instinct for survival has, for now, overpowered my addictions. I cannot do this alone. I will not do this alone. I must not do this alone.

I am not alone. My disease is inside me.

EVENING MEDITATION

I used to create a psychosomatic reason to drink, or a weather reason or a work or relationship reason because for the longest time it just couldn't occur to me that I drank because I am an alcoholic. Then, beyond the deadening effects of an alcohol overload, there was also a sort of placebo effect that comforted me into believing that the alcohol was actually curing something imagined instead of facing the scientific fact that I am an addict addicted to alcohol. Imagined symptoms requiring a drink and the placebo effect which proved it was working.

"Only fools learn from their own mistakes."
– Russian Proverb

QUESTION FOR TODAY

What have you lost when you can't let go?

35. **COCAINE-LACED ICING ON MY RUM CAKE**

"If we had no faults of our own, we would not take so much pleasure in noticing those of others."
– Francois Duc de La Rochefoucauld

MORNING MEDITATION

I was grabbing outside to rediscover something inside. What's wrong with this picture? Stop. Go back. Read that first sentence again. I was grabbing outside to rediscover something inside. Let it sink in. Soak in it. Let it sink in.

In 1970 I stood outside the outhouse outback of my friend's house in the coal region of Pennsylvania, waiting to puke after the square-dance.

In 1996 I knelt outside my first A.A. meeting at the old Atlantic City Detox, literally puking my guts out, cursing A.A. as some kind of fanatical mind control group.

Now suppose that from 1970 to 1996 I had been teleported to another planet.

Just suppose this: I am back. Hear me roar. It was nothing like that. It was everything like that. Except the roaring part. And the teleported part.

(**Sotto**): *Getting sober seems to be like waking up from a dream, the way Jim blurts out non-sense or senseless at times. I half expect to see him rubbing his closed hands to his eyes, like a child awakened.*

Cocaine-laced icing on my rum cake. Wine or brandy in everything I cooked or ate. Quaaludes were an interlude before becoming rude and lewd. It was alcohol in which I stewed. I was the man, I was the dude.

Bragging rights to getting high. A five-star drunken general, I. Cigarette headaches. Dunhill, darling. What I lost, I lost. I could afford it. I wouldn't miss it. I wouldn't miss it. I didn't need it.

But I would always need another drink.

(**Vatchi**): *That's the scary thing, Sotto. When someone gets sober, the mind wants to forget the bad parts. The alcoholic past can seem like a dream, like it didn't happen, like it couldn't have happened, that it couldn't have been as insane as it seemed. Like a bad dream. This is one dangerous door, the door of "it couldn't have been that bad." Relapse remains an insane possibility. Wake the fuck up, Jim. It wasn't a dream.*

I'm in my A.A. bomb shelter, suffering from shellshock. The shellshock of memories' bombardment. Cigarette headaches and credit card headaches from my drunken signature on countless credit card slips, drunk at the Sands Casino, eating alone and drunk with a $40.00 bottle of wine to keep me company with a thousand other drinks. Writing drunken words to music I could not hear, writing music that drinking made me hear. Fear magnified and fear diffused, senseless music from the senseless hemispheres of my brain.

Blackout. Pass out. Time out. Out.

(**Surimi**): *What Jim just described is at the height of his discord, Sotto. You cannot understand his insanity. It does not reside at the intersection of A and B. The insanity of alcoholism, is a moving target or in its own dimension, it does not move at all. Science may one day better understand it. But alcoholic insanity will remain beyond reason, incomprehensible from the outside. And from the inside. He is a very sick person who is now, finally, trying to get well.*

A patient, Michael, heard voices as we spoke, or so he told me on our smoke breaks at the Lakewood hospital. I had heard a voice only once, so I guessed that I could believe him.

One of my many roommates once asked me, "What happened to you?" He was referring to the ghost he'd seen in me, leftover from alcohol poisoning. My face was poisoned, twisted, distorted from alcohol.

My past disturbs me, haunts me. I did not, would not, could not understand what was happening to me then. How could I possibly think that I could understand it now? Is there even anything to understand?

Brought to my knees once again, defeated. A leftover from my chemically engorged past. I cannot let my past succeed in defeating me again. My leftover, hung-over, sideshow, freak show is the language of self-destruction and alcoholic destruction, pure insanity, purely insane, insane, pure.

Help.

Help me. Someone help me. Someone help me help someone. Help someone. Someone help.

EVENING MEDITATION

My 12-step meetings are my new happy hours. They remind me that my desire to pick up must always be measured against my fear of consequences and the pain of consequences. That my future could, once again, be catastrophic is reinforced in every meeting, in one way or another, in our shared recovery.

"When things go wrong, don't go with them."
– Anonymous

QUESTION FOR TODAY

Can and should the healing ever be complete?

36. A.D.D.: ALCOHOL DEFICIT DISORDER

"A man's errors are his portals of discovery."
– Source unknown

MORNING MEDITATION

I was already lost when I found my bottom, or it found me. Debris all around and behind me, nothing ahead. Feeling anything required too much effort. The rooms of recovery call this "emotional bankruptcy" and that just about covers it.

It took me several relapses and then several years of continuous sobriety to begin to fathom the depth of just how fucked up on alcohol and other drugs I had been since the beginning. I have come to realize how much I had romanticized my early years as having been not all that bad. Almost memories. Memories that should have been but are not quite. Since the beginning, there have been almost no dots to connect!

Climbing an invisible, hallucinated staircase, high on an organic flower plucked fresh off the tree by me hours earlier high in the Guatemalan mountains, Gene and I were then arrested on suspicion of substance possession and abuse, awaiting release through bribery. Some memories, like partaking this Guatemalan hallucinogen, bring flashbacks like roll call at reveille. "I am Jim Anders, not all present, not all accounted for, sir." Sometimes I have to surrender to the present, surrender and strive to save whatever little time and mind that I have left….

(**Sotto**): *Vatchi, Jim's realities are stagnant photographs. Is his spaceship just now landing or just now taking off? He is really out there at times. Bring me back to earth, Vatchi. Bring me back.*

I couldn't look Merv Griffin quite straight on. Trying to exhale my alcohol-reeking breath to the left or the right of his face. Below or above. I would be alright if I just didn't breathe on him when I asked him to autograph a book he'd written. Owning Resorts International Casino Hotel at the time, he could have easily fired me immediately, or shortly thereafter, before nightfall.

This was Merv's first meeting with his 3,000 plus employees. And although I would later work with him on several television commercials, this was actually as close as I would ever get to him. Thereafter, I would know what days I was working with him directly and force myself to get drunk as early as possible the night before, so I would reek as little as possible.... (Damn! how I thought there would always be a way to drink, to get necessarily plastered, yet never think to just not drink that one night before any morning after.)

Christ, it must be difficult for large companies to deal with drunks like me.

(**Vatchi**): *You're as fucked up as he is, Sotto. You follow along only to make fun. You make fun because you understand. You understand because you're just like him. You don't like him because you don't like yourself. Circle is squared, Sotto. You think you're a monkey wrench. But you're just a monkey. There is no monkey see, monkey do, because you've done all that. Fuck it. You're both monkeys. Sotto and Jim. Monkeys.*

I didn't think I would ever have a life, not a life without alcohol, anyway. Because all my plans included alcohol, I lived one drink at a time. Is it any wonder that at Alcoholics Anonymous meetings one hears about sobriety lived "one day at a time"?

The life I now live is not the life I could have predicted or even could ever have imagined. Today, I live a life of solitude with a sense of belonging. I never could have guessed how much I take comfort in my sobriety today. Comfort in sobriety was unknowable to me at one time. "Taking my comfort" used to mean Southern Comfort.

(**Surimi**): *Jim is incomplete now because his life was incomplete then. His blackouts were the rude punctuation marks of a diseased brain. And not just alcohol. The chemicals, known and unknown, in Angel Dust, marijuana, and a host of others. The best prisoner is the one who does not know that he is imprisoned. The door is closed and is not locked because no key is ever sought. "Drink me and everything will be alright," whispers the auditory hallucination. Blind loneliness as the final result.*

Stop.
He stopped.

Now what? What next? Where?

To try to tell the story of my life, I see there is no story to tell, just episodes united by the disease of alcoholism. Selective recall. I doubt hypnosis would reveal much more of note as most memories were never formed in the first place during my nearly daily blackouts. Artificial excitement, emotions raised and lowered by drugs and alcohol. Opportunities pursued drunkenly or not at all.

Sometimes I wished I could stop, but I never thought I could stop drinking. Half of my Tower of Babel was my alcohol-induced inability to understand, A.D.D. (Alcohol Deficit Disorder). "I'll gladly pay you Tuesday to stop my alcohol deficit today."

"Time takes time" because so much damage has been done.

EVENING MEDITATION

I do not belong to yesterday. Yesterday belongs to me. I can own it sober or it can own me drunk. Side effects of sobriety may include humility and meditation. Caution: the intersection of solitude and a sense of belonging may result.

> *"I have learned this: it is not what one does that is wrong,*
> *but what one becomes as a consequence of it."*
> – Oscar Wilde

QUESTION FOR TODAY

How can you separate addiction from the pain of addiction? How did alcohol separate you from living? When was the last time you were fully alive?

37. ALCOHOLIC, STRAIGHT OR ICED

*"Every man takes the limits of his own field of vision
for the limits of the world."*
– Arthur Schopenhauer

MORNING MEDITATION

Repeated lies begin to sound like truth, too common, too familiar. Denial can be a trap door, catching me unawares. The familiar surprise of lies upon lies, deny.

It's alright to be empty, feel empty. It's alright to draw a blank. It's alright to feel this and not to feel that. It's alright to feel... nothing. There is this nothing sober and there is that nothing drunk. I will be okay. I will be okay. I am sober today.

This Chapter is empty. My mind is now empty. And I will allow myself. I am simply, simply sober today.

And that is that.

(**Sotto**): *I am here now. I wonder where I'm going.*

The benign indifference of the guru is what I sought when I was younger. But, first, apathy and depression set up their roadblocks. After time, many years, let's say, it didn't matter whether my emotions or circumstances made me drink more or whether my drinking caused my emotions and circumstances to mutate. It doesn't matter how you cut the cake: it's still a cake. And I'm an alcoholic, straight or iced.

(**Vatchi**): *Where can one find home when the very foundation of self has been washed away? The luggage is empty or there is no luggage. No* *children to go home to. No "where have you been?" from family. Nowhere to go and he does not know all the places where he has been. Sotto, Jim is the lost child who does not know he's lost. A drink in his hand is worth nothing in the bush. And nowhere to go. Ten thousand nights. Ten thousand conspiracies of silence.*

Quaaludes stifled emotions and locomotion. I gave up moderation for Lent. Denial was big as all the ocean. My liberation had been spent. One day sober. Today. Today. Today.

My patterns of consumption were a patchwork quilt. Illusion and delusion interwoven. Consumption and alcohol, consumed by alcohol. No quilting bees, no quitting bees, just a buzzing in my head. I thought that the quality of cocaine had declined because I had to snort so much more to maintain a high. No one would believe my lies were not lies, just addictive self-deception.

It's hard to be upbeat when your addictions beat you up.

Giving is the gift. Comfort is for the dying. Giving is the gift. Alcohol would not give me a comfortable death.

I did not drink today.

(**Surimi**): *More alcohol was needed to give the illusion of the same high. But it was not the same high. Could not be the same high. Addiction takes what is lost out of the equation to give the appearance, the trompe d'oeuil of sameness. But it is never the same high that is achieved because the highway of more becomes littered with loss. The equation does not factor in loss because the equation is owned by the addiction and not by the dispossessed.*

Comfort should be for the dying, yet, there is, in the end, no comfort in this. Oblivion is not comfort. Life obstructed. Construct a new life with what's left, Jim. Jim. What will become of him? A simple death, unencumbered by alcohol. Let whatever causes his death be some single cause. Not alcohol. No, not that. Please, not that for him. Give him not that.

Can I even look forward? Will my whole life now be nothing but looking into the rearview mirror? Can I keep my eyes looking forward, steering soberly into an ever more sober future?

Breathe in. Breathe out. I do not know what lies ahead, but it is not a drink today. Breathe in — easy. Breathe out - easy. I did not drink today. I did not drink today.

EVENING MEDITATION

The illusions of others are easy to see. But what about the illusions of me? Delusions of grandeur, cultural delusions. Guises, disguises. I know them all because I have been them all, done them all, lived them all. I lied and then I fell in love with the lie.

"I drank, and then the drink drank me."

"There is nothing more deceptive than an obvious fact."
– Sir Arthur Conan Doyle

QUESTION FOR TODAY

And you, Sotto? What about you? Tell me, Sotto, where do you hurt? Where, Sotto? Where? Who am I to ask and who is asking whom? What the…?

38. **BARTENDER, GIVE ME MY LEVEL OF ADDICTION**

"Simplicity is complexity well done."
– Jeff Jarvis

MORNING MEDITATION

I used to babble. Now, I just ramble. "Progress, not perfection."

Having survived this long, I think of myself as a man becoming old, whereas to those around me, I am already old. Quite rightly, perhaps, I feel like Spencer Tracy in *The Old Man and the Sea*, or, more properly, the old fisherman portrayed by Tracy in the Hemingway novel. Except, instead of the struggle with the fish, my struggle has been with my addiction: A world where so much has been forgotten, because so much was not remembered in the first place.

Here's a perfect example: My older friends (at the time), Lenny and Don, took me on a trip to New York City to have dinner at the famous Friars Club and to meet Jackie Mason, his career having undergone a huge resurgence. The thousand and one memories I should have had about this trip, the amusing anecdotes and charming witticisms that would have entertained whomever would listen, are now in the dustbin of history, like so many whale carcasses upon a beach whose name I no longer remember.

Alcohol, leave me alone.

Whale carcasses. Bones picked clean. Toy soldiers. Dead soldiers. Same thing.

I have surrendered and whatever there is now left, I will savor sober.

(**Sotto**): *I still can hear the echo of his voice. His echo, loud, clear, distilled. I can almost hear him saying "Don't mess with me, Alcohol. Don't." Vatchi, he talks to his disease. He was talking to his disease. Now, that is insane. And I don't think we'll hear him stopping any time soon. He's not through talking to his disease and his disease has not stopped answering.*

There is no Retrospective of my Art, but a Retrospective of my Alcoholism would show that I was always, at each and every point of my descent, always far worse off than I felt I was at that moment and descending ever-more-quickly to an insanity beyond my most fertile imagination. I couldn't see where I was headed; much less know where I had been (including the night before).

(**Vatchi**): *Don't let Jim pull you down, Sotto. Let him work through this. Life is fucked up sometimes. What else is new?*

Yes, sobriety is standing on shaky ground. Standing shaky on shaky ground. Tenuous, fragile, breakable. Drinkable.

Neither faith nor lack of faith could keep me sober. I needed a reason for hope and continued sobriety gave me that. Slowly at first. Mistakes. Lapses and relapses. Learning and earning sobriety. Unlearning my alcoholic ways, sober, yet under alcohol's subtle spell.

So much of my perceived pleasure in drinking, smoking and doing other addictive substances was the anxiety preceding picking up and the relief of getting my fix. Give me my drug and my anxiety and stress were reduced. I called this "pleasure." This must be pleasure, mustn't it? Unknowingly living to satisfy my level of addiction. Is this how and why and what I lived for?

Fuck you, Alcohol! Fuck you!

(**Surimi**): *Jim's past, recollected from the safe distance of a reasonable period of sobriety, seems to promise a release from the pain of living under the influence. He knows the release the alcohol seemed to provide was one of many of his addiction's illusions. A greater emotional balance lies in his future. His mood swings will eventually subside.*
Time takes time.
Shot glasses as prom souvenirs: the culture of addiction.
Time takes time. Time is time.

I don't need you anymore, Alcohol. Slowly, I am outgrowing you, slowly, like I learned to hate you slowly. And when I am growing, there is no need for you. Let me level with you, Alcohol. I don't need a certain level of addiction. Never did. You deceived. I bit your bait, drank your drink, and believed your promises. I lived your life. Past tense. Adios. Adieu. Good-bye. You are dead, Alcohol. I have survived you. Go fuck yourself, Alcohol. I'm through. Alcohol Who....?

EVENING MEDITATION

Like an older uncle or grandfather at a family reunion, beckoned to tell again some infamously funny and poignant story from his own life to a rapt audience of shiny faces aglow with anticipation, the story of my disease takes on a life of its own, a separate reality, these alcoholic memories. Like a mutant cancer cell dividing, dividing, dividing, even memories can forget and a cancer can return and a drink can reach my hand. In memory I can forget what it means to be an alcoholic. My insane memory can become insanity again. And I must not forget.

"We are slow to believe that which if believed would hurt our feelings."
– Ovid

QUESTION FOR TODAY

What is too much when you don't know what you want? Is anything enough? When you do not know, where do you go to find enough of what you do not know?

39. DEADLY, SLOWLY, CONSEQUENTLY

"I don't do drugs, I am drugs."
– Salvador Dali

MORNING MEDITATION
In recovery, your disease will be arrested. Or you could relapse and you might be arrested.

Alcohol is my poison, my prison. A brick wall, a trap door, a cancer, a bad joke, an empty bottle, an excuse, a leaky faucet, a loan shark, a broken promise, a cracked mirror, an earthquake, an avalanche, a train wreck, a recurring nightmare.

Alcohol is my insanity.

(**Sotto**): *Oh, my goodness. I should have seen this coming. Ramble, ramble, ramble. Ramble, ramble, ramble. But I've got to admit it. Some of what he says is at least half-true.*

I swear I used to have some kind of sense when I was drinking that some limousine door of my mind would open for me and an attendant would say, "Mr. Anders, you have arrived." Trouble was, as the saying goes, I was always "a few fries short of a Happy Meal." The illusion that alcohol could take me to some paradise of fulfillment unobtainable in the real world was always just one sip beyond my lips. Under the influence, I was always just this much short of being there.

(**Vatchi**): *Half-truths, half-lies, half lives. The intersection of anticipation and dread. The excitement of readying for a trip and the discovery that it is* *a trip to nowhere. And the mixing in of other drugs: valium, speed, Quaaludes, whatever. Insanity squared. When you've got it, you've got it. Bad. The unintended consequence? Nothingness.*

My poison, my prison. The analogies of addiction are endless. My blackouts were stored in the freezer in a bottle of Absolut, freeze-dried in a tablet of Valium. Wash down the pills with a drink. Wash down the drink with another drink. Wash down. White out. Blackout. Drown out. Shout out. Die out. Cry out.

Continuous undulations of memories.

(**Surimi**): *Some subtle improvement. I'm feeling optimistic for his continuing improvement. Progress in his process of recovery. My fingers are crossed that he continues on his current course, however meandering.*

What alcohol promised and what alcohol delivered. Where did I begin and the alcohol end? Where do I begin when the alcohol ends? Is there something left to salvage? Is there anything left to save?

I did not drink. I could not drink. I did not drink today.

EVENING MEDITATION

The strands of my DNA are curly and long. Generations before me have been powerless over alcohol. A family history of dysfunctional alcoholism has cascaded over me. The strands of my DNA are curly and long and my hair is unmanageable.

"A man is his own easiest dupe, for what he wishes to be true..."
– Demosthenes

QUESTION FOR TODAY

What does normal look like in this insane world of ours? Would you know it if you saw it?

40. THE NEW NORMAL

*"Sometimes you put walls up not to keep people out, but to see
who cares enough to break them down."*
– Source unknown

MORNING MEDITATION

"If at first you don't succeed..." relapse again and again. "Insanity is doing the
same thing again and again..." No wonder time takes time.

There was a time when I was not there, but I did not know it yet. I would
drink to forget, forgetting what I did not know. Not yet. I did not know yet.
Where was I then, when I was not there? For years I lived somewhere
between myself and the next drink. I would drink to forget what I could not
think, halfway to nowhere and another drink. I was grieving and I did not
know it. Someone was dying, but I could not feel it, feel my own dying. I
could not own it because it owned me. Denial is so hard to feel, yet, there it
is, standing next to you. You: Halfway to nowhere and another drink.

(**Sotto**): *He seems in equal part to have been in denial about how much he
hurt people when he was drinking as he is in denial about how much he
needs people to help him to remain sober in his recovery.*

Forty days so far and people are mostly missing from my text. Many of
the people in my notes and my outline are missing. I seem to get caught up
in my own story (and lack of story) and lose track of those around me. Such
a curious lack of people in my adult life. Not many people here. My
alcoholism had become a kind of solitary confinement. People were lost
elephants in the rooms of my alcoholic insanity. Solitary in a crowded

barroom. An empty glass. Insanely alone with my alcoholic infusions, confusions.

Yeh, well, maybe tomorrow will be another day, a different day, a new day.

(**Vatchi**): *You spoke too soon, Sotto. No sooner do you mention other people when Jim chimes right in. It's almost as if he has read your mind. I was unaware that Jim even has an outline for his ramblings. That's a shocker. He has an outline? Can you imagine if he didn't? He thinks there's an order to this crap? Compared to what? His own insanity? Maybe.*

Too impaired to drive, so I did not drive. But my impairment continued without driving, at its own speed, speedometer of addiction accelerating. Crippled, hobbled, humbled by alcohol. And I did not know that I did not know –BAM– denial sneaks in the back door, through the windows, between the smallest crevices.

When I reached a certain level of intoxication, I was at my peak. Not before. Not after. And the duration of my peak performance diminished as my disease progressed. I was a lousy pool player until I had enough drinks in me. I needed so many drinks to function at my physical best. At some point, the new normal was drunk and it was a necessity.

1955: Rosa Parks boards a bus. I'm five years old. Alcohol sits next to me, waiting patiently for me to pick up my first drink.

(**Surimi**): *Jim has cast a wide net over his life and really, all I can see so far is a vast array of correlations. A disparate lack of ability to point a finger at cause. Gentlemen, I'll be brief: The House of Alcohol eventually deteriorates and becomes the "Hodge-Podge Lodge." Cause and effect, out the window. It doesn't matter. It is what it has become, and still is: Alcoholism.*

Yes, this is foreshadowing of a sort, a premonition from the past? I, most certainly, did not know that alcohol would change my life forever. I can see Rosa Parks sitting on a bus in 1955 and I can see myself sitting on a bus in 1955.

Alcohol still sits next to me. Rosa Parks is dead. Alcohol wants me dead. Simple enough? Crazy enough?

EVENING MEDITATION

In recovery, drifting is going backwards. But so is moving forwards too fast. The world of impatience, from Pony Express to Snail Mail - the world we live in - is not especially conducive to recovery. The world we live in, the world of "we want it yesterday," makes recovery difficult. I suppose our culture, changed by the rush of

the global economy and the internet, seems to bring the possibility of a next drink somehow closer. My sobriety is in a delicate balance. Can I remain sober and sane in this insane world? My 'can-do' spirit answers, "Yes, we can." We alcoholics can do together what most of us seem unable to do alone: Be sober, stay sober, live sober. I am never alone. My disease is always with me.
"Yes, we can."

> *"When a person drowns himself in negative thinking, he is committing an unspeakable crime against himself."*
> — Maxwell Maltz

QUESTION FOR TODAY

Do you remember being here last night? Don't you remember? Why don't you remember? And if you could, would you want to?

41. SAFELY CRAZED

"I have come to believe that the whole world is an enigma,
a harmless enigma that is made terrible by our own mad attempt
to interpret it as though it had an underlying truth."
– Umberto Eco

MORNING MEDITATION
When frustrated, it has taken time to turn from thoughts of taking a drink to repeating "The Serenity Prayer" to myself. Time takes time.

I was always a little afraid of pills. Taking one Quaalude and waiting an impatient hour for the effects had, in the past, led me to take a second Quaalude, only to regret it later, after the first one grabbed hold.

Administering the proper dosage of alcohol to achieve the desired effect seemed more manageable. Not strong enough? Switch from scotch and water to scotch on the rocks. Not fast enough? Use less ice. I felt more in control with my alcohol (italicized, because alcohol was my little baby: she never left me down).

Right before my last relapse, after having just gotten out of the hospital for an operation for abdominal hernias, I played Doctor with my prescribed pain medications. I took more than the prescribed dosage because I wanted quick relief. I was in pain. Then I didn't wait long enough for the next prescribed dosage time. Before you know it, I was immobile on the sidewalk, crazed. An ambulance was summoned by a passing stranger (apparently) and back to the hospital I went, having been just released a few short hours earlier.

If it takes eight pills to kill you, I used to feel safe taking six, and then two hours later I'd start wondering if it's safe to take another one or two.

Never was it a case of wanting to commit suicide. I just wanted to get as safely crazed as possible.

After the first drink, there is no other.

(**Sotto**): *Vatchi? He still sounds a little like he wants to be somewhere where he's not. Not a lion seeking his prey, or a vegetarian stalking wild asparagus. Ha! That's a good one! I think he's still looking to get high. Or at least romanticizing his phantoms.*

I know I can never drink again. Countless times, after varying periods of sobriety, I have tried to drink again. The alcoholic insanity always came back and always took over, whether after one drink or twenty. Smoking marijuana, perhaps, when it finally becomes legal? I really don't know. I just fear that other drugs might retrigger my alcoholism. I don't think I can do any drug socially now. If ever.

"Just for Today," as I've heard in Narcotics Anonymous, "just for today, I will not pick up." It has taken me nearly sixty years to say "I'm okay," and mean it and know what that means. That might never have happened were I not an alcoholic. Who knows? All I know is... I'm okay, "Just for Today."

(**Vatchi**): *You don't have to be an alcoholic to romanticize your past, your present, or your future, Sotto. Everyone daydreams and has wishful thinking. It's just that these are shark infested waters for an alcoholic and perhaps a more idyllic paradise for those who aren't.*

A relapse would be a reinvestment in a past that is already broken and can never be fixed. I take that back: can be fixed, but a drink won't fix it. I'm done wallpapering over my past, then repainting it, then, then, then. That was then. This is now. Today I'm sober. Holy cow!

(**Surimi**): *Experiences are the balls on Charlie Brown's Christmas trees. Or arrest warrants for public drunkenness. Needful things, hurtful things, sleep. Experiences poisoned by alcohol. Over-medicated when it is not medicine that is needed at all, at all.*

Alcohol says, "I'm going to kill you" and they, the alcoholics, listen in disbelief.

"You've said that before," they say, drinking themselves to sleep, to the illusion of sleep, to passing out. And then dreams, dreams of turning wine back into water, then back again to wine. This is not a momentary madness. Alcoholism lasts a lifetime, sober or drunk.

I have to pace my sobriety just like I used to try to pace my drinking. But I paced my drinking for all the wrong reasons. To please others and to kid myself that I was not powerless over my drinking, that I had some kind of control. Pacing my sobriety means slowing down, focusing, finding patience, persistence, reassurance, confidence, conviction.

EVENING MEDITATION

The old math was calculating how many more drinks I could have and how many less hours of sleep I could sustain to come to with alarm clock blaring. The old math was calculating how many hours it would take the next day before I could continue the vicious cycle again. My old math measured time in ounces and quarts, in urges and surges and blurs, blaring and bounces, bangles and jangles and booze.

This new math is sane and sober: one is one is won.

> *"Life is short, so we must move very slowly."*
> – Thai Proverb

QUESTION FOR TODAY

Where is your recovery taking you today? Where are you taking it?

42. **OPTIMAL DELUSIONS**

"Don't be afraid to take a big step if one is indicated.
You can't cross a chasm in two small jumps."
– David Lloyd George

MORNING MEDITATION
Life, liberty and the pursuit of sobriety...

Addiction is godless, headless, insane. It rejects faith, reason, feelings. Addiction is heartless, the blackest night. No light. No sun. No stars. In its nothingness, we feel nothing and accept that nothingness is acceptable and true. "Cunning. Baffling. Powerful."

(**Sotto**): *Good Book. Big Book. Bad Book. No Book. Vatchi, can a person be sane in all other respects, but alcoholic still?*

I'm no longer looking for pity. I had enough self-pity to spare. My cup overflowed with self-pity. I have quite enough. Let me share. Go ahead. Take one sip from my pity cup. I must warn you though: it's not very filling. Like Chinese food. You'll be hungry for more in two hours, max. Care for a free refill? My pity cup is endless.

Getting sober seems to have leveled off most all my negative emotions and increased the positive. Sobriety is the drug with no negative side effects.

I can feel empathy today. Pity and empathy are not the same. Alcohol turned me back into myself and killed my empathy.

(**Vatchi**): *"Sane in all other respects, but alcoholic still" you ask, Sotto? You can take the alcohol out of the alcoholic, but I think there is residual* *insanity, even for those who started out being perfectly sane. Alcohol changes everything. One bad insanity spoils the whole bunch.*

I love my optimal delusions. Here's a good one: When I drink, from the outside, all that others see is my selfish motives. That's an illusion. From the inside, I am empty, an emptiness which alcohol promises to fill, but never does. Illusion: One bar I worked in sold a draft beer for less than a glass of soda. The illusion is that it is cheaper to drink beer. For an alcoholic like me, the illusion is obvious: One five dollar soda or a three dollar beer turning into a three day blackout-binge. And the guy who buys the bar a round of drinks just likes spreading the fun around? Illusion. Usually, but not always, he is a chronic alcoholic who knows, or denies knowing, that misery loves company. I deserve a drink? Illusion. What goes up, will come down.

I paid $600.00 for my own "personal" mantra in 1974, partly because "om" wasn't good enough for me, but maybe Transcendental Meditation was. But by 1996, other people's cigarette butts were good enough for me. Illusion: Jim thinking he's not funny. There's Alateen for teenage children of alcoholics. I wonder if there's a Nico-teen? Illusion: Jim thinking he is....

(**Surimi**): *Guys, guys, guys. For someone like Jim, the questions you ask may be interesting, but leave that to science. A.A.'s Big Book says something like "more will be revealed" somewhere. Let scientists have their factual revelations. But for Jim, one fact is clear. One drink leads to ever-worsening catastrophes. Believing the world is flat does not make it flat. Just because the majority of the world's population can drink safely, does not mean that Jim can drink safely. He must not. Ever. For him, the world is bigger in absence of alcohol. His world must be round. And sober.*

Old fears reemerge like a whale coming up for air. Old fears re-emerge, like a bad habit. Old illusions and delusions of alcohol's charms beckon.

My first relapse, after attending A.A. for over a year, seemed like alcohol's plan for me. I don't remember thinking that I wanted to drink. A drink was in my hand and I had already half finished it before I even noticed. I did not decide to drink. I did not decide to drink the first half of that first drink. But I did decide to finish it. Click. Clack. Back on track. Right back on track. Let me have another and another and another. Click, clack, clicketty-clack, drink, drank, drunk. Sometimes habits are hard to break until you yourself are broken.

I did not drink today. Once again today, the Cult of Survival has won out.

EVENING MEDITATION

My oblivious drunkenness was obvious from the outside. In my sobriety it seems that it is the most subtle changes which are the most profound. The shock and awe of my outward drunkenness has been slowly replaced by just a subtle, inward, sober awe.

"You desire to know the art of living, my friend...? Make use of suffering."
— Henry F. Amiel

QUESTION FOR TODAY

How many rocks from your past must you overturn before messages change meaning, before enough of them have seen the light of day? How many before rocks become bridges instead of walls?

43. MY BATTLE, MY BOTTLE, MY BRAIN

"The child is father to the man."
– Gerald Manley Hopkins

MORNING MEDITATION

Breaking old patterns, forming new patterns: That's how I bake. That's how I break. That's how I roll. That's how I grow. That's how I know.

The battle with my brain. Thinking that I could win the battle with the alcoholic part of my brain. Never realizing, or admitting, or being in denial about this one basic fact: There is no one part of my brain that is alcoholic. My entire brain, my entire being, my entire life, is one of alcoholism. I'm either living in my disease or I'm living in recovery.

I cannot win the battle against alcoholism alone. Alone, despite an abundance of knowledge and experience, my brain seems to take me like a rat through a maze back to that first drink. That first drug. And after that first one, there is no other. Continuous craze at the end of that maze. Just one drink puts me there. Immediately, if not sooner. One and done.

(**Sotto**): *What's that old saying about one man crossing twenty bridges or twenty men crossing one bridge?*

Now my head feels like it's swimming in alcohol. Don't know what year. Best guess- 1980. A drunk like me crashed at my apartment in Ventnor, the next town down beach from Atlantic City. Climbing up three flights of steps in the middle of the morning. He was from Philly, I think. I can't remember now. He couldn't remember then. And here's what he could not remember - crashing at my apartment two nights in a row. Walking up three flights of steps in a Ventnor apartment building two nights in a row.

"You were here last night, remember?"

"You're kidding?"

"I'm serious." The conversation went something like that. Never saw him again.

I was always swearing that I would stop drinking if I got this or I got that and then, when I did get this or that, it was always, like... I'll quit drinking if I ever get this next thing or that next thing. But the only next thing I ever got was another drink.

The new fucked up happened so slowly it felt like an old shoe by the time it sank in. I'll never get like that.

Until I did, and then it was still okay.

(**Vatchi**): *Listen to him! "If I got this or I got that..." He's fucked up. He's still telling lies to himself sober. Who does he think he's kidding? Not me. Himself only. He is full of himself and he's full of shit. The only reason he or anyone else who is an alcoholic stops drinking is because of negative consequences, if then. You don't win the lottery and suddenly say, "I guess I'll quit drinking now."*

"Bring it on!" is more like it. "Bring on the booze."

Jim, if you could hear me, I would say, "Get REAL!"

I did not drink today. I will not drink today. I cannot drink today.

I can conjugate a drink. I just don't want to contemplate one. Find something else to do, Jim. "Live, laugh, love." Not "drink, drank, drunk."

(**Surimi**): *Yes, Vatchi, Jim may be kidding himself, even sober. The denial part of his alcoholism seems to have pretty much receded. His old triggers are slowly becoming things he's dealing with on life's terms. His new triggers propel him forward in his sobriety. The trigger of sobriety itself to seek more sober and satisfying things. Call it the anti-trigger, if you will. Now, when his expectations and outcomes don't match, he no longer seeks solace in the drink. He's no longer in a war on drugs. He's living in the solution. In recovery. Bar Rooms, his "cathedrals of consumption," are part of his living memory of his past.*

"Doing nothing is not an option," as he's heard expressed often enough in his recovery groups. Addiction is a patient disease. I think he has finally learned to stick with the winners.

My battle with my brain rages on incessantly. My brain against my brain. Clearly, there can be no winner in this war. I may as well drink. You see? It's like that. "One alcoholic helping another" does seem about my only hope for a continuing recovery. "We have seen the enemy and he is us" is about how Pogo expressed it in Walt Kelly's comic strip. My brain is lame. Hence, thus, therefore: lamebrain.

Suffering for my art ends here. Recovery for me starts here. I did not drink today and that is that.

EVENING MEDITATION

On Land's End, the edge of a lake in Mays Landing, New Jersey. In a drunken stupor a couple of relapses ago. I don't think I consciously chose to be a dying drunk at the water's edge. Each grain of sand along the water's edge could have been an epiphany if I had had the power to feel. Survival of the fittest seemed to have taken over when I was no longer able to fight. Sweet surrender: what I could not yet know.

"One's destination is never a place, but rather a new way
of looking at things."
— Henry Miller

QUESTION FOR TODAY

Can my past, too, be infinite or are all the stones already carved?

44. **SWEET OBLIVION, PRETTY POISON**

*"How come if alcohol kills millions of brain cells, it never killed
the ones that make me want to drink?"*
—Author unknown

MORNING MEDITATION

Abstinence is cold and lonely and wants a drink. Recovery moves the human heart
forward, fulfilled (Yes, I lay it on a little thick sometimes). Sometimes.

An avalanche and then forgetful snow. This is how I would die. Death by
alcohol. It would seem to comfort as it killed...

I've said it before and I can and I will and I must say it again. Repetition
ever reminds me that I must not repeat my actions. I repeat again that
alcohol is my poison, my prison. A brick wall, a trap door, a cancer, a bad
joke, an empty bottle, an excuse, a leaky faucet, a loan shark, a broken
promise, a cracked mirror, an earthquake, an avalanche, a train wreck, a
recurring nightmare.

Alcohol is my insanity. Yes, I repeat myself. Over and over. I repeat the
words so that I do not repeat the actions. Retrain my brain. Repeat the
words. To learn, to unlearn, to relearn. To live sober. Over and over.

(**Sotto**): *I like Jim's use of words here. Words as approximations of facts.
Analogies of addictions. Whistling in the dark: half-prayer, half fear. But
Vatchi, I sense a sort of reckless solitude here on his part, don't you?*

"At least I'm not an addict." That's the sense of moral superiority I once
had. Today, that statement would be sadly laughable. Too hung over to
carry a bar tray full of drinks without spilling them. Asking co-workers to

141

place the straight up martinis in front of the customers' placemats because my daily shakes wouldn't allow me to do so without spilling. Spill. Spill. Spill. Spill. Spill. Avalanche.

If alcoholism isn't addiction to alcohol, what the hell is it?

Spill. Spill. Fucking spill.

(**Vatchi**): *Sotto, that's why the support of others is so critical in recovery. Without support, especially, I guess, for people like Jim, that half fear, half-prayer could turn into a full shot glass. Solitude can turn to loneliness without that support that Jim is finding in his A.A. meetings. Loneliness can be a big trigger. Alcohol separated him from the world in his addiction and loneliness can take him back out there.*

Who doesn't pack vodka?

I have to stop right here. My sister, Betty, blew her brains out with a shotgun. So her body wasn't at her funeral.

Who doesn't pack?

I have to stop here.

Who doesn't?

I have to... stop.

(**Surimi**): *You're right, Sotto. Alcohol can look like a pretty poison, praying for change, fearing that one cannot. A snake pit. Jim didn't list that one. The poison, the potion, the venom, the snake. And Vatchi, I think you hit the nail on the head with loneliness being one of Jim's biggest triggers. Alcohol took him out of himself, but eventually left him with nothing. No one ever knew he needed help because he was so good at hiding it from himself and from others. Sweet oblivion. Pretty poison.*

I guess it's no wonder that when you get to the point where you can't hold a drink without spilling it that you also can no longer hold a job. Not that I'm making excuses, but it just seems that once you slide so far down into your alcoholism after so many years, you are so entrenched that it seems the only answer is another drink.

My life, condensed and frozen on the walls of my brain, could not be papered over. Scrape bottom, seek help, change. Of course, that was not my hallucination at the time.

EVENING MEDITATION

So much is known and so much unknown about addiction and recovery. But I do know this much: If my very first rehab had not allowed me to continue my addiction to smoking cigarettes as I tried to remain sober, I most likely would have bolted out of there, no fourteen day stay. I would have left, I would have smoked, I would have had a drink, and I may have died. Trial and error is frightening when you confront the fact that one small error can change the entire course of your life. Today, not drinking and not smoking are mutually reinforcing. Lose one and I would most certainly lose both.

I did not smoke or drink today.

"Humor is just another defense against the universe."
– Mel Brooks

QUESTION FOR TODAY

Where do you turn when more is too much, too empty, too lost?

45. **ALBINO GRUBS**

"Fear is an emotion indispensable for survival."
– Hannah Arendt

MORNING MEDITATION
I fear faith that preaches fear. My defense? Ignore ignorance.

Trapped in the state of being, everything is as it seems: You cannot find your dream. You want to turn the wheel on which you're turning: You want to become. You want to be real, but find it disagreeing, really so unpleasing, when everything is as it seems. You cannot break the seal, it's so uneasing, trapped in the state of being: You cannot find your dream. You want to turn the wheel on which you're turning: You want to become.

A shopping list of memories piles up like snow. Waking up to snow. Numbed by snow. By memories... Smoking cigarettes on the balcony in Hartford, Connecticut because Trent's mother had only one lung. Waiting for my hangover to go away so that my desire to get drunk again would return. Being able, at one time, to afford all the chic places to eat and drink and still not fitting in. Having anonymous sex in a fur vault, in an abandoned building, and here and there and this and that. The memories pile up like snow. Adding to the list, adding to the list, drinking to oblivion.

(**Sotto**): *Isn't it ironic? This listing of memories, as Jim is doing it here, once again, seems very much like he's trying to gain some measure of control over his past (over his alcoholism?). Lists seem to do that. Some sense of tidy order made out of disorder. Powerless over his past, he feebly attempts to make a list, to regain some illusion of control, taking back some power now that he's sober. Maybe it's not ironic. Maybe it's just sad.*

Here's a real list for you, Vatchi: every bar in Atlantic City Jim went to, every liquor store he got thrown out of, every job he got fired from, every apartment he got evicted from, every roommate he ever had. Every spill, from one hospital to the next, one rehab to the next detox, spill, spill, spill, spill to the last cascade.

Read that list, Vatchi. Feel that power, Jim. At least his sobriety is a better illusion than the content of his lists.

Isn't that ironic, Vatchi?

"Jim, how is it that you don't have a hang-over?" That question was typically asked of me by anyone who had the misfortune of spending the night with me. Whomever it was, and there were many, did not understand that I did not have a hangover because I was still drunk. In fact, drunk enough that I would find a way to stay drunk all day (typically a Sunday after a hard-liquor Saturday night). Mimosa, Bloody Mary, Champagne Cocktail. Two or three of those at a Sunday Brunch would tide me over before the groundswell of hard liquor would return later on Sunday afternoons.

There would be no hangover when I remained drunk.

(**Vatchi**): *Sotto, Jim is fucked up. And that I, at times, understand him, that is the irony.*

I don't have to overturn every rock to see what albino grubs live beneath them from my long gone past. I just have to not drink. No. That's not true. Just not drinking isn't the solution. Just not drinking is not recovery. Recovery is action. And interaction. I need the interaction with other alcoholics that I find in my A.A. meetings. There. I've said it. I need the interaction with other alcoholics that I find in my A.A. meetings. And I've just learned something else. I will search under each rock of my rocky past, in due time, but I must also turn over some of the rocks since my sobriety began. Sober realizations of my newly sober life. The albino grubs of my most recent sober past need the light of day, too.

"More will be revealed," is how it is sometimes expressed at my A.A. meetings.

"Albino Grubs Seek Daylight," my mental newspaper proclaims. My stupor slowly fades.

(**Surimi**): *Guys, Guys, Guys. Sotto. Vatchi. Jim's brain has been hijacked for dozens of years. When that alcoholic plane/brain crashed, his life, his brains, were splattered on the runway. The plane, obliterated. And Sotto, your comments about Jim's lists? That's part of his brain's inventory. He's starting a new life. He's picking up the pieces. This is the deconstruction and* *reconstruction of a new life for him. Jim is Humpty Dumpty putting himself back together again. With the help of others who are like him. That's not irony. "One alcoholic helping another." That's survival of the fittest. Survival for all who band together against a common foe: Alcoholism.*

I remember seeing magazine ads with Ronald Reagan, then the actor, hawking Chesterfield cigarettes, the glamour of addiction unperceived, the calming effect of a cigarette suggesting the simple fact that every puff would return me to my level of addiction. Smoke cigarettes and play pinball across the street from my high school – that's what I did. I was never cool, no matter how many signs of coolness propped me up. Crutches of coolness in my terrible teens. In terms of growing up, my groundwork had been laid by the culture that surrounded me. It was all I knew. Smoking and drinking for me were inevitable.

Today, I do not belong to yesterday. Things can change. Perhaps I can change, too.

EVENING MEDITATION

"I" am the eye of this life's storm.

"It is one of the most beautiful compensations of this life that no man can sincerely try to help another without also helping himself."
– Ralph Waldo Emerson

QUESTION FOR TODAY

Do you hear that inanimate thing, that drink, calling your name? Do you hear the drumbeat of your heart, of that drink? Can it, will it, ever be just a memory? Can you outlive it? Can you survive it? Can you live sober?

46. **IMPLOSIONS**

*"I don't think we get more alcoholic. I think it just shows
more as time goes on."*
– *A New Pair of Glasses*, Chuck "C"

MORNING MEDITATION

When I first got sober, there was no pleasure in sobriety. Red was gray. Yellow was gray. Blue was gray. My brain was unable to experience pleasure. Too gray to cry. Too gray to try. Too gray to die.

Before Tina Turner rocketed to superstardom with "Private Dancer," I wrote these lame lyrics for her, which she wisely rejected.

"Get Me Out Of These Clothes"

This life that I'm living's
Called just getting by
On a pint of gin,
On a loaf of bread.
It's a nowhere life
And I feel half dead.
Ain't no kind of living
When you're just getting high
On a pint of gin,
On a pound of food,
On a dead end street,
In an empty mood,
With no one to give to.
Make love with me, Baby.

It's your love that can save me
From this dead end battle,
From this bread without gravy.
Make just a little,
Make just a little love,
A little love, Baby.
I'm only real when you touch me.
Can't you feel when you touch me?
Get me out of these clothes.
Get me out of this mood.
Get me off of this street.
Get me out of this life.
Make love with me, Baby.

(It goes on and on and on, just as badly, and worse. But that's all I can handle right now, truthfully.)

(**Sotto**): *Jim obviously is a hopeless romantic. His sentiments seem to speak, "Love conquers all," but that, frankly, seems not to be the case when he's in the drink. Addiction trumps love. All bets are off. Alcohol is the winner and the winner takes all. Love be damned. Case closed. Vatchi, he expresses things well sometimes, yet doesn't seem to have a grip on things himself? How is that?*

One drunk offers another drunk, a total stranger, a line of cocaine while standing at the urinal in the men's room of a favorite watering hole. I was the one stranger accepting the free line of coke from the other stranger. Most drunks, the ones I knew anyway, would gladly accept a free line of coke from a friendly stranger. In fact, I rarely bought coke. It was offered to me free of charge often enough. Pleasure, like misery, loves company. And addiction loves company, at first, at first, at first.

In many ways I was fortunate that I had always ignored offers of free crack or heroin. I had already been entrenched in my addiction to alcohol by the time those offers were made to me.

(**Vatchi**): *Even Jim's somewhat inept ability to describe human frailties is at least partly due to his own frailties. Experience trumps talent. At times not understanding the depth of his own remarks, and at other times, over-estimating himself completely. Like you mentioned before about list making and the illusion of being in control, all of this, all of this, all of this is about Jim coming to grips with himself, with his life, with his alcoholism.*

Whistling in the dark. And then... enter, stage left, "King Alcohol."

2011: I heard the announcer on TV say that that year was the Twenty-Fifth Anniversary of the 1986 Challenger Tragedy. "Everyone remembers where they were when it exploded," he said.

I was in a bar thoughtlessly waiting for the empty coffin of myself to implode.

(**Surimi**): *Implosion. No fireworks. No Fourth of July. An entire life crumbling in upon itself. Like a black hole, so dense that no light can escape. There are no rubber-neckers to implosions. Implosions are not cause to celebrate. There is nothing to see. Not communal. Nothing communal here. Solitary. Alone. Entirely alone.*

If one, then, survives this implosion, I suppose that there is some hope of finding a way out. What would be Jim's bid for any kind of normal? Do I hear "one"? Do I hear "zero"?

People, places and things. Not only am I an alcoholic, but I am also part and parcel of the culture of addiction. More than alcohol would have to go if I were ever to stay sober. Part of who I was lived in the thoughts of those around me. Some people can remain sober when their spouse still lives in their addiction. Some other alcoholics can tend bar in sobriety. I tried tending bar in my first sober year but it was the culture of addiction I was surrounded by which was my downfall finally. One day a drink found its way into my hands and I drank it without thought. That was that and several years went by, drinking, drinking, progressing and progressing, backwards, downwards and out.

So much for people, places and things for me. So much more time lost, tossed, apple-sauced.

EVENING MEDITATION

I tended to believe in my expectations, in the good times drinking promised to deliver as it once had done. I accepted what I wanted to believe. But the cold, hard facts were that the results of drinking, that eventual brick wall, did not and could not and now never would, live up to my expectations. Expectations and I got smashed. We, oui and whee!

> *"The way to love anything is to realize it might be lost."*
> – G. K. Chesterton

QUESTION FOR TODAY

What signposts did I pass by on my alcoholic highway? What wouldn't I ignore for one more for the road?

47. ALCOHOLIC BONSAI BASTARD

*"Whatever you think you can do or believe you can do, begin it.
Action has magic, grace and power in it."*
– Johann Wolfgang von Goethe

MORNING MEDITATION
Getting freed from my past is getting freed for my future.

When I drink, the only world there is, is alcohol. I will drink until I blackout and I will continue drinking until I pass out. More is the only word I know. More, until I blackout and then still more until my body shuts down and I pass out. And somehow, even then, more is not enough. My disease cannot ever be satisfied. When there is nothing else, there is always more.

More is everything… and nothing.

I will never be like most normal folks.

When I drink, the only world there is, is alcohol.

(**Sotto**): *I don't know if I can feel as empty as Jim has felt. Knowing the cause does not erase the effects of his emptiness. I don't think I've ever felt an emptiness quite like his.*

This street on which I live, this street which is my mind, now clean, now calm, now well-lit, could not have been imagined considering all I've gone through to get here. This journey forward that I am on will continue to set me free. I will turn over my fears, let go the falling leaves of time. Let snow begin to fall.

(**Vatchi**): *Empty is a good starting place when you want to start over, Sotto.*

You may feel empty, but the things that got you there may still be hanging around, like the drink, always within arm's reach. Emptiness is a feeling, lack thereof, and an illusion. "People, Places and Things."

Hope snowballs. Recovery seems possible. I am becoming a person, a sober person, still young in my sobriety, still getting older in years. Like an alcoholic bonsai bastard, I am clinging to this rock, well-weathered, alive. If I have a drink, I won't have a snowball's chance in hell. A bonsai bastard am I.

(**Surimi**): *How is it that you can have such misplaced emotions? Sotto, you persist at differentiating yourself from others. Allow yourself to identify. Even allowing near similarities will allow you to become more of a person. "Mr. Gorbachev, tear down this wall!" is how President Reagan said it, Sotto.*
And you, Vatchi! Lighten up! Too many of your trains of thought point to death and dying. At least Jim's self-deprecation is only a small step backwards in the undulations of his moves ever forward. Trust in Jim's recovery. I think he's beginning to.

The effects of alcohol addiction on me have been many and various. I say "bonsai bastard" because, like a bonsai, my growth has been stunted by years of alcohol use. And "bastard" because I cling tenaciously to my sobriety, like a true bonsai in nature might cling to an outcropping of rocks, a life in miniature. Another alcoholic analogy. There must be thousands.
The intelligence of trees, deformed.
Emotions eroded by the flow of alcohol through my veins stunted my maturing process. Much, if not most, of sobriety has been simply learning to grow up no longer under the influence. Addiction's lies appearing bigger than the truths that they obscured. Fragile, unverifiable, contaminated, directionless, I was delivered to the doors of the rooms of recovery powerless over my addictions, frightened, a pathological and tragic figure at best. The cage door of addiction was always open and I was afraid of freedom from addiction because it was incomprehensible and seemed impossible and was never even considered.

EVENING MEDITATION
Like a scene from The Exorcist, there was a time when I felt as equally possessed by Alcoholism as Linda Blair's character felt possessed by the Devil. At one point, we both would have done anything to make it stop. What makes alcoholism and other addictions even worse is that for most people, hitting bottom is a complete nightmare and each successive relapse is a recurring, worsening nightmare.

*"A tough lesson in life that one has to learn is that
not everybody wishes you well."*
– Dan Rather

QUESTION FOR TODAY

*How much of isolation is self-imposed after the King, Alcohol, has been
deposed? How much of blame is well-deserved and how much not? How
much, how much, how much, how much is enough?*

48. **THIS PICKLE MUST CHANGE**

*"Go confidently in the direction of your dreams.
Live the life you have imagined."*
– Henry David Thoreau

MORNING MEDITATION

Ancient in origin, the "well-trodden path" did not seem to be the one I was on when I first got sober. I had a lot of vine hacking to do to stay sober. And it took a while for the trail from my drinking to grow over and this new path called sobriety to be my foothold. My path to sobriety would be my own, yet I could not, would not, did not do it alone. "Well-trodden" to others, yet unique to each and all. Ancient drums beating in the distance, my newly sober heart straining to hear and follow.

A man jumps out of a burning building, his clothing consumed in flames. Ripping off his clothes, some of his skin and burning flesh comes off with the shirt he was wearing. The blisters are now just forming, the smoke and stench of burning hair in the air. Paramedics struggle to put him on a stretcher, his arms and legs flailing from the pain of his suffering, his screams drowning out the screams of the sirens. Suddenly, he breaks free from the paramedics and runs back into the burning building, the walls now consumed in flames.

This is the insanity of alcoholism. This is relapse. And this will happen again and again, each time just a little bit differently, each time progressively worse. Insanity, according to Einstein, is "doing the same things over and over again and expecting different results." The insanity of my disease wants me to cross through the threshold of that door, cross back to drink, to think that more is more.

(**Sotto**): *Like you said earlier, Vatchi, Jim is, in a sense, whistling in the dark. His themes, his dreams, his drunken days, repeat themselves and he repeats them back, a drumbeat, trying to survive.*

The drink wants me. There's a crazy, crazy part of me, when I'm feeling lonely and a little bit sad that says, "The drink still wants me." That is as insane as I can admit at this time. The drink is like a hand puppet and I listen and I believe. Believed and deceived. Insanity. Insane. Hand puppet. I cannot feel my hand. My lips are numb. Alcohol numbs my lips.

The drink still wants me.

(**Vatchi**): *That's a bald truth you've just expressed, Sotto. Illicit drugs, illegal drugs, prescription drugs. Jim's drunken days still beat in his ears. When he's listening and when he does not listen.*

I would drink before going into the movie theater and drink immediately after, but it never would have occurred to me to take a bottle or a flask into the theater with me. Eventually I reached the point I couldn't go two hours without a drink. so I stopped going to movie theaters altogether. I'd take out free movies from the library once in a blue moon (I didn't have a VCR and would watch movies at a friend's apartment). One night, after coming home drunk near dawn, I lost the key to my apartment (again), I fell asleep (passed out) on my doormat and woke up (came to) with my movie having been stolen from right under me (literally my pillow).

When I couldn't pay for the lost movie, the library (my former employer) revoked my library card. On my downward spiral, it took several relapses and several job firings to scrape together enough money to pay the library fine and reinstate my privileges.

I followed rules so well, did what was expected of me for so long, broke very few laws. Change that to "got caught breaking" very few laws. Years sober and I still forget that with the exception of alcohol and tobacco, obviously legal, all the drugs I did were either illegal or prescription drugs I didn't seem capable of taking as directed by the physician. My brain seems to seek all drugs, legal and illegal, prescribed by a doctor (or someone else's doctor) or not.

(**Surimi**): *Jim must wear his sobriety "like a loose-fitting garment." Not a Halloween costume or mask. He used to get really drunk. Authentic sobriety is far away for him, still. Like French, Spanish or Chinese, living sober is akin to learning a whole new language, a new way of thinking, being and doing. Dynamic change. "You can't change a pickle back into a cucumber." Indeed. And yet. And still... This Pickle Must Change.*

It did once seem my brain was a Geiger counter in search of alcohol or other drugs, metallic clicking increasing in volume and frequency as I neared my score, my sip, my slug, my drug. The pleasure of anticipation (false emotion, this) seemed to precede the drug. The pleasure was not really during and after the high. The high would eventually bring pain. Before the drug the pleasure came and then the pain. The pain would always come and always wanting more. How insane is this, was I? There was no reward. There was only addiction and the insanity of addiction. How insane was I?

EVENING MEDITATION

Murder in the first degree, premeditated murder. "Alcohol is out to kill you." That kind of murder. That kind of murderer. Just short of paranoid, I felt alcohol was out to get me when I first got sober. I would meditate to block the beast, to find peace. Meditate/Premeditated. It makes some insane senseless sense. Anxiety, then, serenity, find me now.

"What do I know of man's destiny? I could tell you more about radishes."
– Samuel Beckett

QUESTION FOR TODAY

Are you a one-trick pony? Will you ever learn to be free?

49. MY HIROSHIMA, MY NAGASAKI

"A mind stretched by a new idea never shrinks back
to its original dimensions."
– Oliver Wendell Holmes

MORNING MEDITATION
I used to resent when someone at an alcohol or drug addiction recovery meeting would suggest that you could use anything as your higher power, 'that door, anything.' Then someone else pointed out that 'that door' was willingness.

Don't get between me and the next drink. When I'm drinking, that is dangerous territory. And my disease was a great coach. It taught me how to use my charm as a weapon. To get what I wanted. When I wanted it. People, Places and Things (potential triggers in my recovery) were tools in my addiction. The forests were the trees in my disease, Louise.

Please, oh please Mr. Bartender, just one more for the road? Please?

(**Sotto**): *I like Jim's "And my disease was a great coach." I can almost hear 'the coach' saying things like, "Okay, Jim, shoot a few more baskets and I'll take you and the rest of the team out for a pizza and some pitchers of beer." Easy, peas-y. Not too disease-y.*

"Warning: Alcoholism Ahead" - There were no signs posted on the roadway my life was taking as I grew up. Even the supposed 'cultural revolution' of the sixties (and early '70's): the Beatles, Ken Kesey, Timothy Leary, Women's Liberation and that whole ball of wax. No Warning Signs there. Or ignored, at best. Alcohol was not only socially acceptable (as was smoking cigarettes, really), it was expected in the neighborhood I grew up in. Alcoholism, like a thousand and one other subjects, is a taboo subject, still, in much of American culture. The rooms of my childhood and adolescence were not big enough for all the elephants in those rooms. And the elephants in this room, the room that I am in right now, may only be recognized by me in retrospect. Self-justification becomes a way of life.

(**Vatchi**): *Such a great coach alcohol is, indeed, Sotto. The invisible coach cheering you on to victory. Except other people know who's coaching you before you do. And the victory you imagine is actually an illusion that will drive you, finally, to complete defeat, thinking you still could somehow win. Until there's no hope left and booze stops working. Still, you will continue to drink. The biggest of the people, places and things is that thing in your mind, the mind itself and its invisible coach, King Alcohol.*

To me, celebration and alcohol were synonymous. In fact, "celebrate" was a euphemism for drinking, a part of my culture, my denial. The celebration of a New Year is synonymous with the popping cork of champagne bottles. My Hiroshima and Nagasaki (euphemisms for hitting bottom and relapsing time and again) would come later. Christ, why could I never surrender to my disease? I intellectualized or did nothing at all. Hilarity did not ensue. But unnecessary chaos did.

"Side Effects May Include...," did not include "You Will Not Listen." My bragging rights to consumption would drown out "You Will Not Listen."

Salt on the rim of the Margarita glass, salt on the wound....

"You Will Not Listen." Ouch. I did not listen.

(**Surimi**): *Pain is a great motivator, coach, if you will. "Get out there and fight" or "Get in there and fight."*

Forty-eight flavors and they're all alcohol. The prize is the punishment. The prize is the punishment in that insane world. The prize is the punishment. It's "Here, this'll cure what ails you." And it's "Thanks, Coach. Thanks, Coach." And there is no goal-to-go, Coach. Done. Done. The game is done. The finish line. And no one won.

"Thanks, Coach. Thanks."

Thinking of my disease when I was in my disease was a pleasing cul-de-sac at times. Trapped, but a drink would fix all that. My deadened thinking somehow allowed me to separate myself from my disease and being separate from it in many ways allowed it, encouraged it. The courage to be discouraged. Some such insanity. Separation from reality allowed its separation. Insane. Too much saki. Too, too, too much saki. Too much, too much, Nagasaki.

Insane.

EVENING MEDITATION

When addiction co-opted the pleasure system of my brain, my irrational thoughts and fears became a perpetual motion machine whose purpose for spinning was spinning to spin. The waterwheels and windmills fueled by the self-sustaining powers of alcohol. Eternity seemed complete in my alcoholic delusion. At least for twenty years or so.

"I have an everyday religion that works for me. Love yourself first, and everything else falls into line."
– Lucille Ball

QUESTION FOR TODAY

Did being medicated prevent you from seeing the downward progression of alcoholism? Was your truth too difficult to bear? Free of gravity, there is no down. What other illusions have you found?

50. SAFETY IN NUMBERS

"It is possible to store the mind with a million facts and still be entirely uneducated."
– Alec Bourne

MORNING MEDITATION

Even when I feel helpless, I can still help someone else. Remembering this can get me out of a funk. Relapse prevention: mine or theirs. I have to stay connected with this sober crowd in order for me to remain sober. Over time 'have to' became 'want to.' A subtle perceptual shift.

"Oh, wait. What? Alcoholism is an illness? Addiction is a disease?" Ignorant disbelief. Early on in my alcoholic descent, no matter how bad my hangover in the morning, I could always find an inescapable reason to get drunk that very next night, no matter what. No matter how strongly I may have told myself "never again," the disease of alcoholism would dissolve my resolve before the liquid night called alcohol would dissolve my brain again.

Alcoholism and drug addiction seem to be our culture's biggest cancer (double the cases of biological cancer, so I've been told). Add ice, stir, ignore. Ignorant disbelief. It took me decades to admit that I am an alcoholic and another ten years to learn to say "we".

"We are alcoholics." There, I said it. ten years of discontinuous sobriety, then, finally, "We...".

(**Sotto**): *"We," he said. "We." He said it and I'm repeating it. "We." "I need help," brought him to his knees. His disease. His "I need help." Recovery. Relapse. Recovery. And finally, "We..."*
Or am I hearing things, Vatchi? He did just say "We," didn't he?

159

Jail might be a place to sit, to sort things out. My ivory tower self fantasizes the grateful solitude jail might have been, could yet be, knowing full well the isolation would just let my alkie brain stew and stew, machination upon machination. Mere absence of alcohol in the body does not erase the alcoholism in my brain.

I have come to understand how recidivism and relapse are intertwined. Isolation is not solitude. Comfort and security can lead to growth or stagnation.

I can't seem to herd the cats within my brain. How the fuck am I going to stay sober? Hey, doggie, herd them cats my brain.

(**Vatchi**): *Sotto, Jim's very doubt here, doubting he can stay sober shows me that I don't think he fully gets it yet. Remember, he just admitted that it took him ten years to say "we" after it took him decades of alcohol abuse for him to hit bottom and finally admit that he's an alcoholic.*

"I get drunk, we stay sober," is how it's been expressed in the rooms of recovery. He just needs to embrace the "we" part of his recovery program. His knowledge can be fleeting and doubtful. "Trust in the program." "It works if you work it." All these statements are true for him. For anyone. Everyone. For Jim.

There's the mental illness that is alcoholism, the disease of my mind that tells me to drink more despite negative consequences. The disease of my mind that had me continuing to drink long after I had shifted into blackout mode. There is the mental illness that is alcoholism and the mental illness beyond alcoholism that my alcoholism has caused. Hitting my bottom brought on a state of severe clinical depression. There is the insanity of alcoholism and the further insanities that alcoholism sometimes cause. Parallel and co-existing insanities. Survival and addiction meet at ground zero. In the white light outside the emergency room in the dead of night, in a drunken epiphany, I hit bottom, the sum of all memories undisclosed by alcohol, a life of alcoholism, my resentful teacher.

(**Surimi**): *When Jim said, "We are alcoholics," I was so pleased. Safety in numbers to those who understand the power of alcohol and the powerlessness of the alcoholic. And for those who decide that the herd instinct with all its negative connotations is not for them, I would have to say that, except for rare instances, the help of others is almost always needed in the battle with addiction. How could the same unaided brain disease called alcoholism recover solely under its already diseased power? I don't know, Sotto, Vatchi, but some few can. Alcohol is "a subtle foe," indeed. And Jim? Subtle? Not so much. Not very subtle at all.*

Herd the cats in my brain, my alcoholic brain. Another 'cat' sits next to me at my A. A. meeting. He's herding the cats in his brain, his alcoholic brain. Perhaps together we can shepherd these cats together, in turn and together, herding cats, herding our brains, alcoholics all. The alcoholic melting pot of herding cats. Call this recovery. Let me call this recovery. Let us.

EVENING MEDITATION

I should hope that somehow my self-sorrow will end. But it has not ended yet. It exists within my current self, my sober self. It is a sorrow and a pity for my younger, drunken self, that self near dead, containing a dormant predator. This predator waits for me to let down my guard. Yet today, self-pity is one of many baits my predator disease lays out, a mouse trap in my recovery maze. Relapse will always be a possibility. There are traps and I must be vigilant. I see my younger, drunken self this world over. I must remain vigilant.

> *"I'd like to live as a poor man with lots of money."*
> – Pablo Picasso

QUESTION FOR TODAY

Are your always and forever more important to your yesterday or your tomorrow? What remains to be finished? Is anything best forgotten? What?

51. ONE TRICK PONY, DISMOUNT

"Luck is a matter of preparation meeting opportunity."
– Oprah Winfrey

MORNING MEDITATION
I accepted being powerless over alcohol when I was drunk because being drunk killed the pain of being powerless.

My brain knows my disease. My brain loves my disease and my brain will never forget my disease because my disease has carved permanent grooves into my brain that no amount of sobriety can ever putty shut. The grooves in my brain lay waiting for me to pick up again so that the grooves can progressively deepen. I must depend on the help of others. Acting alone, I will be devoured by my disease. For addicts, alcohol will devour memories of the past and anxiety about the future, drowning them in the unreal, insane world of addiction. A living lobotomy. A blind man descending a spiral staircase leading to nowhere. No past. No present. No future. Addiction will survive by eating you alive.

Now, in recovery, I'm learning how to thrive.

(**Sotto**): *Well, isn't that fucking beautiful? The guy gets sober and finally life is like a goddam Broadway Musical. He's delusional: One nut short of a Cracker Jack box.*

The myth of Sisyphus, that eternal hell of pushing the exact same rock up the exact same hill, only to watch it roll all the way back down every time. There's a whole lot of hell going on there, but at least Sisyphus knew the score. With alcoholism, I had too much at stake to admit this reality.

The Legacy Effect: I had too much at stake. I had to put a higher worth on my worthless efforts. Protect what was destroying me because my identity was immersed in alcohol.

I wonder if Sisyphus drank?

Rolling Rock, no doubt.

(**Vatchi**): *Sotto, sometimes I think you get so caught up in the words that you miss what's behind the words. You just commented on Jim saying, "We are alcoholics," and you totally missed that he moves two steps forward and one step back. His progress in recovery is slow and tedious and now you're mocking and oblivious. He'll hold up the truth for all eyes to see, then hide himself behind some joke.*

Jim's still in the holding cell. He's still hurting. He still lives in fear. He still uses ego as a weapon. Sotto, look behind his words. Not only is Jim an adult in recovery from alcoholism, he is still, too, a child growing into an adult.

I couldn't stop drinking. Who in their right mind would wake up after spending a fortune while in a blackout and continue drinking? The "Fucked up Stops Here" never happened. The instant my blackout would start, I was feeding my disease and nothing else. If alcoholism is insane, blackout drinking is even more insane.

It's so easy after a few years of being sober to wonder why I didn't stop drinking sooner. And it became so easy after a few years of sobriety to forget how insane it was. That is why, for me, connection with other alcoholics is so key to my continuing sobriety.

"Staying stopped" – that's the trick. Please, lucky horseshoe, let me be a one-trick pony.

(**Surimi**): *Now, that is funny. "One-trick pony"? He's had countless relapses, fallen off the wagon, gotten back on his sobriety high horse, and now he wants to be a one-trick pony. But listen up, guys. When he says "one-trick pony," I think he means "from this day forward." You know, like a wedding vow, except this time it reflects a commitment to sobriety. If fear doesn't overtake him. Or his ego, past or future. Or some misaligned need for instant gratification. Then he's got a shot, guys. I think he's got a shot. And I mean a shot at sobriety, not a shot of scotch.*

One-trick pony on the carousel of life. That's what alcohol was for me. When I'm sober, the calico carousel keeps turning, waiting for me to remount. The clock keeps ticking and drinking or not, I am an alcoholic. I am the pony. The pony is me.

Dismount.

EVENING MEDITATION

Alcohol eventually crushed my ego. Akin to a black hole in outer space whose gravitational pull prevents even light from escaping its grip, alcohol had me. Humility crushed in upon me. As corny and impossible as it may sound even to my sober self, sobriety has made what little degree of humility I possess become expansive, connecting, life-affirming. I think I'll throw up now. But seriously, folks....

"To speak ill of others is a dishonest way of praising ourselves."
— Will Durant

QUESTION FOR TODAY

On what level of drunk did you perform your personal best? And, oh, how different is life sober? Changing, changing, changing, can you feel the change? Now? How about now?

52. SIMON SAYS STAY SOBER

*"Learn to say no. It will be of more use to you than
to be able to read Latin."*
– Charles Haddon Spurgeon

MORNING MEDITATION
Smug indifference is not acceptance. Change is not born of indifference. Change starts with acceptance. Indifference does not. Repeat. Repeated. Repeat.

"John Lennon has just been shot!" That's what we heard on the radio as we left the recording studio. I say "we," but I can't really remember who the driver was. The simple fact is that at the time of John Lennon's assassination, I was the co-owner of an advertising agency and had stopped driving cars years earlier after being unable to find my car on several mornings after several nights before.

I was apparently smart enough to know I shouldn't drive while drunk, but not smart enough to understand the implications of always being too drunk to drive, every single night without exception. I had ripped my Pennsylvania driver's license into six little rectangles after one day spending four hours walking in ever larger concentric circles in the neighborhood of my apartment looking for my car, left God knows where the night before.

Back to John Lennon. Any of several people could have been driving the car from one of several recording studios I had used to record various radio and television commercials I had written and produced. I can't tell you which recording studio, which commercial, which driver. I guess time doesn't travel in a straight line for alcoholics like me. Time travels in circles, like I did when looking for my car that final day after that final night before.

Time does travel in a straight line for the police. And police cars travel in a straight line when you call 911 at six o' clock and ask them whether it is 6:00 a.m. or 6:00 p.m. because you have just awoken from a binge and have no clue.

(**Sotto**): *Vatchi, I'm beginning to see how Jim's biography has no time sequence. He's not saying, "I did this and then this happened. And I did that and then that happened." Time is like, "SPLAT!"– Shot from a paint gun. No dates. No consecutive order. Random chaos. Ping-pong balls shot through the tube in a State Lottery drawing. "And the Powerball number is... Alcohol!"*

Christ, when I was drinking, I couldn't remember anyone's name because I was always drunk. But now that I'm sober, it seems like everyone in recovery wants to remain anonymous. Alcoholics Anonymous: now, there's an irony. Wanting to remain anonymous sober and not being able to remember anyone's name when drunk!

(**Vatchi**): *Sotto, "Time is like, SPLAT!" – shot from a paint gun, for an alcoholic, just like you say. Waking up the next day... Make that coming to the next day and "What the fuck? Where the hell did this paint come from?" And the collateral damage, Sotto. "Look what you did last night, Jim." And now that Jim's sober, all that chaos, all that unreality, all that insanity. It just doesn't seem possible to the rational mind. Making amends for shit you can't even remember. Can a normal life even become possible?*
We're both so lucky, Sotto.

I thought I was the wolf in sheep's clothing, on the prowl, playing it cool. I really only got lucky when I met someone as drunk as I was. The wolf in sheep's clothing was really my alcoholism.

Why did my drinking have to keep getting worse? There was a time when it was troubling and painful, but there would have been a certain level of comfort and sustainability if it hadn't kept progressing. Of course, I'm minimizing here. That's what alcoholics do. Damn it! Why did it have to progress and why couldn't I see its progression? Why and when and how did it turn from getting high to staying high with an ever-increasing list of negative side-effects?

Brain disease. That's what I have. Oh well, but now, instead of "what the hell, I may as well drink..."

(**Surimi**): *Jim just proved it. You can't reason with insanity. And alcoholism is insanity. "Doing the same things over and over and expecting different results." That's insanity, alright. And the worst insanity, which Jim has expressed, is that it always gets worse. You can't reason with a disease* *which defies logic. Jim needs help separating himself from his disease. That's the start of recovery for him. Separating himself from people, places and things. Alcohol uses chaos as a weapon.*

"Clean and Serene." That's a Narcotics Anonymous expression. A serene mind will not pick up a drink. A blackout is not serenity. Jim's brain soaked up alcohol like a sponge. His recovery will be porous, too, but involve more than his brain. It will be porous and involve all of him, connected and serene.

I cannot betray today, the sober days leading up to now, this certain resiliency which I have somehow obtained, this gift. One drink would toss that all away. I'm invested in my sobriety now as I once was too invested in drinking as a means of self-definition. Moving forward in my sobriety actually feels good today, natural. My ever more painful relapses have brought me through these rings of fire to my current calm and sober place, a recovery enhanced by the routine miracle of breath.

Simon says, "Stay sober." "Simon Says," the schoolyard game, "Drinking game Over."

EVENING MEDITATION

Some people get sober and stay sober for the rest of their lives. Not so for me and the vast majority of alcoholics and addicts. My progress from drunk to sober has been accompanied by setbacks. For me, progressively longer periods of sobriety have been followed by progressively shorter periods of relapse. My next relapse could be my first death. "One is too many and a thousand never enough."

> *"The trouble with the world is that the stupid are cocksure and the intelligent are full of doubt."*
> – Bertrand Russell

QUESTION FOR TODAY

It's not a question of right thinking returning. When will my right thinking begin? When?

53. ACCOMPLICE TO MURDER?

"Absence of proof is not proof of absence."
– Source unknown

MORNING MEDITATION
In some ways, being sober is more selfish than being drunk. In the end, I drank for addiction's sake, but now, I'm staying sober for me.

I sat near the end of a long conference table. I was being questioned by two detectives in some office in Northfield, not far from Atlantic City. They thought that I had been witness to a murder, and that possibly I had been an accomplice. If I had known that at the time, I would never have agreed to meet with them without an attorney present because I didn't know what the hell they were talking about when they first approached me.... Until I saw the videotape of what looked like me coming out of the apartment complex at New Hampshire Avenue and the Boardwalk on the night of the murder. And it did look like me, even to me. Same height. Same weight. Same gym bag slung over the shoulder. In those grainy images, the only way I knew it wasn't me was that I never carried a bag on my right shoulder and the shoes were of a different color than any I had worn at that time.

Prior to actually viewing the video, I had admitted that I frequently was in that building to visit a friend on the ninth floor (several floors above where the murder was committed) and that although I was a blackout drinker, I only and always blacked out after leaving the building (I was sure of this because the girlfriend I always visited always passed out from over-indulgence, whereas I had only been priming the pumps, and would not blackout until much later).

I was scared. They were trying to torture a confession out of me. I had to beg them to stop so I could go outside and smoke a cigarette in the parking lot. I also drank about a half pint of vodka right out of the bottle while puffing furiously (I always 'carried' - a bottle, not a weapon - by this point, which was, like, after my third relapse, like, man, what are you talkin' about, man?).

(**Sotto**): *An indefinable sense of guilt. It's underneath his words here, Vatchi. I think I see his ploy here. I don't mean to second guess him. "That's how alcohol made me feel." Is that what he's going to say next?*

Sitting here, right now, completely sober, my drunken past seems like a distant memory, a dream. To remember that I could not remember (blackouts almost every day and night for years) only makes me sad now. I must not forget that so much of my life is beyond memory. Sins of omission. I need other alcoholics to remind me of my losses, those I can remember and those that I cannot. My brain seems to want me to forget both. And all.

(**Vatchi**): *I guess Jim would have to have an indefinable sense of guilt. He did those things. They were his life. There would have to be remorse, loss, a million emotions dealt with and not dealt with as a result of his disease. It's no wonder that most alcoholics need to help each other find a new life, a sober life, a productive life.*

The scariest thing about being a suspected murder witness is that because of my alcoholism, if not a witness to this particular murder, I could have witnessed another murder and never known it. Those more religious than I might be inclined to say that that was God's will. I'm more inclined towards pure luck on my part. It's bad enough that I was the intended murder victim on three different drunken occasions over the years. Intent and outcome unrelated, at least not always a case of cause and effect. Cause and effect are almost immaterial. Were not alcohol in the picture, it's more than likely that none of this would have happened. But, damn it, alcohol was behind, in front of and next to everything I did. The important thing here is to remain sober, make a daily commitment to sobriety and to continue to live a sober lifestyle.

(**Surimi**): *I think you're right, Sotto. I think Jim does feel an indefinable sense of guilt. He did not witness the murder, but he knows he could have, given his blackout history. And, in a certain sense, he is both the murdered and the murderer, the victim and the perpetrator. Death of self, with the weapon, alcohol. Alcohol is his poison, his potion, his perpetrator. His problem.*

Tumbleweed blows down an empty street. Now, what is left? Angel Dust. Angel weed. PCP. Tumble. Mumble. Dead.

Those two detectives were trying to torture a confession out of me (just like when alcohol had me down for the count and tortured an admission of powerlessness out of me). They were trying to find a way of making me contradict myself, catch me in a lie, get me to admit. Let a name slip out: the name of the murdered, the murderer or his accomplice. But I didn't have a clue. Mr. Green in the Laboratory with a Rope? I really had no clue. Finally, they gave up and released me. But alcohol did not release me. Alcohol did not stop torturing me, punishing me, hurting me, then helping me get over that hurt. Insanity. I should have stopped sooner. Shoulda, coulda, woulda.

Jim Anders, in his Life, with a Bottle. Stop.

EVENING MEDITATION

Even an imaginary power greater than myself is better than the real power greater than myself, which is alcohol. Any belief will do except "I believe I'll have another cocktail (W. C. Fields)."

> *"I am an agnostic; I do not pretend to know what many ignorant men are sure of."*
> – Clarence Darrow

QUESTION FOR TODAY

What does your spirit need except to be discovered? What does your blindness need except eyes?

54. THE GOD OF FROZEN YOGURT

"Silent gratitude isn't very much use to anyone."
– Gertrude Stein

MORNING MEDITATION
I am smart, but I am not smarter than my disease. No one is. No one alone. At least, not me alone.

Alcohol has changed my face. The face on my body, the state of my life, lost, doped, hopeless. Apartments, lost. All the jobs, lost. Love lost. Opportunity lost.

My un-defining moment was being plastered and bowling a 276. Seven drunken strikes in a row in my bar's bowling league. At that time, I really did do my best physically when I was drunk because drunk had become the new normal. My brain was used to drunk. My brain needed drunk to be in familiar territory. The liquid I had become used to navigating through was alcohol. Liquid me in a liquid dream swimming through alcohol. Alcohol bathed each and every cell in my body, separately and lusciously. Caressing each cell like a little warm oil rubdown at an expensive spa. Alcohol, the ultimate masseuse. I bowled a 276, plastered, shortly blacked out and still drinking, swimming through alcohol like Marlee Matlin swimming in stunning silence. There was no before or after, only this oblivion.

(**Sotto**): *He's making me a little uncomfortable here. A little too enticing. An attractive numbness. I'm shifting my feet. Is this the place where fear starts, Vatchi?*

Zombie waiting lines. I'm standing in line for my cafeteria tray at the

Lakewood Hospital, my first real rehab. High on Librium, looking and feeling like death. Dragging my feet with my body following and my mind two steps further back. I am on my way to discover my new god. My new god is frozen yogurt. When more was not enough, that was the avalanche of alcohol. More is not enough: Alcohol. More is enough: Frozen Yogurt God. Zombie trudge. Trudge, fudge, nudge, drudge. Left, right, left, right. Zombie feeding time. Mmmmm. mmmm, God.

The yogurt seemed enough, was enough, until the Librium wore off. Then the God of Frozen Yogurt melted. So maybe it wasn't the frozen yogurt at all that was my new god. My new god would be, could be the Librium until every cell in my body had mourned the death of alcohol. I kept switching gods: alcohol, Librium, frozen yogurt, and then back to Librium.

If only getting sober meant only getting sober. Oh, how easy it would be. But that is not how it is writ. A few days sober doesn't change too much of anything. When the Librium wore off, all I wanted was another drink. And to stop melting.

(**Vatchi**): *That attractive numbness enticing you, Sotto, that is not where the fear starts, Sotto. That is where the fear is buried. In that dumb numbness. Like the child beaten by a punishing father. Loving the person who just beat you down if for no other reason than he is your father. A child's forgiveness. The alcoholic, too, forgives the punishments that Alcohol metes out. "I will forgive you, Alcohol. I am the bad one. Give me now your love, your forgiveness, your soothing. Numb me now with one more drink." That is part of what is behind Jim's words, Sotto.*

Zombie yearnings. Is that all this zombie yearned for? An answer to the more of something? For what? The Zombie does not ask or answer or yearn. The Zombie plods forward.

This is all just so unimaginable.

My mind, burnt toast, seeks the God of Frozen Yogurt. Zombie security. Zombie peace. Where am I? Am I around this next corner? Zombie have no answer in this cavern of my mind. The stalagmites and stalactites of my mind are irregular and repeat without pattern. Zombie step. Zombie hear doomsday clock. Zom. Zom. Zomb

Be

(**Surimi**): *The guilt known and the guilt unknown, memories lost, never to be returned. Memories never stored in the first place. Blackout drinking. Blackout living. Blackout dreaming. The electrical storm in Jim's brain. The electricity will go out. His frozen yogurt will melt. His sobriety can never restore what was never stored in the first place. His studying alcoholism* *does not create his sobriety. Nothing is retrieved. Nothing can be relived. The storm is over, Jim. This storm is over.*

I do not know why all of this sounds so good to me. I do not know if it is part of my disease or part of my recovery. This avalanche of frozen yogurt or the gods who melted so soon after. This god is dead. Long live this god. Chocolate, chocolate, chocolate.

EVENING MEDITATION

Cocaine was one of many forces which sped me to my bottom. Less blackouts, more binges. I might have died a horrible death years and years later from alcohol alone. Cocaine and other drugs sped the progression of my alcoholism. Thanks, Cocaine & Company!

"Defeat may serve as well as victory to shake the soul and let the glory out."
– Edwin Markham

QUESTION FOR TODAY

How long does it take to discover a re-emergent self, a self already here, always here?

55. DOWN FOR THE COUNT

*"Human beings are perhaps never more frightening than when
they are convinced beyond doubt that they are right."*
— Laurens Van der Post

MORNING MEDITATION

In a twisted way, I feel like I'm becoming the person sober whom I wish I had been drunk.

[EDITOR'S NOTE: The following lyrics, eventually modified for Joe Frazier, boxing champion turned vocal performer, are from Jim's only recording contract]:

"Storm Warning"

Now I say hear me out and hear me loud and clear.
I say I'm storming out and I'm gonna make you hear....
I say I'm storming out, storming far and wide.
I say I'm storming out and there's no place left to hide....
There's no use crying out, crying out with pain.
There's no use screaming out that love's a crying shame.
There's no use running out, 'cause you're running out of time.
There's no use holding out, 'cause I'm gonna make you mine....
Storm Warning....

(**Sotto**): *Vatchi! Dig this: Joe Frazier, struggling to remain in the limelight. Struggling to get back on his feet. Not in the boxing ring. On his feet, in the limelight, singing, performing. And Jim, going down, knocked out by the alcohol, not even knowing he's down for the count. And he didn't even know* *it yet, man. What a scenario!*

Admitting that I might need some kind of continuing psychiatric help after leaving Lakewood Rehabilitation Hospital was a real breakthrough for me. I broke through the social taboo of ever admitting that I might need professional psychiatric help. Don't worry though: my defenses were such that as soon as I discovered a chink in the armor of any professional psychiatric facade, I was quick to see through their shams of perfection. As soon as I would see that any professional person was as human as I, my deduction would be something like, "they need help more than I do" and then I would start missing scheduled visits to their offices and sooner than later stop going altogether.

The present informs my past. I remember standing inside the Rodin Museum, not far from Philadelphia's Art Museum. Frozen in my alcoholism, like an insect trapped in amber, its destructive powers gave me a certain strength. Entrapment, the permanence of my disease, gave me an insane sense of indestructibility. Dying from my disease, that is what I might have known of eternity, what I should have felt, if I could have felt. The present informs my past. There is a connection here. The god of alcohol led me to the god of frozen yogurt.

"I feel like a piece of burnt toast dropped on a shag carpet landing butter side up." That is how I felt when the Librium wore off.

(**Vatchi**): *Jim was down for the count. Knocked down and knocked out by alcohol. He was toasted. Is toasted. By his own admission. I can't help but imagine Spongebob Squarepants in the boxing ring. But instead of Spongebob, it's burnt toast and the toast is Jim.*

Instead of nervous laughter, this is how I feel: just nervous because there was only one hero here. Joe Frazier is a hero. Jim Anders is not. Alcoholism is not. Is not, is not.

The Librium wore off. The after-effects of alcoholism are lingering within me these many years later. Coming of Age. Now. Coming to terms with my disease. Now. Learning to live. Now. To struggle. Now. It seems like the world around me is changing. But I am also changing as the world changes around me. I'm thinking of Charles Darwin's assertion that it's not the strongest or the smartest species that survive, but those which best can adapt to change. And sobriety is the biggest change this dyed-in-the-wool alcoholic faces. When I drank, I slowly turned to stone, a fossil. Each molecule of me replaced by a molecule of alcohol. Petrified in that true sense, replaced by alcohol, bit by bit.

(**Surimi**): *Ossified, fossilized. Down for the count. Toasted. Burnt out.*

Clarity does seem to be returning to me. Relative to my former blackout state, my mind's clear. Time will wash my past away; this fleeting moment will, too, soon be gone. Our future will obliterate into star dust. Or a black hole sucking in all eternity. Or something else more, or perhaps less, dazzling.

The Riddle of the Sphinx I could figure out. But this riddle? Catch this moment. Hold this moment. Then, let this moment go. Joe Frazier was a good man.

I do not know whence I go.

EVENING MEDITATION

Back in the Old West, the Pony Express was called express because it was fast for those times. Today, our Postal Service is jokingly called snail mail because it is perceived as slow relative to the instantaneous nature of the internet. The fact is that snail mail is far faster now than the Pony Express ever was then. By far. And a drink is fast. Far too fast for me. A drink is far too deadly fast for me. Too Fast. Far too fast. Deadly, deadly, slowly, slowly fast.

> *"Peace of mind is that mental condition in which you have accepted the worst."*
> – Lin Yutang

QUESTION FOR TODAY

Why don't you paste your hatred on me?

56. EXPRESS SNAIL

"The ego could be defined simply in this way:
a dysfunctional relationship with the present moment."
— Eckhart Tolle

MORNING MEDITATION

Habits vs. Addictions. Habits are like going to recovery meetings on a regular basis. Addictions are like what you go back to when you stop going to recovery meetings on a regular basis.

The walnut tree stood outside the witch's house. When you are ten years old, there is the distinct possibility that someone is a witch. English walnut or black walnut? I'm not so sure. Black. I like to think black. Her old house was unpainted or the paint had peeled and the wood was bleached by the sun. The wood was gray from age and the weather. And the witch sat in her living room on her rocker and she was gray from age and the weather. The sky was gray. My thoughts were gray. But not the newly installed picture window that separated us. The glass was new and clear and unscratched. Perfect.

In this scene I stood by the side of the road as if I were part of the picture I am now painting. Scatter small flakes of yellows and greens, small shimmers, like wind chimes in a soundless landscape.

Oh, yes. And her hair was gray, like piano wires.

(**Sotto**): *He's going off here. Why's he going off? Piano wires? Where's he going with this? He can be freakin' scary, man.*

My clearest memories of my childhood are not cerebral, to be sure. They

177

are mostly solitary sensory memories. If an apple fell on my head, I did not declare, "Gravity!" I would say, "Ouch!," and that would be the end of it.

It is so easy to romanticize the past, I guess. But clearly, the life of my childhood was easy. I really did love staying at my Uncle Paul and Aunt Edith's farm for one week every summer. Milking the cows by hand and collecting the eggs from the henhouse. Playing the broken piano that sat on the back porch. Rusting piano wires.

(**Sotto**): *Piano wires again. What's with the piano wires?*

(**Vatchi**): *Clearly, he's getting off track here. Christ, he needs a fact-checker. What does this have to do with anything? Sotto, I don't know if this is some diversionary tactic of his or what. He doesn't know about us, so this must be some kind of delusion or flashback. Just have some patience. He'll come back around. He's not totally derailed.... yet.*

Son of a bitch! Maybe my childhood seemed so great, not because I was a child, but because it preceded the onset of my alcoholic catastrophes.

(**Surimi**): *Maybe romanticizing the past isn't really romanticizing at all. Jim's romanticizing a past that preceded the onset of his alcoholism. Seeking sobriety by exploring the prehistoric record. And, by prehistoric, I'm referring to all the life that preceded his very first drink.*

B.C. (Before Catastrophe), A.D. (After Detox), D.P. (Downhill Progression), E.S. (Early Sobriety) - I could alphabet soup my entire life, put it into chronological order. But there can be no Autobiography of this life. It seems as if it can only be the way it is: slow, tedious, order imposed after the fact....

(**Surimi**): *It is a wonder that Jim has survived at all. Luck as much as anything. Not beginner's luck, but luck, just as well.*

"Whee!" declared the snail riding on the back of the turtle.

EVENING MEDITATION

My recipe for disaster was doing whatever I was doing whenever I was drinking, which was always. Short term disasters, long term disasters. Before, during and after any disaster there was always the drink. In an odd way, it's no wonder that I didn't blame it on the alcohol. Certainly, I sometimes mouthed the blame on alcohol when it served some purpose. Jim - alcoholism's latest victim.

From victim of alcohol to living responsibly in recovery. Now that's a recipe.

"Every wrong attempt discarded is a step forward."
– Thomas Edison

QUESTION FOR TODAY

Have you conquered the art of madness?

57. FINDING PEACE

*"The only way to heal the pain is to embrace the pain.
The only way out is through."*
– Fritz Perls

MORNING MEDITATION

To me, "One Day at a Time" has come to mean a life-long daily commitment to recovery. It took me many days to learn that daily commitment to sobriety is both necessary and finally, rewarding.

No doctor ever questioned me about my drinking habits. No stern warnings. Too many times I'd wind up in the emergency room, fill out papers and sit there or fall asleep, or get sent to detox or get hospitalized or... or... or... Dozens of dead ends, "Sick and Tired of being Sick and Tired." That's how you hear it at an A.A. meeting.

Whale-watching in Provincetown: The beauty and grace of these huge animals gliding to the surface, diving, reemerging. So unlike my resurfacing from a blackout in the emergency room. What kind of crazy life was I living? A whale leads a whale's life. Was this a human's life I was leading? This life I led was absolutely insane. A diseased life. A drunken life. All humanity must most certainly scream out against it. But not my brain. Even at its worst, or perhaps even more so at its worst, all my brain wanted was another drink. A drink to kill the pain caused by drinking. Insane. Turn it over.

(**Sotto**): *Jim reminds me of one of those paddles with the rubber strand and ball attached. Or the cup attached to a stick with a ball and string. Child's play. His attention is diverted easily. Not attention deficit disorder. Just* *attention diversion. He is a precocious child whose alcoholism never let him grow up. He's sixty something, just now sober enough to grow up. Maybe.*

Anticipating the next change that is sure to come to my sober self is so different from the endless more of drinking. It is such a fleeting occurrence and of little consequence compared to that nagging "must have" for the next drink. A blind drunk, blinded by my own drinking, myriad blindness. Blind to addiction, my physical and mental prison without walls. Self-deception, believing my own lies.

(**Vatchi**): *Sotto, Jim's logic is lame at times. Unfocused. Inane. But I guess inane and sober is better than insane and drunk. His progress has been slow. And his imperfections, glaring. He's still rewiring his brain: Coming soon! To a theatre near you! A new, improved Jim! A blind drunk discovers the Braille of Recovery! For mature audiences only.*

Most of my physical alcoholic overhaul was achieved in a few days. No permanent liver damage. Vital signs apparently somewhat normal. Three hernia operations coincidentally related to my alcoholism. My real healing is mental change. And that has been slow, steady and progressively better. I've even come to accept my many relapses as part of my recovery progress and process. The physical obsession to drink has long gone and now I have just the occasional battle with the thought of a drink, minor skirmishes, really. I have been learning to participate in my own recovery.

I can't fuck with this. And helping others truly does seem to help my own recovery and mental rewiring. This is one double-edged sword that's been easy to carry: hope as a weapon.

(**Surimi**): *Sotto, Jim is in a race to make peace within himself before his last breath is sucked out of him. Race, race, the human race. Jim, please slow down. The race is over. Peace will come slowly, in its own time. Just breathe.*

Responsibility, such an odd notion from another planet. Responsible for my own sobriety. Here I am old and sober, just one notch above dead and drunk. But I really, really can't do this alone, no matter how sober, no matter how long sober. Being responsible is neither a command nor a suggestion. I am a novice in November, the November of my years, learning so late in life to live soberly. I am living responsibly today. One day these clothes may fit more loosely, less restrained. Freer. Just not quite yet.

EVENING MEDITATION

Rest and relaxation. Exercise and action. The ebb and flow of life. I could have none of that balance in my drinking life. Alcohol was my clock. The time between drinks was not the time spent drinking. Blackouts: black lines where the time should have appeared on a train or bus schedule. Alcohol does not stop at this station. The train does not stop at this station. Please proceed to the club car.
Wake up. Go home. This is the last stop.

> *"When we allow ourselves to feel our feelings, what should*
> *be intolerable becomes intolerable."*
> – Kenny Loggins

QUESTION FOR TODAY

Should I include the appreciation of possibilities in a description of reality? I hope so, I really hope so. Or should I hope for something more? Can I? Should I? Must I?

58. ALCOHOLISM DISCONNECTS, RECOVERY CONNECTS

"Sobriety is my new addiction."
– from *Intervention*, the TV Series

MORNING MEDITATION

When I drank, many promises I made were broken. In my sobriety, the promises of recovery are slowly being realized.

Is all of this doing me or anyone else any good? Should I care? Should I persevere? Do I really need the help of others to stay sober today? I did before, but do I still?

Sick of myself. Sick of my disease. Go ahead. Paste your hatred on me. Use those childish scissors so that you do not hurt yourself. Paste your hatred on me. Cut dark red, dark blue and dark green construction paper. No yellow, never any yellow. Open that big, white plastic jar of white glue, dried on top from exposure to the air. Use that horse hair brush to break through to that soft, white, gluey center beneath. Paste your hatred on me. Use short brush strokes. Paste it until you can taste it.

(**Sotto**): *Gone. I'm outta here. He's crazier than a bedbug. How did he get this way? This can't be good. Can't be.*

There is too much hatred in this world. Hoping, wishing it were not so would not change that. I have my doubts that praying could change things. Is there power in positive thinking? Maybe not for the world. But, maybe for my world. Connectedness. That's what it is. That's what it takes.

Alcoholism disconnects. Recovery connects. The gathering of eggs in the morning at Uncle Paul and Aunt Edith's farm. Climbing nearly to the top of the old pine tree at the bottom of the gravel driveway. Up there where the birds fly. Pinecones. Hickory nuts. Walnuts. Chestnuts.

Fuck it. Everything's one if you make it one.

Alcohol broke my world apart. Humpty Fucking Dumpty. Put me back together. Connectedness. Sobriety is connecting the sober dots. The dots that are left. Connect the dots. Collect the eggs. One half of my brain is fried, the other half is scrambled. Am I such a bad egg? Connect the dots, the remaining dots.

(**Vatchi**): *Dipsy-doodle, apple strudel. He is a little nuts, I guess. He most certainly does have "lapses in his synapses." I think Jim gets unhinged once in a while just to reshuffle his own cards, his remaining brain cells.*

Sotto, don't go anywhere yet. It's not over 'til the fast synapses singe.

Connect the sober dots. The dots that are left. Punch holes in these papers to put in a three-ring binder. Collect the dots left that the paper punch makes. Collect the dots and connect the dots.

"For this I am responsible."

How odd and true this new sobriety feels, this learning to live responsibly, without the drink. The old hat comfort of the first drink has become an ill fit. My thinking is changing. This is a beginning. Connect the dots. Move forward, move on.

(**Surimi**): *Vatchi? You have a lame sense of humor. "Dipsy-doodle"? At least both of you can now appreciate that he is slowly regaining and developing a sober sense of humor. Humor heals health and hope. Or something like that. His uncertain humor is a means of attraction. His way of saying, "Like me, please like me." He was known as "Rusty" when he drank, for his Rusty Nails (Scotch and Drambuie). He's looking for a new name and a new face now. He's still trying reality on for size.*

Why did the sober chicken cross the road? Because he did not yet know that he did not yet know.

Giddy with hope - that's how I feel in these new feeling clothes called sobriety. Not the manic of manic-depression. Giddy with hope - that's how I feel sometimes, when I can leave this train wreck of my life momentarily aside.

Is hope but a useful fiction? Perhaps. Perhaps it is my state of mind now that the fog has cleared, the debris has cleared, this accident is over. I could never have foreseen this new point which I have somehow now reached.

Abstinence is something less than sober. And sobriety is something more.

EVENING MEDITATION

When change is in order, there should be order in change. When I first got sober, I guess I wanted immediate change and my impatience seemed to wear away the very foundation of my sobriety. I have to protect my sobriety today, as much as ever, and I sometimes don't know where my patience hides or to where it seems to disappear. Going from beat up by alcoholism to upbeat about sobriety did not happen overnight. Addiction is a culture of inevitable failure. My sobriety feels like a 'me' today instead of a feel for one more drink.

Plain English: I just feel good sober.

"A book must be the ax for the frozen sea within us."
— Franz Kafka

QUESTION FOR TODAY

Like a leaf floating on a lake and drifting off, can you live through your emotions and just let them go? Can you?

59. DOUBLE-VISIONARY

"Remember always that you have not only the right to be an individual; you have an obligation to be one."
– Eleanor Roosevelt

MORNING MEDITATION
Addiction steals power by stealing everything except the illusion of power.

Group therapy, I remember thinking, in a grey, grey kind of way, keeps you busy, keeps you distracted, kills time. Kill some time instead of killing yourself with alcohol. Sobering up is about as exciting as watching paint dry. Green paint. Hospital Green. Stand close to this wall. Closer. Stare at it, then relax your eyes. Everything, the world, fades away. The Librium Shuffle. Shuffle down the hospital corridor with fifty-some other shufflers. It took me awhile to realize that this was a farm factory, a conveyor belt of recovery. Henry Ford would be proud (or would he?). Enter Stage Left on Day One and Exit Stage Right on Day Fourteen. Numbers moving along in a Librium Shuffle toward sobriety.

Recovery is a process, alright. I was cow #43. I was American cheese. No Port wine cheese. No Wire Hangers. No reason left to live. Too burnt out to care one way or the other. Kill myself? Why bother? Librium Shuffle and the God of Frozen Yogurt.

Recovery Factory. Like Sesame Place, but for chronic alcoholics and drug addicts. I fit right in like a tonic and gin.

Whack a mole. Whack a mole. Guacamole.

(**Sotto**): *Librium shuffle, at the bottom. Brain cell shuffle, out at top. If there's something to get, I've got it. If there's something to forget, forget it.*

186

There seems to be a certain art to madness, to Jim's madness. Construction paper and art class paste. Congratulations to Jim. He has just graduated the seventh grade. Alcoholism is a developmental disability. Slowly, Vatchi, I almost hate to say it: Jim is slowly getting a little better, day by day.

Accomplishing next to nothing. When I was one day sober, a smirk was too much effort. One lip, one corner or lip, slight curl. My hair would hurt if I knew how to let it. This evil fog lifts slowly. Surrounded by bodies immersed in this fog, in this fog themselves. Slowly this fog is replaced by fear. This story of my life is hardly a story, barely a life. Emotions hollowed out by addiction. Every day is Halloween out there, nothing in here. Am I all that I have left? Fear, then forgetfulness. Am I less than what is left? Fog, fear, forgetfulness. What next, what left?

(**Vatchi**): *Some of what Jim remembers best is what he remembers least, Sotto. You say he's getting a little better every day. Compared to what? Alcoholic insanity? I'll give you that one, Sotto. But some of his empty places have been filled in by fear. And fear of emptiness.*

Am I less than forget? Am I fear? Am I bread, unbuttered and dropped on some psychiatric floor? Am I manners? Mannerisms? Is this all that is left when the alcohol is taken out? Omitted. Dignity omitted. None or one or three hot meals and a cot. Dignity, that ugly shoe. Is that the only thing left hanging over my head like a hangman's noose? Stolen, lost, broken. In too many hospitals that have names and some that don't or didn't or can't or won't. The old memory is gone. Asleep or awake, it's the same disaster. Visionary, double-visionary, disaster. Crippled by alcohol. I am crippled. No monologue, no dialogue. Dead, but not dead. No relief seems left. Possible.

(**Surimi**): *Sotto, Vatchi! Don't let Jim pull you down when he gets lost in thoughts of his own mindless past, his path. But let me add here, Sotto, I like what you just said about alcoholism being a developmental disability. You've said a mouthful. And as Jim just said, it is crippling. Alcohol has a crippling effect on alcoholics, slow erosion, years in the making, the unmaking, the taking.*
And Vatchi, please, Jim has hope, or at least, let me say this: I still have hope for him.

I must change. I have changed. I am changing. I must conjugate my recovery. Recovery as a verb, as action. I used to get drunk. And then I was a drunk, a drink, and then nothing. Blind. I was blind. The eye that could not see itself and then could not see at all. Blind drunk, ten ways to someday.

I must change. I have changed. I am changing.

EVENING MEDITATION

Before I got sober that first time, I could only picture myself dying with a drink and a cigarette in my hand. Some weird sense of "nobody gets out of here alive" was my only thought. I would most certainly die a miserable alcoholic death. I would die in separation, a separated death.

> *"The secret of life is to appreciate the pleasure of being*
> *terribly, terribly deceived."*
> — Oscar Wilde

QUESTION FOR TODAY

Drunk and proud. Which of a thousand oxymorons am I?

60. AN UNREMEMBERED EMPTINESS

"Possibilities and miracles are one and the same."
– Anonymous

MORNING MEDITATION

At first, I thought I could learn how to get sober. And I did. But then I relapsed. Then I thought I could learn how to stay sober. And I relapsed. Now I know that only living sober is sober.

I've been robbed of my gratitude and my optimism by a chemical concoction, a chemical addiction. Killing me and wanting more. There was never a thought of letting go, of quitting. Quitting? That would have had to include admitting defeat and the alcohol itself seemed (and somehow still seems) smart enough to prevent the possibility of thinking, simply, "I give up." How is that even possible? For me, it simply was not. And the people from my alcoholic past are strewn like corpses along the side of the road. Or, not alcoholic like me, still drinking and happily planting daffodils along the path of their lives.

Memory. Memory. Memory. My life has been so much an unremembered emptiness.

(**Sotto**): *What the fuck? Is any kind of new life even possible for Jim? Is he permanently disabled? Does his future hold hope or is it only hope?*

Everything that alcohol did to me in the end seemed impossible. Like some magic trick. Wait. How'd he do that? Alcohol, the magician, pulled optimism out of my ear like a gold coin which then vanished in his hand. Wait a minute. How'd he do that? Delusional reality? Mirrors, baby, mirrors. Alcohol, the magician. How'd he do that? Money, poof. Up in smoke. Smoke and mirrors. Smoke disappears. Mirrors disappear. I disappear. There used to be a time when it felt like there was a right way to drink and drug. How did that time disappear? When did time disappear? Fuck. How'd he do that?

(**Vatchi**): *(Speechless, shuffles his feet)*

I don't know if I can do this. I just don't know if I can do this. I just don't know if I can do this. I just don't know if I can do this. I just don't know.

(**Surimi**): *(Speechless, sighs)*

"A long deep sigh." That is what I say. That is what I feel. That is what I will just now do, sigh. Good night.

EVENING MEDITATION

The final irony is that at first I drank as a way to break that ice until what melted the ice broke me. Alcohol, the tool I had used to connect with others, ultimately separated me from others. It would be through connecting with other sober alcoholics that I would break that chain. What will fix this brokenness? Being human is my glue.

> *"Hatred is never anything but fear – if you feared no one,*
> *you would hate no one."*
> – Hugh Downs

QUESTION FOR TODAY

Can I remain sober under any and all conditions? Can doubt be used as a tool to solve unanswerable questions? Can love solve what alcohol dissolved?

PART III
THE RECONSTRUCTION

61. DEPRESSION AND ANXIETY (DISSOLVE)

"It is well to remember that the entire population of the universe,
with one trifling exception, is composed of others."
– Andrew J. Holmes

MORNING MEDITATION
Don't burn bridges behind you; concentrate on building the bridge that is before you.

I would have refused "tough love" had anyone tried to force it upon me in my early sobriety. But I am learning now that I must perform some kind of tough love on myself if I am to survive. I have to keep my sobriety on a very short leash, as I've variously heard it described at my 12-step meetings.

(**Sotto**): *Vatchi, Who is he? What will become of him? I don't know what. A cartoon figure of his former self? What is left? Who will Jim become?*

Let me go back two homeless times ago, before my second stay at John Brooks (known then as The Institute for Human Development). I.H.D. couldn't admit me until Monday and I was able to stay sober over the weekend at the Rescue Mission 'on a wing and a prayer.' I had made the decision to get help. No one can tell my story but me, and being so fucked up, it's nearly impossible to tell. But like some dream image from the collective unconscious, I found a dime bag of marijuana on the sidewalk

191

fifty feet outside the Atlantic City Rescue Mission door on my way to being admitted to I.H.D. Like the head buried beneath the flowerbed in Hitchcock's Rear Window, I buried my dime bag in the ground cover near Bally's Park Place Casino parking garage.

(**Vatchi**): *But what's underneath all of this, Sotto? A dime bag buried? Worm holes? Nothing? Not even a cartoon continuum of his former self, Sotto. Everything will have changed. Even one iota's change changes everything that ever could have been. Jim's future is an unturned stone. The Fifteenth Stone, Sotto.*

When I rebelled against this thing or that thing, in favor of the drink, a rebellious nature became my habit. A habit caused by drinking. The power of the habit turned rabid. It's the old "problems caused me to drink more and more drinking caused more problems." That routine had to change. Habit rabid and rotten routine. I've got to keep changing if I want to keep staying sober. "The man I was will drink again." That is the blessing and the curse of sobriety for an alcoholic. Change or die.

Change is good. And yes, change is frightening. And yes, I did not drink today.

(**Surimi**): *You two amuse me. Your perspectives on him, at times, are as uneasy as his steps. He's not choosing his emotions. He's trying to live through them. Emerge on the other side, I think. But he doesn't seem to know how to let go. Hopefully, he can learn how to embrace his sobriety, live in today instead of through yesterday. One step at a time. His brain is used to waiting for the next drink. He's remembering his past, the feelings he had while waiting for his perpetual next drink. Let it go, Jim. Let it flow.*

One persistent complaint I have about my 12-step meetings is a very anti-intellectual mindset so prevalent there. "Don't think. Don't drink. Go to meetings." That's a commonly heard anthem. Religion is talked about in a roundabout 'spirituality' kind of way. Psychiatry and the medical community are not wholly admonished. But at no 12-step meeting have I ever heard anyone recommending going to a library to learn from a book about this disease called alcoholism.

Knowledge may not keep you sober, but ignorance most certainly may keep you drunk.

Done. Another burden has been lifted.

EVENING MEDITATION

My relationship with myself is much better sober than drunk. That damn Alcohol sure got in the way of my relationships, including my relationship with myself.

"Everything should be made as simple as possible, but not simpler."
– Albert Einstein

QUESTION FOR TODAY
What do you know of love that searching has not taught you?

62. A PACK OF LONERS, ALONE

*"They say that God is everywhere, and yet we always think
of Him as somewhat of a recluse."*
– Source Unknown

MORNING MEDITATION
Ego is the crack cocaine of recovery.

At some point in what I thought would be later described as a glorious drinking career (I had accepted that I would never stop drinking and that I would never let it get worse), I had to up my game by introducing other drugs to improve my skill, my cunning, my power, my control. Once, I was so proud of being admired for being totally annihilated and yet, like a cat thrown into the air, able to land on my feet again. I was a walking miracle. I was the baffling magic man. "How does he do it?" Everyone asked that. I did not know then that my drinking career would soon make me implode and that eventually, once I got sober, my ego would have me implode again and put a new, first drink into my hand.

(**Sotto**): *Vatchi. His ego is tied up in his damn disease. Proud drunk. Drunk and proud. What a man! What an asshole! Does he ever listen to himself? False pride? Vatchi? Is this false pride?*

Every drink is the first drink, and no drink is the last drink. This is alcoholism. This is "all bets are off." That first drink seems to flip a switch in my brain, the "more" switch, the no turning back switch, the river of no return switch. Speaking personally, the only way I have ever stopped drinking, through multiple, multiple relapses, was through eventual alcoholic poisoning and hospitalizations from near fatal overdose. Some people make a decision to stop drinking. Not me. The best I can do is to make a decision to not start again after I have been forced to stop through my inevitable hospitalization. I have finally realized that I have a disability: I can't drink and that's about as brilliant as I can get.

Here's the really fucked up part: When I'm sober, I sometimes have a hard time understanding other peoples' relapses. Quite simply, that is why I need my A.A. meetings. I need near daily reminders of other peoples' weaknesses and consequently, my own. The consequence of my not participating in my own recovery by going to meetings is always the same (and worse): relapse.

One day at a time. One death at a time. Every single part of me has Jane's addiction. She is dead. I now own a little part of "we". "I" has become a part of the "we" of recovery, sadly, from surviving the death of others who could not take the heed.

(**Vatchi**): *False pride in transition, Sotto. Through his many affirmed relapses, he learns. He learns, not from drinking, but from the consequences of drinking. He's hard-headed. Pride. I guess it is pride. Losing yourself and then finding yourself. Jim could hold his liquor. The bigger question is this: Can he hold his sobriety?*

Sometimes my recovery group meetings feel like packs of loners bound together by the hopes of another day sober, despite society casting us off and under cover, like a leper colony. Hated and full of self-hatred, blamed and full of self-blame, we are freaks to be reviled, mislabeled and misunderstood. All that the world scorns in us, we scorn in ourselves as well.

When the alcohol dries up, the dust that remains can be self-pity. This is a dry drunk. Through several relapses, I guess I, too, have been a dry drunk at times. Gratitude, humility and the interconnectedness I find at my recovery meetings keep me alive. Meetings are my "oxygen network."

Today, I can breathe and my breath is free of alcohol. And for this one moment I am free.

(**Surimi**): *Can he hold his sobriety? Can sobriety be held? Or is it like a champagne bubble that will burst when held? Or does sobriety go flat, like stale beer? Daily renewal, daily reprieve. The tide comes in, the tide goes out. Sobriety is Now.*

Too much money and too many years were invested in my "alcoholic lifestyle." Alcohol filled the emptiness and created more emptiness. Ego was my shield, protecting me from the truth.

"Surrender to be free." The chips are down. The game is up. This Russian roulette has been terminated.

EVENING MEDITATION

The world cannot be only as I see it, though it does seem that way sometimes. The doctor who prescribed 100 Oxycontin to me: Did he know that I'm an alcoholic who after my surgery for a stomach operation was furtively seeking an alternative high, an escape from self in pill form? Or did he suspect, knowing that I did not have any health insurance at that time that I could sell those pills on the street for an incredible profit? Sometimes the world is exactly as I see it. Sometimes not. The world, it seems, indifferent, does not know that I still just want to get high sometimes. Alcoholics each other we must help.

"Birds sing after a storm. Why shouldn't we?"
– Rose Kennedy

QUESTION FOR TODAY

What can't you remember from that first primordial ooze? Why can't you touch the origin of all life imprinted everywhere? Why can't you touch with your mind all life's beginnings? Why do you deny this, all of this, any of this?

63. INJECT ME SLOWLY, TRUTH

"Independence, like honour, is a rocky island without a beach."
– Napoleon Bonaparte

MORNING MEDITATION
Only in retrospect am I beginning to understand that alcohol merely muddied my emotions. Alcohol was not a solver of problems; it was a solvent of emotions.

Slow the injection of truth. Insert the needle of truth into my vein, into my brain, slowly. First, hold the needle upright. Squeeze out any air. Leave only the clear, the liquid, the truth. Inject me slowly. I want to want to watch that crystal clarity enter my vein. The truth, too fast, could only scare me. Inject me slowly, or quickly watch me die.

(**Sotto**): *Don't tell me he shoots up, too? Isn't it a little late in the game, here, to be making that admission? What else has he left out? Nothing makes him blink. I swear.*

"Bartender. Bartender."
"Jim."
"Rusty."
"One for the road over here."
When I first got sober, I tended bar for one solid year. It was a year, anyway. And apparently, not too solid, or I would not have relapsed. Some people get sober and can tend bar and stay sober. Obviously, I couldn't. And now, I wouldn't even want to: the thrill is gone.

Partly being sober. Partly growing older. Maybe growing up? Hopefully, growing up. "Forty Year Old Virgin?" Try this: Sixty Year Old Teenager.

(**Vatchi**): *He lives in a liquid/solid dream world, skating on thin ice. "A solid year sober." Not a very funny pun. I don't know if his self-esteem has returned yet, but it seems his 'steam' has. See? I can be punny, too, Sotto.*

Sober long enough to finally realize that I have truly become a different person than the person I became after decades of non-stop drinking. Too proud, too independent to learn from the vast history of others' failures and successes at sobriety and relapse, finally, I found that mustard seed (or apple seed!) of faith and hope and charity.

From drooling self-aggrandizement to finally the metamorphosis into this, then SLAM! Some old nostalgia enters my mind to entertain the thought of a drink. How good was it, how high was I, powerless when high? My head in the clouds and my feet on the ground today. My past is crumbling and falling off this edifice of self. How high was I, really?

(**Surimi**): *Good doubt. Bad doubt. Without a doubt, doubt plays heavily in Jim's life, the life of all alcoholics perhaps, perhaps all people, Sotto, Vatchi. There are, I am sure, unintended meanings in much of what he says, just as there were unintended consequences to his "alcoholic lifestyle."*

He has the nerve to ask, "How high was I really?" Intentionally ambiguous or not, I wish that I could squelch that doubt for him. Forever powerless. Of that, there can be no doubt. None whatsoever. Permanently powerless, the high, in any meaningful sense, can only be an illusion. Was he as high as he was powerless? I would say not.

A diseased high. A poisoned high. Daily surrender to my alcoholism always meant another drink. Daily chipped away by my disease. And what was left of me when the chipping away stopped? Not Mount Rushmore! My brain fragments on this sculptor's floor. The dust of my disease. The oxygen masks, the intravenous drips, the sedatives.

How, having barely survived all of this for years on end, can I have come out on this other end today, feeling whole, joyful, alive?

I cannot doubt this good and goodly end result. Gratitude.

EVENING MEDITATION

I stand before the firing squad and am asked if I would like to smoke a cigarette before the execution countdown begins. "No thanks, I'm trying to quit." This is my insanity. Part of my insanity. Addiction has rearranged reality. The new normal is insane still, if substance-free. Insanity will forever be part of my new sanity.

"No thanks, I gave at the office."

"No thanks, I'm trying to live."

"No thanks, thanks."

"Let the measure of time be spiritual, not mechanical."
– Ralph Waldo Emerson

QUESTION FOR TODAY

My fix couldn't fix my fix. Could yours? Could you? How will we ever stay sober? Will we? How? When?

64. MY EXTREME FLOWCHART

"If you don't like a thing, change it. If you can't change it,
then change the way you think about it."
– Maya Angelou

MORNING MEDITATION

I thought drinking could offer me freedom, but I ended up being a slave to it. I have learned in sobriety that freedom without structure is chaos. Drinking had no structure, just destruction, chaos.

I've been thinking about today for three days now. Because I knew it would come to this, the 64 thousand dollar question. How to explain myself out of the paper bag of love. I cannot write this. It was to have been about how in 98 out of 100 one night stands I would tell myself "this could be the one that will last forever." And then, after telling myself and half believing this lie, it was: smoke a cigarette, and good-bye. And now. And now, and now, and now. Going through some of the old, old flotsam and jetsam of my life, I find a long and tedious poem I once wrote:

"Love Is…"

Love is indelicate.
It is not a bird with murmuring heart and fluttering wing.
It is not a ship passing in the night.
It is not a flight.
It is a stone, harder than plutonium.
It is a weight, a downward force
That straps you to immortality.

Love never sets you free.
It is not blind,
Not something that you find.
Love finds you.
Keen sight. Sharp claws. No morals.
Love can tear you apart.
Cut out your heart with the raise of an eyebrow.
No mercy for the hemophiliac.
Cold-blooded, hot-blooded love.
Love is dispassionate, always in control.
Love controls you.
An iron hand. A drug.
Love is a thug.
Is there an end? A paradise?
A time or place where love is nice?
No dice. Fat chance.
Ask the lady to dance and see who gets danced upon.
Love will survive
By eating you alive.
It is a weight, a downward force
That straps you to immortality.

(**Sotto**): *Is that why Jim drank? Or is this where drinking took him?*

(**Vatchi**): *What makes you think it matters, Sotto? The result is just the same either way.*

(**Surimi**): *Isolation, depression, anger, resentment. A thousand excuses for an alcoholic to drink. And the one reason he should not? Because he is an alcoholic. It does not matter where it takes him. It will always take him down.*

I can remember standing on the front porch of our house with my father when I was maybe ten years old. We lived in a small valley and a few miles away to the west was the rim of the valley. This was called South Mountain. We could watch storms approaching from the other side of the mountain. My father taught me how to predict when the storm would reach us by counting the seconds between when we saw the lightning and when we would hear the thunder. The closer the storm, the less time it takes between seeing the lightning and hearing the thunder. It takes a long time, too, when you first get clean and sober to get a clear picture of reality. Relapse now and you may never hear the thunder and feel the rain wash clean the debris of your disease.

My father and I stood on the porch. We saw the storm get nearer, saw the lightning, heard the thunder, the dog and cat beneath the couch because they were frightened and did not understand. And then the rain would come down in buckets, the street still hot, giant puddles of water, the steam rising and sometimes, just sometimes, after the storm, we would see a rainbow.

(**Sotto**): *Gritty. Gruesome. Gory. Dark. Why is love so dark and inaccessible for Jim? And then, Bam! He goes right into the rain. The rainbow. No transitional segue. No explanation. Everything is backwards and upside down.*

Enough mush. I don't know love today. Not romantic love today. That wanting someone badly, just not as badly as the next drink. Or only with the next drink. Never just you. Always the next drink. I do not want you. But I can remember searching, searching across those many barrooms for someone to go home with. The biggest problem was usually finding someone just the right amount of drunk. As drunk as me or as drunk as I was going to get. This usually involved buying them drinks, plying them with drinks. You see, I was always "pre-plied," which, if there isn't such a term, there most certainly should be.

Finding someone attractive was usually not too much of a problem. It was finding someone willing to get equally high. And me not getting too high by the time they caught up. "The spirit is willing, but the flesh is weak" was an alternate insanity. Far too often, it was they're not drunk enough or they're too drunk or I'm not drunk enough. It was sometimes nearly impossible to get me and anyone else to agree, without putting it into words: "We're drunk enough now. Let's go now." There was seldom a now and nearly always just one more drink.

(**Vatchi**): *Extremes, Sotto. From one extreme to the other. Seeking emotional balance. Someday, perhaps someday. Backwards, upside down and sober. At least he's staying sober and seeking balance.*

Alcohol fucked with my self-esteem tremendously. Roller coaster highs and lows, followed by the curves of getting too high, passing out and coming to. My mood swings followed the flow chart of my drinking. It's no wonder I was prescribed anti-depressants when I first got sober. Most certainly, I am neither a medical doctor nor a psychiatrist, but I can see in my own past behavior patterns that years of drinking could be seen through the lenses of Obsessive-Compulsive Disorder and Manic-Depression. The flowchart of my drinking mimicked these things.

(**Sotto**): *Dr. Jim, Neurologist? No. Jim, Neurotic Nutcase.*

My self-esteem issues have become more balanced as I move forward in sobriety.

(**Vatchi**): *Neurotic self-diagnosis. Yes, Sotto, you're right. I think Jim may be heading for trouble.*

(**Surimi**): *Guys, inescapable charm is definitely not Jim's problem. But I think he's finally beginning to realize the big difference between being drunk and sober. Water lifts all boats, but apparently not the same can be said for alcohol. There is no safe harbor when the sea is alcohol. His extremes, his drunken fire and ice. Sobriety, and all that comes with it is more balanced, more centered and less extreme than his active addiction was. His cadence and his rhythm are now more clearly a reflection of his life. Addiction is chaos. Sobriety will eventually have a calming effect on almost anyone.*

I drank myself sober sometimes. My mind would seek to find some equilibrium. Despite my drunkenness, my mind stood at cross purposes with my substance of abuse. I couldn't have known that then, or at least I didn't know that. Did not know that. In the most strange of strangest ways, I finally drank myself sober. And that is that.

EVENING MEDITATION

I can remember when gasoline was 32.9 cents per gallon in the 1950's and when it was $3.29 per gallon after the century's turn. That's a magnitude of ten increase. All things considered, that progressive increase in prices has been relatively sane. The progression of the disease of addiction is nothing like that. It's irrational and insane. That's comparing ordinary apples to insane oranges. My oranges were not oranges anymore.
I did not drink today.

> *"All human evil comes from a single cause, man's inability
> to sit still in a room."*
> – Pascal

QUESTION FOR TODAY

"Emptiness" and "More" and "Me." Is it any wonder that finally I could not juggle? Is it? Is?

65. PHANTOM TOES WIGGLING

*"Success is a lousy Teacher. It seduces smart people
into thinking they can't lose."*
– Bill Gates

MORNING MEDITATION

Wreckage of the past? When I first got sober, I had so much inner debris that I
could not look back or forward. There was humiliation and pain, a full menu of
negative emotions. Change was slow, has been slow, will be slow. Life is different
today. And good. Life is good today.

I seldom remember actively returning to consciousness after one of my
daily blackout episodes. Normally, I would simply drink until I blacked out,
and then continue drinking until I would find myself home again to pass
out. But this one time was different. The lights outside the hospital
emergency room were like the lights on the landing strip of an airport and I
was a helicopter hovering, hovering, hovering. I stood on the street outside
the emergency room of the Atlantic City Hospital. I had been in a blackout
and I did not know how I got there. Finally, a paramedic came over to me,
after 5 or 20 minutes. An hour? I don't know.

"Do you need help?"

I answered, "This is not working. This is not working. The alcohol is
not working. I cannot do what this is now, not working…." I collapsed on
the street like a sandcastle knocked over by a wave. My sand spread out
onto the sidewalk.

I still have phantom memories of my drinking past, euphoric recall. It's
as if one of my legs were amputated, but that I can still sometimes,
somehow feel those toes that are not there. Triggers are phantom toes

wiggling. Don't take the bait. Don't bite. Use your good leg, the sober leg. The bad leg is gone. Let it go. Say your eulogy. Mourn this death and move on. Addiction is a beast that lives within you. You cannot kill the beast. Denial, anger, fear will not kill it. Begging, pleading, blaming will not tame it. Depression, self-pity, doubt: they only feed it. Confront it. Accept it. The beast will never die.

(**Sotto**): *I've got it! He's talking to himself. Whistling in the dark. Saying what he has to say to not pick up a drink. I don't think he even knows we're listening. That anyone is listening.*

How many jobs, roommates and apartments had I had over my drinking career? Workaholic/Alcoholic. Alcoholism became my full time job. Putting together a time-line, going from the primordial ooze to the caveman to homo erectus, as seen in all those cartoons and parodies, became painful to me in my early recovery. Between years of blackouts and job changes and being thrown out of apartments and one-night stands and lost loves and firings and on and on: no time-line was remotely possible for me. But I did the best I could. And it was a tool that helped me stay sober for just one more day. Just one more day sober. That's all I wanted. That's all I was capable of. That's all I could do. And I could not do it alone. Alone, to me, at one point meant only one thing: alone with a bottle.

It is so easy for me to become estranged from my past. After all, the person I had become could never be my friend today. I would find him intolerable, active in his disease. As manipulative and conniving as I was in my drunkenness then, surrounded by enablers (blame them, Jim, blame them), today I would not, could not be fooled. Today.

Half ditty, half prayer: I do not want to go back there. No intervention would have been possible back then. Physical collapse was, has been and most likely could only be this alcoholic's interventionist. Interventionist: reminds me of "The Exorcist." My exorcism could not be of the religious variety. My sobriety would be freedom from alcohol and freedom from religion.

(**Vatchi**): *Freedom from religion? He's an incurable Romantic and an incurable Alcoholic. Alcohol was his one and only because, finally, all else no longer existed. Even when Jim thought that he was done, silently, his disease was waiting, waiting, waiting. His drinking became unsustainable. Then, too, so did his sobriety.*

Five piers used to jut out from the Cape May Coast Guard station years ago. Over the decades, somehow they were destroyed and only two remain. Without pity, merely as a comparison of magnitude, I feel as if I, too, have sustained several generations of damage, not like the time and tides on those Coast Guard piers, just the sustained damage from alcohol wave erosion. Wave after unforgiving wave, the mind that time forgot, broken, damaged.

Please let me save what little I have left and build on it.

(**Surimi**): *Vatchi, I think you're on to something here. His unsustainable sobriety, thinking he was at one time a functioning alcoholic eventually did not work for him. And finally sober, over and over, Jim relapsed, ultimately learning that his sobriety was unsustainable without daily vigilance and work. He learned that there would be no "Eureka! I've got it" moment. As A.A. literature clearly explains, the paradox is that "in order to keep it, you've got to give it away." No more beer in the shower. No more marked bottles. No more detoxes. No more rehabs. Just for today. Breathe in. Breathe out. Say "Good night," Jim.*

From alone with the bottle to alone without the bottle. I could not be alone, alone. I could not be alone. I could not be. I could not. The death of one part of me to allow the life of another part of me. Ritual sacrifice. I've got blood on my hands from this phantom beast who will not die. This near death to prevent more death. This life thing will take some time. This sober thing. This thing.

EVENING MEDITATION

I was Peter's Sponsor in our 12-step recovery program. Once he said to me, "Jim, every day I pray that I never have to go back to prison."
"Pray instead," I said "that you learn how to stop doing the things that put you there."

> *"Talk doesn't cook rice."*
> – Chinese Proverb

QUESTION FOR TODAY

Is there always a lesson to be learned? Relate or relapse? Is that my lesson? Is it?

66. INSANITY CUBED

*"The human heart in its perversity finds it hard to escape
hatred and revenge."*
— Moses Luzzatto

MORNING MEDITATION

I must not let my being an alcoholic be an excuse to manipulate others through emotional blackmail. I want to stop being a victim of alcoholism and this should include not making others victims of my sobriety.

The only thing unusual about me drinking beer in the shower was the low alcohol content (compared to my usual Scotch). Dr. Jim (that's me) prescribed a drink in the shower for its medicinal sobering up qualities and its effervescent lilt. Beer was the common man's brew. Dr. Jim only drank beer in public as a way to show that he flowed with the sea of humanity (or was too drunk to drink anything else). "Lather. Rinse. Repeat." I thought I could follow directions. But my direction faded. I and alcohol and fear went down the drain together, clockwise, north of the equator, yet directionless.

(**Sotto**): *Moon walking. That's it. Appearing to walk forward while sliding backward. Michael Jackson's move. Drinking beer in the shower to get ready for work. Eureka. By Jove. Good Golly, Miss Molly. Jim's moon walking! (laughing out loud) Drinking in the shower.*

Everything was distorted, twisted out of shape when drunk. A minute, an hour, a day. An inch, a foot, a yard. A dream, a hope, a fear. Twisted, Mr. Alice in Wonderland. One drink, twelve drinks. "One drink makes you larger, and another makes you small." Time. Quality. Emotions. Everything is fucked up… and I don't care. Hitting bottom, emotional breakdown. That place where infinity and nothingness meet.

(**Vatchi**): *Sotto, you're drunk sober. Laughing like a damn fool! Sotto. Maybe the Michael Jackson behind the mask, his mask, this disease. Alcoholism, so misunderstood, has a persona, too, Sotto. The one mask fooled Jim. Alcoholism's other mask is the stereotype that fools almost everyone.*

"Cut in half or double almost everything an addict says," one therapist once said to me. That would make a foot and a half more like nine inches or a yard. And four could be two or eight. To an addict. And I can't much disagree with what my one-time therapist said, "Addiction distorts." I am an addict. Addiction distorts reality. Distorted reality is the new normal. Insanity is normal. I am sane, the world is insane. When I'm drinking, it feels like reality would suck with or without the drink. So, what the hell, "I may as well drink." The insanity of this insanity is that even after a sustained period of sobriety, for me, that "I may as well drink" thinking returns. Even after relapse number one or two or three. I am Insanity Cubed

(**Surimi**): *Insanity cubed? If I didn't know better, I'd swear Jim's talking about you two. You could both use a dose of reality and a dose of empathy. There's no empathy in heaven. There's no empathy in hell. Empathically, telepathically, empathy is here and now. Michael Jackson.*
You're both nuts!

Half insane. Twice insane. I am Insanity Cubed. No wonder then, no wonder when, I'm sober long and strong, a disease whispers and I do not know I hear, "It could have been different. It shouldn't have been, it wouldn't have been insane, if only, if only, if only...." Somehow, then, I picture the captain of the ship, tied to the masthead, so that he would not bring his ship aground upon that ever-beckoning shore, the Sirens calling him. It is myth that keeps me sober, some life force which wants only to replicate itself in abundance. The dance of abundance, this will to live, this myth that keeps me sober. Amen.

EVENING MEDITATION

The leech of letting go: that's how I sometimes think about problems. I want to surrender, let go, move on. But my problems seem like leeches sucking the life-blood out of me. I try to let go while the leeches still cling on me. And when I'm happy I may not notice: the leech of happiness.
Jim, Jim, Jim. You're being silly now.
Oh. Really?

"Science without religion is lame, religion without science is blind."
– Albert Einstein

QUESTION FOR TODAY

Have you not yet noticed that the progressive nature of addiction is just another of life's algorithms? Rhythms? Isms? Insanities?

67. MONKEY FROCKS

"Alcoholism isn't a spectator sport.
Eventually the whole family gets to play."
– Joyce Rebeta-Burditt

MORNING MEDITATION
Sobriety is a gift. Recovery is earned.

Rehab and Recovery and Relapse and Rehab and Recovery. I've been in several detoxes and rehabs and programs and group therapies - several times each. For my second time in the Institute for Human Development (which is now the John Brooks Recovery Center) I was again in a Librium fog, stretched out on my cot, listening to the two guys two cots down talking quietly with each other about their addiction to heroin. They talked about how they would not have a problem with the heroin if they had the fame and money of rock stars. They professed that they didn't need the right people, places and things for their recovery because they really believed that with the right people, places and things, they wouldn't have a problem with their heroin.

There was a time when I had a false sense of the superiority of alcoholism over other addictions, and this false sense helped allow me to continue with abandon. "Oh, the humanity," the announcer exclaimed as the Hindenburg went up in flames. "Oh, the insanity…" of any and all addictions. Always wanting more and feeling empty, left out, done. And not done.

(**Sotto**): *I feel like the priest in a confessional. He is talking, but I cannot hear the sin. The sin is inside of him. He is not the sin, he is its container* *and the sin is emptiness. Vatchi, this makes me feel sad. Alcoholism. His disease is emptiness. '*

My alcoholism has most certainly been influenced by cultural beliefs and expectations. I had, and most probably still have, a sense of my addiction to alcohol being somehow culturally superior over the addiction to other, illegal, addictive substances. Meth, crack and heroin, as well as a slew of other street drugs are illegal. Addiction to prescription medications is perceived differently by society than alcohol use. Clearly, I had some sense of alcoholic superiority over other addictions.

Looking for excuses, the denial part of my addiction to alcohol is different from all of the above. The bitch part is that since 90% of people can drink socially and are not addicted to alcohol, my alcoholism is far too often seen as a moral weakness rather than a disease. It is no small irony that our culture's denial of alcohol's addictive potential plays a part in relapse. After a sustained period of sobriety, it is no wonder that people in recovery think that they can begin drinking as the rest of the non-alcoholic world drinks.

Once I start drinking, I can't stop. Whoa, but were it so simple. It's staying stopped, living sober, that's the problem. A program of recovery, a sobriety maintenance regimen, is what time and relapse after relapse have finally taught me. "A daily reprieve, that's all I have." That's A.A. lingo and my experience has shown it to be true. Staying connected with other alcoholics keeps me connected with my disease and the disastrous effects of my "built-in forgetter."

(**Vatchi**): *Sotto, I know you have an ankle bone and a thigh bone. I didn't know you had a feeling bone. Alcoholism: "the disease of emptiness" - I like that one, Sotto. You should allow yourself to feel more often. Instead of dissect. At least allow yourself to see and feel the whole. Then tear it apart, bonehead. Sotto, the feeling bonehead. Step right up, Ladies and Germs. Only 25 cents. Meet Sotto, the Magnificent Feeling Bonehead.*

I didn't want to leave the monastery. Oh. I'm so sorry. I mean, the rehab. I didn't want to leave the rehab. You see, there was, for me, a sort of monastic quality about this rehab. Shuffling along, feet dragging along the tile floor and simultaneously hovering two inches above the earth. Giving up my worldliness, like a monk. Separated from "people, places and things." The hospital gowns like monkly frocks (or monkey frocks). Living this aesthetic life, not even sacrificial wine would touch these rehab lips. A living saint was I, sustained on the holy water of an intravenous drip. Each patient nun and monk holier than thou. Here comes another needle. Ouch! And ow. And om. And wow. Not high on life. Not now. Inject me slowly....

(**Surimi**): *"Ow!" becomes "om". Pain becomes serenity. Change becomes eternal. "The disease of emptiness." Sotto, Vatchi and me: that makes three of us. Agreed. The glaringly obvious, the subtly insane. One never quits, one simply lets go. Jim's no longer using, just addicted. No longer using, Jim is still an alcohol addict... in recovery.*

But things are different now. After several years of sobriety "The Lakewood Factory Shuffle" has been slowly replaced by the serene sanctuary that my continued sobriety has at times allowed me. I hover now two inches off the floor, "clean and serene" as they say in Narcotics Anonymous. Time takes time. One shuffle replaces another. One relapse replaces another. Finally sober, sustained sobriety and "Bolero" by Ravel weaves through my mind, melodious and gentle. The cool breeze of its wind instruments mindful of my sobriety's harmony. Chaos is not gone, but the insane chaos of being in the drink is now a memory to be remembered only, not relived.

Shuffle me sober. Monkey frock sober and then some. Not numb. Hum.

EVENING MEDITATION

One-day-at-a-time sobriety somehow has me feeling lost, directionless, rudderless. That feeling, that looking for a drink feeling, sometimes returns, even when it's not a drink I'm looking for. Some purpose, any purpose can keep me moving forward. There are many different kinds of one day at a time and they're not all good.

"Success is liking yourself, liking what you do, and liking how you do it."
— Maya Angelou

QUESTION FOR TODAY

Does your pulse know the difference between fears real and fears imagined?

68. EPIPHANY-DEPRIVED

"When we're connected to others, we become better people."
– Randy Pausch

MORNING MEDITATION
Escape from reality is OK, just so long as it isn't escape back into addiction. Change it up, break the monotony, free from alcohol and drugs.

Then there was the Christmas where every gift I received, I re-wrapped and gave to someone else. Getting much. Giving nothing. Having nothing. That's how it felt. Why does it sometimes seem that everything that happens in life is some goddamned lesson to be learned (again, and yes, again)?

Fired from my first job sober. Ain't that cute? Over-medicated on prescription anti-depressants. Have they no anti-self pity prescriptions? What must I do to not feel screwed? Emotional brick walls. Pills for everything except for who I am. The self as brick wall and not knowing which side you're on. No pill for that. Salvation Army. First job sober. Fired for being too slow, you know? You know.

What is left when nothing's left? A drink. A cigarette. Ten thousand more.

(**Sotto**): *This is getting better? This is what getting better is? Going through the laundry list of failures, large and small? What good can come of this? Have I seen any breakthroughs in him? Jim's an epiphany-deprived bastard, Vatchi. Or is it me?*

Let's play "Blame the Parents." Let's play "Blame the Blame Game."

Let's play "I am Virtuous and True." Let's play "Screw You." I can't blame my parents for much of anything, I guess. They did the best they could. My Mother was sixteen and my Father was twenty-one when they married. They grew up as they raised us kids. They both lost their fathers in their early childhoods.

Alcoholism is in my genes and in my jeans (excuse the bad pun on the nature/nurture controversy). Alcoholism was inside me at birth and the world I grew up in was surrounded by alcohol, swam in alcohol. Regardless: the progression of alcoholism is slow and torturous, regardless. Regard. Regard. Sober today, I have learned to grieve the death of my old and drinking self and celebrate the emergence of this new frontier, sobriety. My old self may have died for all sense and purpose, but my disease will never die. The zombie-killer lives within. Waiting to strike, to catch me off guard. But I cannot be off guard. The zombie-killer awaits. This is but a daily reprieve.

Have a nice day, mother fucker. See you in my dreams.

(**Vatchi**): *I don't know what good, if any, can come of this, Sotto. But I'm beginning to recognize an emotional resonance in Jim here. Like the ping! Tuning fork. Ping! The big waves and the small waves of emotion are beginning to have some commonality. Ping! Do you hear it? Ping! Emotional resonance.*

The fear I felt coming back on the bus from the Lakewood Rehabilitation Hospital was palpable. I was afraid I could not do it. I would not be able to stay sober. I had tried before. My history reeked of failure, leaving the emergency room of the Atlantic City Hospital or another detox and immediately I would pick up a drink. The simultaneous insanity of me and I, myself and absence of self, my hand, this stranger's hand, attached to this arm, my arm and a glass comfort, a cold-warm comfort, a drink, this drink, insanity in my hand and down. Down. How did I get in here? This is the only thing I have left, the only thing that I can do, what I am. I felt fear on the bus. A killing fear. I didn't know if I could do it. I fought fear and fear fought back. Every emotion I had had a drink in it.

Off that bus I poured my fright-filled self.

(**Surimi**): *It's no wonder that for Jim, and many like him, after decades of drinking, first day sober occurs again and again. It's the other side of relapse. Coming out and finding one day sober, swearing, "never again." And again and again, "never again" happens. "This is getting better?" Sotto? Sotto. Yes, Sotto, for Jim, this might be getting better. His relapses are further and further apart, and his periods of sobriety are getting progressively longer. Today may just be the day he "gets it." "Ping," to you,*

Vatchi. Emotional balance. The rules seem to keep changing, but Jim appears stabilized today. Sobriety being fine tuned. Resonance resounds all around, all around. Virtuous effects compounded.

On the edge of now, between yesterday and tomorrow. Between vigilance and serenity. Between fear and doubt. I seek balance, not on a tightrope, but balance on a "broad highway." Less extremes, more calm. Give me that. It's that that I seek. No more next drink. No next drink. More of this. Just this. This.

EVENING MEDITATION

Some people hide behind their bottle far beyond the scope of their addictions. Some people hide within the rooms of recovery far after their obsession to drink leaves them. Sometimes, I am some people, too.

> *"Toleration is the greatest gift of the mind; it requires the same effort of the brain that it takes to balance oneself on a bicycle."*
> – Helen Keller

QUESTION FOR TODAY

Who is your god's god? What is your god's addiction? Who does your addiction worship? Where is my recovery now?

69. MY LAST RELAPSE

"People don't like change, but they like to have changed."
— Will Bowen

MORNING MEDITATION

I've heard of miraculous recoveries and miraculous discovery (of a higher power), but I've never heard of a miraculous relapse (I am no longer an alcoholic and can now drink like a normal person). Never, ever, heard of that one.

Why it has taken me quite so long to mention my last relapse has slipped out of my mind, but I do remember that a nurse at the Atlantic City Rescue Mission's AtlantiCare Health Clinic diminished the impact of my last four-day binge (which put me into the hospital and ended nearly two years of continuous sobriety). She called it "a slip."

Here's what happened and what I learned from it. I had been living in a "safe house," which is to say that all four members living in the house had several years of sobriety: Rob, Herb, Alice and me. Rob was dying of brain cancer. After his death, his surviving sister put the house up for sale and I was forced to move to a room a block away. My brain, my disease and I moved into a single room across the street from historic Boardwalk Hall. I was quite happy and quite sober, living by myself, and felt quite secure in my sobriety. Then I started having troubles with my job. The details are unimportant, but suffice it to say I was pissed at my boss when two days off from one workweek and two days off from the next workweek fell back to back. Thirty-five dollars sat in my bank account and I was pissed. (That I can't remember what I was pissed off about shows me that I may have just been looking for any excuse or that my disease was looking for a chink in my armor). What I did not know, when I made the decision to drink away my last thirty-five dollars over this four day period was that my new landlord had been out of the country and that all the weekly rent checks I had been giving his secretary sat undeposited in his desk drawer.

By the second day I had spent the entire thirty-five dollars and wondered if between loose change lying around my room and whatever was left in my bank account I might be able to scrape together enough money to buy one more bottle of vodka (even a half pint would have to do) before straightening out and resuming my sobriety. (Who would know?)

Long story short: I called the bank's automatic teller to find out what my balance was. I sat there drunk hearing that I now had several hundred dollars in my account (my undeposited rent checks)... If you're a drunk like me, you know what happened next. I went on a bender, one A.T.M. cash withdrawal after the other, until all the well-intentioned rent money was spent and I ended up in the hospital.

Yada. Yada. Yada. Same old story. So much for some new miracle of control.

(**Sotto**): *Finally, he's describing something factually: Push the stone up the hillside, Sisyphus, and it rolls back down. Push the stone up the hillside again and again it rolls back down. No wonder he finally got drunk. This shit really does get boring, especially when looked at from the outside. From the facts. Jim should have known better.*

But I've made the decision now. The decision to remain sober. My near deaths and the near deaths and actual deaths of others and the always disastrous, catastrophic effects of picking up a drink or drug have finally become painfully obvious and the potential joys that only my continued sobriety can bring have brought me to this moment. Life, for me, now, can only be good in a state of continuing, deepening sobriety. "Time takes time" and I'm good to go. Two feet firmly on this sober ground or six feet under. Hardly a question or an option, is it?

Sweetly obvious: I did not drink today.

(**Vatchi**): *Sotto, I think you're right. He's almost talking like a "normal" person now. Enough chaos has preceded this. Jim should be grateful for what he has now and grateful that his past, horrible as much of it had been because, finally, has brought him to this point in his sobriety. Jim has become "worthy of his sufferings." He must learn to accept this or I think that he will be primed to become a victim of his past once again, Sotto. Are you feeling me yet, Sotto?*

Sweetly obvious, I'm done.

(**Surimi**): *Ping. No Pong. Virtuous effects resounding. All around. All around. Good, new story. Good. He has a chance now. Everyone has a chance.*

Not today. Thanks for asking. I'm not interested in what you have to sell, Dear Alcohol. It is in the here and now that I dwell. This sober life. No thanks, I'm good.

EVENING MEDITATION

Once upon a time, admitting I am powerless over alcohol or anything else seemed impossible, un-American, unmanly. "Drink like a man" made more sense to me than "I am powerless." But, after several relapses and multiple self-realizations, saying that I am powerless over alcohol and that I am an alcoholic has not only become easier, it just "ain't no big deal."

"Contentment makes poor men rich. Discontent makes rich men poor."
– Benjamin Franklin

QUESTION FOR TODAY

Could your hollow bones not support the added weight of alcohol? Could you not fly?

70. THIS IS PAGE ONE

"You alone can do it, but you can't do it alone."
– Dr. Ron B.

MORNING MEDITATION
Even when lost in this beautiful, new reality called recovery, I must remember to keep one foot on the ground, just like I used to do when the room spun around and around on a roll.

This is one of many nows, this now. This sober day. This is a day of living where sobriety is a routine, a change of habits well-rehearsed, a life reversed. This is what is left when the last tremors of the earthquake have subsided. This is where the illusion of illusions has melted.

This is Page One.

(**Sotto**): *He is insane. This must be his insanity. Sober, but insane. One insane moment after the other. One paw print at a time until the beast is revealed. Vatchi! He's making me nuts now, too.*

Fear sat somewhere in my near immediate future, a crouching tiger, always ready to spring forward. I could feel and yet not feel the alcohol and its absence. Towards the end of nearly every relapse, anxiety attacks would consume me. I couldn't move forward because I was frozen in fear and anxiety. Those drunken, imaginary and insane fears were no less real than the factual fears of a knife at my throat, a gun in my back or the rest of my blah, blah, blah, blah, blah, drunken reality. Fear, a beating in my head when I had no drum. Pounding. Pounding.

Sobriety has helped me rid the imaginary fears so that I can better face the real ones. Alcoholic friends (in sobriety) instead of an alcoholic drink in my hand. It really took me about five years of sobriety for it to begin feeling comfortable, sustainable. I stand a chance in recovery when I maintain some sense of we. When it's just me, it's never just me. Alcohol and my alcoholism are always here. Beside me and inside me.

(**Vatchi**): *One foot in front of the other. I feel Jim struggling to sustain his sobriety and I feel empathy for his wavering emotions. Surimi, I sometimes get caught up in his emotions, too. So much so that I sometimes lose track of his words, actually. The only feelings he had left, towards the end, it seems, were the sensations of alcohol itself and nothing else. No other sensations. A throbbing test tube for alcohol. Jim, if you could hear me, I would say, "We are beginning to understand."*
Sotto, "the beast revealed" is Jim, moving forward in his sobriety.

To say the least, I was reluctant to stay sober at first, as my several relapses stand witness to. It has been life-changing, this new (less than ten years sober is new to "old-timers"), sober routine. I have developed and built upon the remnants that remain. It has always been possible only through the acceptance and support of my fellow "suffering alcoholics" and "grateful alcoholics" and all of those honest enough and brave enough in between. The cycle of stubborn independence I clung to had to be broken. It took sustained periods of sobriety for me to realize the illusion of independence, the laws of gravity (one person helping another), a new way of life, of living.

Let me be clear here about my alcoholism, this taboo: It is a cultural conspiracy of silence. And like the AIDS slogan from the 80's, "silence = death." I count myself fortunate to live in an age where alcoholism and addiction are coming out of the cultural closet. It could be worse. Taboos can be broken. Change is possible. I have learned that my alcoholism is treatable, manageable. Sobriety, sustainable. And I did not drink. Today. We did not drink today. We are not drunk. Today.

(**Surimi**): *You know, guys, even after bringing the skeletons out of the closet, you've still got to put some meat on them bones. "Dem bones, dem bones, dem crazy bones." The confluences of many events and emotions have led Jim to this point. Many causes or no causes, it hardly matters. One of many cycles has been broken. One of many cycles has begun. The earth is no longer the center of the universe, but the world can still be his oyster, all kidding aside. The conspiracy of silence that was with him has been broken. And I think I just heard the dog yawn, a constellation in the starry night.*

The tide comes in, the tide goes out. Solitude and serenity find their interludes. A recovering alcoholic is who I am and who I will remain being as I wend my way in sobriety. I am beginning to find my way. Wounded, yet in the process of healing, I reluctantly admit that helping others sustain their sobriety also helps me. Neither a hero nor a healer, I push myself forward. The tide comes in, the tide goes out. No bottles washed ashore.

EVENING MEDITATION

Alcoholism is identity theft. The old "the bottle in front of me became a frontal lobotomy" is more than partially true. Even if I were famous, any sense of capturing some sense of an autobiographical self would be impossible.
Believing I am sober does not make it so. Recovery accrued.

"For fast-acting relief, try slowing down."
– Lily Tomlin

QUESTION FOR TODAY

How many new normals have I had? How many possible futures postponed by another drink? How many pasts must I remember to remain sober? How many whys must I stop asking? How many questions have I still to ask?

71. VIRTUOUS CYCLES OF PROGRESS

"No price is too high to pay for the privilege of owning yourself."
– Friedrich Nietzsche

MORNING MEDITATION
Stagnation = Relapse

Addiction is a god. Worship. Fear. Ceremonies. A culture. A belief. Idealized. Idolized.

I truly feel as if I have turned some mysterious corner here. No one has pronounced, "Let there be Light!" or anything of such Biblical proportion. But here is a certain lack of darkness, barely felt, and the darkness, complete darkness is gone.

Now, at last, sobriety is becoming familiar.

(**Sotto**): *Vatchi? Who is the god of my addiction? Where is this god, Vatchi? Where can this thing called god be found, Vatchi?*

I've tipped the scales between my addiction and a better life. My God, which was addiction, is now my demi-god, forever struggling for a return to power. The God of my addiction has not been replaced by a Santa Claus God or an Easter Bunny God or any God whatsoever. Sobriety Itself whispers in the wind and I heed its call. I've tipped the scales between my addiction and a better life. I now favor a philosophy of living clean derived through my desire to survive.

I hold that thought, then gently let it drift on by....

(**Vatchi**): *Virtuous effects compounded, Sotto. Unvirtuous effects compounded, Sotto. These are your gods of recovery and addiction, Sotto. Don't even say or think 'god.' Or 'higher power.' Stick with virtuous effects compounded, just as Surimi recently stated. Stick with virtuous cycles of progress, Sotto.*

Like a bird flying past the boundaries of North and South Carolina, unknowingly, I was crossing borders, thousands of them, the borders between active addiction and sustained sobriety. Flying above the myths, the prejudices of perception, the taboos, I feel one incontrovertible fact, the irony of survival being the prize of survival, the everything that is nothing, the enigma which occurs when struggle becomes effortless. Life is cool. No drink, no sweat. I hold that thought then gently let it drift on by.

(**Surimi**): *"Virtuous cycles of progress." I like that, Vatchi. It's life beyond the myth, the foregone prejudices of myth, the unnecessary, the non-thinking. The irony of consequences with unattributable causes, because the causes are too many, too varied, too complex. Somehow, the victim has become the survivor. Virtuous progress or virtual hell? Do people know what they're asking when they ask, "Why doesn't he just stop drinking?"*

The prize for surviving is surviving. Simple, easy, like breathing when breathing is easy. Nothing good, nothing bad, could be made better by a drink. I would not have believed that forty years ago. For thirty years I could not have believed. "I came to believe," as they say in A.A., that nothing would be better with a drink, be made better by a drink.

EVENING MEDITATION

In sobriety, I stand guard outside the prison gates of addiction in a proactive stance to block my entrance back in, my picking up, to block, to stop insanity, to stop. That a prison guard, too, is in prison is one of the ironies of sobriety that I shall have to abide. Stop. Do not go in there. Stop. Do not go in there. This prison guard is somehow free.

> *"I thank God for my handicaps for, through them, I have found myself, my work, and my God."*
> – Helen Keller

QUESTION FOR TODAY

What became of the world that I thought only LSD could give me? Am I there now, along its infinite borders? How many borders am I crossing right now? How many borders have and will be crossed?

72. INSANITY'S BOUQUET

"Success is going from failure to failure without losing enthusiasm."
– Winston Churchill

MORNING MEDITATION

Instead of "One-Day-at-a-Time," it's "I've got to do something, and I've got to do it today."

Jane's addiction decided for her that she had suffered enough. The pain was enough. The pain of being unable to feel the pain was enough. The unbearable pain of the struggle to be free of her addiction was a giant wave whose undertow drew her back to the ocean of her addiction. She could no longer live free. No longer free. Under she went. The undertow of addiction drowned her.

Jane's addiction could not undecide her death.

(**Sotto**): *He separates himself from her death with his words. He is using his words to separate himself from addiction. Not from his own inevitable death. He's using his words to give himself one more day. Vatchi, his Jane is gone and he has no tears, but he is bringing a tear to my eyes. I wish he could know that I can sometimes feel his words more than he can. This is his disease, his side effects, his butterfly, his domino, his avalanche.*

Like force-fed fowl grown fat before their bones have had a chance to grow, alcohol altered the maturing process and crippled me. My hollowed out bones could not support the weight of alcohol. My head was a pumpkin carved from the inside. Collapsed. No candle ever lit. Slow motion implosion.

A building destroyed before it was completely built. I hit bottom, left with this ruin. I must pick up the pieces left living and build a new life. Destruction, deconstruction and reconstruction. It is all possible, so long as I keep moving forward. So long as I don't pick up.

(**Vatchi**): *To be honest with you, Sotto, I am only now learning to understand what we have in common: Two men walking over the same bridge (Thank you, Wallace Stevens). Alcohol, that bull in the china shop and the tiny pieces left behind. Some people actually do become stronger at the broken places (Thank you, Ernest Hemingway): One alcoholic helping another. Connectedness.*

Why is it so difficult to let go of a past I can barely remember? And blackout after blackout with no memories at all. I was zero. Those around me enabled me or ignored me. I ignored myself (alcohol did not ignore me). Poison. Prison. Nothing. (Can you smell the steel, the stench of nothingness?) Insanity's bouquet.

(**Surimi**): *Sotto, there's a certain truth to what you're saying about Jim using words to separate himself from reality. The symbol, the word, can be a kind of substitute for the reality it is trying to describe. Worse than non-alcoholic beer. Words are signposts along Jim's road to recovery. I think you're right though, Sotto. His recovery lies beyond his words, beyond Jane's death, within the birth of his sober self.*

Insanity's bouquet is not of different colored roses, or different flowers of various sorts. It's a bouquet of weapons, destruction, defense and offense, all wrapped in lies and gin-soaked tears, false laughter, hollowed-out bones. This is insanity's bouquet. Hot steel, cold steel, nothing. I will fill the black holes of my memory with a retrained brain. Live my way sober or lie my way drunk, powerless victim or sober victor. One foot in front of the other.

EVENING MEDITATION

Sometimes the present seems worse than the past. The present has fresh wounds, more hurtful than mere memories of wounds past. But one thing I know for certain: I want no drink before my final curtain. A drink, for me, can no longer heal my wounds. Only cause them.

> *"Anxiety does not empty tomorrow of its sorrow... but only empties today of its strength."*
> – C. H. Spurgeon

QUESTION FOR TODAY

The door of more leads to another door. Won't you, don't you, adore the door?

73. THIS SOBER ROAD

*"The foolish man seeks happiness in the distance: the wise man
grows it under his feet."*
– James Oppenheimer

MORNING MEDITATION

Actions have consequences: drugs, laws, morals. Sometimes, that's a tough pill to
swallow.

The universe seems to welcome life. A forest, destroyed by fire, completely
rejuvenates from the necessary ashes. Life replenishes itself and I am
replenished when I remain open. There is splendor in sobriety, in all of life.
I could not have appreciated this in my drunkenness.

(**Sotto**): *Vatchi, life seems to have given Jim another chance. He does seem
to be on the proverbial road to recovery, doesn't he?*

God strike me dead if I mean any mean to Bette Davis in this
apocryphal anecdote: Bette was seen entering the stall in the Ladies' Room
of an exquisite Beverly Hills restaurant. Through the walls of the stall she
was allegedly heard loudly and drunkenly exclaiming, "Corn? When did I eat
corn?" Hangovers, when I still had them, were like that to me: "I said what?
I did what? I went where?" And on and on.

(**Vatchi**): *Reality is coming to him, in doses large and small, as his sobriety
continues. I think he's improving, slowly, step by step as each day passes,
proverbial or otherwise.*

Now sober, I hope the world can now well see that seventy-five percent of my insanity has been contained. I'm still working on the other half (more corn).

(**Surimi**): *There's a certain discipline to remaining sober, living sober. Regrets, losses, self-hatred, an alphabet soup of emotions. Jim needs, and to a certain degree has established, a network of sobriety for himself. Being sober is a new normal for him now. To tell the truth, I'm surprised he's not more fractured. His emotions, his sense of self-destruction and helplessness. Change will happen. An even more new normal awaits him. "Time takes time."*

I value my sobriety today. "Armor-piercing" bullets, cop-killer bullets, that's what one shot is to me today. One shot of booze would be like a gunshot to my brain. Negotiating the twists and turns of sobriety is not easy. Alcohol magnifies or diminishes or twists all reality for me. There is no balance, for me, in the drink. The useful tool that it once was, was short-lived, turned long and twisted.

The progressive punishment from alcohol sold me on A.A. as my means of escape to reality, then alcohol blind-sided me once again, then again and again, into thinking I could somehow gain control over it, somehow, someway. No way. The irony of painkillers causing pain does not elude me. I value my sobriety today.

EVENING MEDITATION

At one time (for real, for real) it was believed by many that sex with a virgin is a sure cure for AIDS, or so some such rumors spread. Turned out that it didn't stop AIDS. Didn't cure AIDS. But it did do one hell of a job of spreading AIDS. And fear. And violence against women. "Here, this will cure what ails you," the bartender says. Turns out drinking alcohol will not cure an alcoholic.

Today I must insist on abstinence. A drink would be violence against myself. ("Why doesn't he just stop?")

> *"Make the best use of what is in your power,*
> *and take the rest as it happens."*
> – Epictetus

QUESTION FOR TODAY

Confidence, addiction's handmaiden: Under-confident, over-confident. Are you confident that confidence is addiction's lie?

74. TAKING A BREATHER

"Everything we see hides another thing; we always want to see what is hidden by what we see."
– Rene Magritte

MORNING MEDITATION

When I've been confused about my feelings and I've been willing to listen, I have heard through others' voices the feelings that I had somehow been blocking from my consciousness, a new clarity. Getting better by osmosis: People, places and things turned inside out. Batteries recharged.

Unlearning emotional insanity and learning emotional sanity. Are they opposite sides of the same coin? This is talking to myself. I'm talking to myself right here. A drink wouldn't shut that up. I know that now. A thousand drinks would shut that up. I know that now. One drink is a thousand drinks. One meeting is not a thousand meetings. I know that now.

(**Sotto**): *Love Addiction. Sex Addiction. Drug Addiction. Alcohol Addiction. Attach any adjective to this noun, addiction. It is an empty well that cannot ever be filled, fulfilled. Jim's story is beginning to wear on me.*

Is sanity control? I know insanity is not. Thinking to myself instead of talking to myself. How can I practice what I preach if I am not preaching?

(**Vatchi**): *His wheels are still spinning much too fast. Jim thinks that he has changed much more than he really has. I think he needs to slow his pace even more here.*

I am an old carnival man now. A Carnie. "He could have been good, once." "Too many spills on life's tightrope without a net." "Too many spilled drinks." "Too many stained carpets." "Too many sweat-stained armpits." "Too much blood in the gutter."

(**Surimi**): *If Jim can squeeze ten years of good living on top of thirty years of drunk living, then that might be the best that he'll be able to do. He can't make up for lost time, but if he can really learn to appreciate the time he's got, then he'll be just fine.*

I am less than an old Carnie. I am an old Carnie's dog, seven times older, my blood a sea of alcohol.

Rest now, Rover, rest.

EVENING MEDITATION

The universe can be seen as elegant, on one hand, or a slagheap of human suffering, on the other. All of that is secondary to the drink for me. For me, for me, for me, I must stay connected to my sobriety or some final separation will occur. That final separation is a drink. And for me, to drink is to die.

> *"The man who never alters his opinion is like standing water*
> *and breeds reptiles of the mind."*
> — William Blake

QUESTION FOR TODAY

I chased alcoholic illusions and delusions as I drank. Has the chase ended with the end of alcohol? Where does my sobriety begin? Let us share our fears, shall we? Can I stay sober just this one day? Can we? Where does our sobriety begin? When?

75. BROKEN RECORD

*"If you keep saying things are going to be bad, you have
a good chance of being a prophet."*
– Isaac B. Singer

MORNING MEDITATION
Relapse is rationalized insanity.

"The phenomenon of craving" is how Dr. William D. Silkworth separates the alcoholic from the social drinker in "The Doctor's Opinion" Chapter of A.A.'s basic text, Alcoholics Anonymous.

When I drink, it seems this craving is what qualifies me as depraved. Guilt, shame, self-pity, and a host of other emotions are all mine when this craving for more takes over. Even in a blackout state, my brain seems to crave, no, require more alcohol than my body can process. More until I blackout and more until I pass out. More until I find the hospital door. Or it finds me.

This craving, if it were to be described as a sin (as many societies, cultures and religions do), would neatly fit within the "Seven Deadly Sins". The Sin is Avarice, the craving for more. The Sin of Avarice is its own punishment, hell on earth, as it were, because more is never enough. More is never enough. Never. Enough. Move on.

(**Sotto**): *Vatchi, I'm getting better at understanding Jim, now. But understanding can be somewhat of a vacuum. Something always seems left out. Unsaid.*

Money. Money. Money. Money. Money. Christ. When I had my

business, early on, an employee stole checks from toward the back of the company checkbook and cashed a few checks for a few hundred. Forged signatures, but not enough for jail time. Another employee made a zillion long-distance phone calls (all over this continent as well as most of Europe) when my partner and I went out for lunch. I knew nothing about employees stealing from me. I would never have thought of stealing. As I heard someone at an AA meeting once say, "I only stole emotions." Drink. Drink. Drink. Drink. Drink. End of that story.

(**Vatchi**): *Sotto, sobriety is a balance of emotions and reason. Jim is a toddler on the sobriety tightrope. He can't be expected to express what he does not yet understand.*

The old joke used to be "this job gets in the way of my drinking." Twenty jobs and thirty years later, the new joke is "this job gets in the way of my recovery." I like both jokes equally well, especially since I'm on the sunny side of sober. A sunny smile now. The teeth are now false, but the smile is real. Funny somehow (but just barely) that as alcoholism drained happiness from my life, I did an equally terrific job of letting my teeth rot out of my head. When you're an alcoholic like me, steeped in your addictive tea called alcohol, healthcare falls by the wayside. Had not a senseless, drunken and violent crime against me broken out all my front teeth (and broke my jaw and punctured my lungs), I might have let my teeth rot further as I drank each endlessly continuing drink. A blessing in disguise, I guess, but it was one big mother fuckin' disguise.

I need this damned jukebox brain reprogrammed, man. Livin' on bar snacks. Same old, broken refrain. Arm broken, needle rusted, record warped, spinning, wobbling, warped. Wednesday. Thursday. Friday? WTF.

(**Surimi**): *You both give Jim too much credit. When he speaks with any kind of authority, his knowledge is merely a pretense, a shield, another form of denial. Not denial of his alcoholism, but his denial about not knowing a whole hell of a lot more than anyone else. A defensive smokescreen. One doesn't have to be talking of God to come off as "preachy." Jim's pedestal is stemware with a martini glass base. It's all part of his recovery process, finding his own sober middle ground.*

I have kind of, sort of, learned to keep my ego in check. I (my camel-sized ego) strive to pass through this narrow, narrow eye of the needle (narrow to my eye), my gateway to recovery. Can I ever fit anywhere, sober or drunk? It was and has been a necessary part of my recovery strategy to find a new fit. It seems that different parts of me are getting well at different rates of speed and on different levels. The alcoholic tremors, the

DT's, only lasted a few days, but the rest of my recovery has been a long, long haul. Coming soon to a theater of self near you: a re-integrated personality. Eyes wide-opened, mind half shut.

I'm still bad with money but financial planning is no longer just a cruel joke. "Progress, not perfection." Money can't buy happiness, but its mishandling is most certainly not happiness. Like our broken financial institutions, my finances need some kind of regulation. I'm tired of these bubbles bursting.

EVENING MEDITATION

I felt rejected because I was rejected. That's the plain truth. And alcohol could or would or was a way to deal with rejection. Alcohol was an easy tool to use but it answered no questions and solved no problems. Even short term, it was effective at nothing. Alcohol: Short term, long term, nothing. It cannot now be how I ever thought it was.

> *"The cause is hidden, but the result is known."*
> – Ovid

QUESTION FOR TODAY

Can contentment be contained? Or anger? Rage? Resentment? Or can nothing be sustained (The only constant is change)? How must I, will I, contain?

76. SELLING A DREAM, BUYING A NIGHTMARE

*"Suffering in and of itself is meaningless; we give our suffering
meaning by the way in which we respond to it."*
— Viktor Frankl

MORNING MEDITATION

In our recovery meetings, we speak one at a time. Sometimes, when I listen
carefully, I hear a symphony of sobriety.

Bad joke, so let's just call it "an imaginary conversation":
"Why do you drink, Jim?"
"I drink to forget."
"What are you trying to forget?"
"I don't remember.... You see! It's working!"
How can I painlessly segue into this next most painful, but true
anecdote? I can't. I dive right in. Like a sharp knife entering flesh. Slouched
in my seat at the end of the bar, not nodding to sleep, just nodding in a
drunken stupor after a three-day binge, I was approached with, "Excuse
me, but didn't you used to be somebody?"
Why did I drink? To forget I used to be somebody.

(**Sotto**): *Vatchi, who is this somebody anyway? A lot of smoke and mirrors
and distorted feelings. American idolatry. The ego as God. The Wizard of
Oz, false god. Who is this somebody? Who is he, this Jim? Haven't we heard
this all before?*

Drunk beyond the point of recognition and barely recognized. A
garden-variety drunk, finding neither fame, nor my true self. Just a me

reaching. Just a reaching. Just a shelf. Any bottle on any shelf. Just a battle. Just a battle that I could never win because there was less and less of me left to put up a fight. Give me another fucking drink above all else. Any shelf.

They called me "Rusty" because I drank Rusty Nails. They called me "Rusty" because that is what I was. I was my drink. And when you are your drink, you are nothing. Fuck you and give me another drink. Moonshine trumps sunshine. Drink until I black out. Drunk until I pass out. Fuck. Any self. Any shelf. Fuck.

(**Vatchi**): *Smoke and mirrors. Snakes and ladders. What does it matter, Sotto? Jesus walked on water. Jim walked an liquor and the illusion fell through. And Jim fell through. Fell through. Through. Overly confident, overtly confident. Confidence man. Con man. He fooled most people for a long, long time and then finally, only himself. And then and then and then nothing and no one, not even himself. Jim's crash to the bottom can be easily forgotten. He had humility. There. At his bottom. Can he stay humble as his competence at living sober increases? Competence trumps confidence. Place your bets. The chips are down. Way down.*

My advertising career and my bartending career had similarities. Selling the dream. Selling a dream. With advertising, I sold the dream through the print, radio and television ads I created and produced. With bartending, I sold the dream through Johnny Walker, bar snacks and shot glasses. I could sell what I didn't believe in (advertising), but what I did believe in (alcohol), sold me. Our consumer culture did not consume me. It was alcohol, that vulture, that picked my bones clean.

(**Surimi**): *Selling a dream, being sold by a dream. Most people are one or the other. Or both. Jim's dream of completeness included alcohol. Had to. He's an alcoholic – 100%. Like being pregnant, you are or you aren't. Now, just how far downhill this progressive disease's slope was he?*

Selling and buying a dream with no winners. You can con a con – at least alcohol can. But, at last, alcohol didn't. At least, not today. Alcohol lost today.

I cannot, cannot pick up a drink today. I have a solid fear of hitting bottom again. The only bottom I think that's left for me is death and I can't afford to have myself proved wrong. Being a blackout drinker, as I was, were I to pick up a drink, my final drink would be never coming to or worse, an alcoholic twisted pain beyond any and all I've already had, just worse and final.

Sometimes gratitude sucks. Even when I cannot, must not, do not drink.

EVENING MEDITATION

Do not define me by my absence of your faith. My lack of your "brand" of religion is an absence only of your understanding. I have values, moral precepts, beliefs. Let the doors of recovery be wide enough for all to pass through. Sermon over.

"We cannot solve our problems with the same thinking
we used to create them."
— Albert Einstein

QUESTION FOR TODAY

Have you considered the epiphanies of now? Not the rearview mirror, not tomorrow's hope, just the epiphanies of now. Have you? How about now, then? Now?

77. RESENTMENT

"The inner fire is the most important thing mankind possesses."
– Edith Sodergran

MORNING MEDITATION
Faith without works is hot-air hypocrisy.

I thought I had stockpiled a limited amount of knowledge of food and wine in the restaurant and bar businesses, but parlayed with my hospitality and advertising experience, I had buffaloed my way into the peachy job of restaurant critic on a four-minute television segment known as "Time to Dine" on WWAC-TV 53's Friday night evening news broadcast. My show didn't even last their full last broadcast season "due to budget restrictions," but the unconfirmed possibility exists that my alcoholism was strongly in the picture. Although it is true that I had had no prior broadcast experience in front of the camera, it is the emotional truth, the alcoholic truth, which I want to get at here. How others correctly diagnosed me as an alcoholic from the outside did not fit my feelings and identity as an alcoholic on my insides.

On a windy day, standing outside whatever restaurant it was that day, with camera rolling, I can remember talking out of the side of my mouth, as I habitually did in order to prevent my alcoholic breath from wafting into the closest set of nostrils. Never mind that this was not "Smell-o-Vision" and that no one could have smelled the alcohol on my breath on the other side of the TV screen.

We taped the "Time to Dine" segment several days earlier on location at the various Casino and non-casino restaurants, and I can guarantee, come Friday night, when my segment aired, I was already plastered. At that time, it was not uncommon for me to arrange to be in the office of one of my favorite advertising clients around four o'clock on a Friday, drinking scotch on the rocks in Andy's real estate office, high above the Atlantic City Boardwalk. Andy was a good twenty years older than I was at the time (this was 1984 or 5) and I marveled at how rich and successful he was and still able to belt down scotch like a perfect gentleman. I imagined that I would one day be able to be successful, like him, and to be able to drink successfully, like him, but I was chasing the illusion of all alcoholics that somehow, someday, my drinking could be, would be, better and different. This was before several relapses finally taught me, that for an alcoholic like me, I could never drink successfully, and that, no matter what else happened, or how long I went without a drink, it would always and could only, end worse. The best I could do was to imagine that my drinking would be manageable.

(**Sotto**): *Some imagined future vision of our selves. We hold it up to the light like a snifter of fine cognac. And yet, others judge us by our past, like a child's lemonade stand. Our own sense of self includes our as yet unfulfilled potential. Jim thought that one day his drinking could become more manageable.*

"I'll show them!" drinking has always been my most catastrophic. All it has ever shown "them" is what a chronic alcoholic I am. My last "I'll show them!" drink resulted in a four-day binge that got me neatly strapped into a hospital bed and nearly fired. "Just for Today," "One Day at a Time" and a dozen other catch phrases from Alcoholics Anonymous (most significantly, "The Serenity Prayer") have been my roadblocks to "I'll show them!" and dozens of other triggers. One circumstance after another presents itself as another reason that I can't drink.

(**Vatchi**): *All we have is now, Sotto. The drunken TV show host is gone. The anonymous drunk and disorderly nuisance is gone. Jim clings to these memories to keep himself fearful. The sirens are calling him to drink 'on the rocks.' "Surrender to win" is a tough, tough sell. Until the alcoholic learns that there is no alternative. And with the first drink "now" ends and the old insanity begins again.*

When I was young and not too good looking, I didn't pay too much attention to my appearance, not because I was young and attractive enough, but because I was young and looking. Looking for good times (and I had many) as most young people do. But then my alcoholism took over. Dental and eye care went the way of the horse and carriage. I didn't care. And I didn't care that I didn't care. Yada, Yada, Yada. Now I'm older and sober and caring how I feel and how I look. But all of that is the byproduct of this package deal called sobriety.

(**Surimi**): *Sotto, my mind is still lingering back to your lemonade stand, that childhood past, image of hope, prosperity. Jim got smashed. Alcohol took over. Now he's starting over. Sober. A lemonade stand. Make lemonade, Jim. Stay proactive, Jim. Not reactive. No more "I'll show them!"*

I could never drink in moderation. Now sober, moderation in thought and action have become among my biggest tools for staying sober. That Zen-like middle road called balance. The simple rewards of sustained sobriety gently squelch any thought of a drink. Sobriety now quenches my thirst.

Except in dreams, I did not drink today.

EVENING MEDITATION

Life seems sometimes irreducibly complex. An abundance of caution and the ability to let go seem irreconcilable. Life seems a paradox wrapped in a riddle in a kettle playing fiddle. I can't settle for less than complex and a simple letting go.

"The effort to understand the universe is one of the very few things
that lifts human life a little above the level of farce,
and gives it some of the grace of tragedy."
– Steven Weinberg

QUESTION FOR TODAY

How many times must sobriety and insanity cross paths before serenity feels familiar? How many degrees of separation will it take for me to begin to feel whole? How long will it take to let go of my drunken self? How long until there is no more more and enough is enough?

78. THIS IS WHERE WE FIND OURSELVES

"Doubt grows with knowledge."
– Johann Wolfgang von Goethe

MORNING MEDITATION

Gratitude. Serenity. Humility. These are the things you discover you never really lost, you just lost touch with. Rediscovered, uncovered, revealed, restored.

Smoking cigarettes as if there were some kind of comfort in continuing to smoke. Living when living seemed to have no purpose and the only meaning might be found in this smoke. Meaning, rolled up in paper and exhaled. There is nothing left but yellowed fingertips.

Brown. Brown fingertips.

Here you are drunk and walking the hallways of the Taj Mahal Casino, picking cigarette butts out of ashtrays. You break off the filters and re-roll the butt ends with new cigarette papers. This is a way to survive, to think that you're surviving. This is when the only food is the juice in this vodka and cranberry. This is when it takes you two solid hours to get out of bed and put on a pair of shoes. This is when there is no next drink, there is just this one long drink that goes on forever. This is where there is no up or down and you can only move sideways. This is where waking up is like falling through a stage prop wall. This is where you carry your addictions in a cardboard box as if you were moving to another location. This is finding no location and the box is empty. This is standing and not being able to move. This is drunk and crashing, falling, falling through a bottom, tumbling. This is where a hospital wakes you up and you do not know who you are or where you are.

(**Sotto**): *This is where Jim gets lost in his past and I get lost with him. This is where I ask you to help me, Vatchi. This is where he traps me in his past, Surimi. This is where I want to get out.*

My father was a wood carver. He carved ducks out of wood. Like Michelangelo searching for the block of marble that contained the statue he would sculpt, in a block of wood, my father searched for a duck. He had the right tools. He was motivated. He was inspired.

For years I never had a reason to quit drinking and by the time I had a reason to quit, reason no longer had anything to do with it. I drank for escape and I ended up being unable to escape from drinking. Now, years sober, I have found many of the tools of recovery. There are those who have inspired me, motivated me. Slowly, patiently, I must carve the frustration, self-pity and despair out of this block of wood. Carve out the envy, anxiety and intolerance. File down the burrs of hatred, jealousy and resentment. Chisel out the suspicion and sarcasm, the mistrust. Get rid of the apathy, the remorse, the self-deception. Cast out the doubt, the blame, the fear. Scrape out contempt and cynicism. Smooth out the rough edges.

A.A. has given me the tools. There are those who have motivated me, inspired me. Someday I hope to walk and to talk like a duck. And I pray that I will float.

Drinking kicks you down the steps. The 12-steps lift you up. Now, let's go fishin'!

(**Vatchi**): *Jim is sober at last. This is where he starts over, Sotto. This is where his life begins, Sotto. This is where the future is now, Sotto. This is where we find ourselves, Sotto. This is now. This is today. This is sober.*

False comfort in a cigarette. False comfort in a drink. False comfort in a Southern Comfort. Just don't let me think. "Obliterate me," I would sometimes think and, thought or not, obliteration was the usual result. Cause or no cause, the effect was always the same. Drinking is a game I cannot win. Drinking I cannot. False comfort. False comfort. I slid down the drain. Down and out.

(**Surimi**): *There is no starting over. Or there is only starting over. He has been through all this. He has survived this insanity. All of this. A star explodes. This end is this beginning.*

I cannot hear. I cannot focus. Nicotine and alcohol cannot quite satisfy my reptilian brain. Tweet. Tweet. I cannot hear it. Too many Katrinas, too many cyclones, floods, disasters, relapses. Too many. I cannot hear. I cannot focus. I cannot find my footing. I must not lose my footing. This is not, is not easy.

EVENING MEDITATION

Without the sorrow and suffering of sliding and slamming my way downhill, I couldn't have ever entered my current state of contentment. So much of recovery may not be visible to bored onlookers. Consequently, recovery doesn't have the appeal of an action or disaster film to them. My current "estate of mind" may lack "curb appeal" but I'm not ready for any trade-offs today. Not today.

> *"The worst sin towards our fellow creatures is not to hate them, but to be indifferent to them; that's the essence of inhumanity."*
> – George Bernard Shaw

QUESTION FOR TODAY

How long after the last hit or last sip will addiction's momentum continue? Clean and serene, is addiction a perpetual motion machine? Can I stay clean? Where am I going? Where will this all end?

79. A DAILY REPRIEVE

"Not to be absolutely certain is, I think, one of the essential things in rationality."
– Bertrand Russell

MORNING MEDITATION
Gratitude does not anticipate: It simply is.

I turn over my fears as I'm walking down the street one cloudy day. The autumn leaves turn over themselves on the sidewalk before me. And then I hear something. Far away I hear a literal bird singing. And then it hits me. This is what turning over my fears and my addictions has finally given me. My hearing. My unfocused hearing. After three years sober I turned over another addiction, my addiction to cigarettes, and here's what I noticed: not that I would live longer, but that I could live more fully in the present. Yes, I could taste better and smell better without the tobacco and liquor in my mouth and on my breath. But the real reward is not delayed for some unforeseen future. It is lived in the present, not focused on the next drink of my addiction and the next smoke of my addiction. I simply am. And in that state of merely being, I could hear then what I could not hear before, this bird singing in its simultaneous being. It wants no more. Nor did I. Nor do I.

I can live more fully in the now. Clean and sober. I turn over my fears as I'm walking down the street. The autumn leaves turn over themselves on the sidewalk before me. I live more fully in the now, in the present that lies before me.

(**Sotto**): *What has not died, what has survived, is a life to be lived more fully,*

Vatchi. I will give this one to Jim. I will go so far as to affirm his sobriety. He has become more than sober. Not a dry drunk. Alive and sober, this different kind of more, in the absence of alcohol. More. This more. Sober.

Diminishing returns. When drinking started in my late teens and early twenties, the positives outweighed the negatives, and by a long shot. If I weren't an alcoholic, when the scales tipped in the other direction, I would have been pro-active in cutting down or stopping drinking altogether. But that's not how addiction works. Drug abuse (alcohol is a drug) continues despite and sometimes because of negative consequences. The poison is the potion. But there's something pervasive about diminishing returns in recovery, also. When I first got sober, the positive changes were stark, bold, immediate. Then, as time went by in early recovery, the changes became less visible and more subtle. It was at this point that my gratitude for sobriety seemed to lessen. It would be at this point in my recovery where I would find myself singing, "If that's all there is, my friend, then let's keep..." drinking.

(Vatchi): *Yes, Sotto, yours is an honest affirmation. Jim's recovery has an ebb and a flow, degrees of being unsure, degrees of gratitude and impermanence, degrees of insanity. Sotto, you too, are given a daily reprieve, if not from alcoholism, then from any one of many things. Death. If only a daily reprieve from death. Accept it graciously, Sotto. Jim is but an example. You are but an example, Sotto.*

The smaller changes (those barely noticed, and so many do go unnoticed) that sobriety has continued to bring me are subtle to the nth degree. Subtleties, are more important to me now. My advancing age and continued sobriety have mellowed me out. Life is sweet. I see now that letting go is not complacency.

(Surimi): *The rage of addiction. A raging fire. A raging madman. Jim goes from raging alcoholic to the subtle innuendoes of continued sobriety. Some people have said that A.A. employs brainwashing techniques. Guess what? I think Jim's brain needed a good washing. His greed for chemical relief has faded. He's gone green. Fresh. Fresh coat of paint. New glasses. New ears, too, by his account.*

Loneliness, anger and resentments are all a part of my sobriety, but these and others and all emotions are more manageable sober without an unimaginable, unmanageable drink overhead, in my head. Let it go. Let it flow. I can do this. I never could have known this. Today I am sober. Sober.

EVENING MEDITATION

The doctor diagnosed my condition as a sinus infection and gave me a prescription for antibiotics. Knowing I would be well in ten days made me feel subjectively better instantly. Nothing changed but my faith in the knowledge that things would change for the better very soon. If I can learn to apply this kind of trust to everything in my life, then I will feel better now and feeling better now will guide me into feeling better in my future. Of course, this is a hard concept to hold onto and an easy one to let slip out of my hands, but I just have to keep repeating it until it becomes my heartbeat, my heartbeat, my heart.

"The older I get the more I trust in the law according to which
the rose and the lily bloom."
– Johann Wolfgang Von Goethe

QUESTION FOR TODAY

Can you admit that life is looking brighter sober, despite this slowly dying of the light?

80. MY SECOND INSANITY

"In quarreling, the truth is always lost."
– Publilius Syrus

MORNING MEDITATION

Isolation is my enemy. My addiction speaks in shouted whispers. That's right. You heard me. Shouted whispers.

My first sobriety was my second insanity, as I think I've already stated. My first job first time sober was at the Salvation Army. I was over medicated on antidepressants and was consequently fired for moving too slowly. I was quickly rehired by a bar I had worked at several years before. As any bartender can tell you, in most bars, a good proportion of regular, daily grind customers are alcoholics in various stages in the progression of their disease and in varying degrees of denial. For this alcoholic, at that time, I really thought I could work in that snake pit without being bitten.

A good time was not had by all.

One regular, Morris, had a distended stomach from alcohol-induced liver disease. His liver bled into his body, or so it seemed from his bloated belly. I don't know. I just know that his liver was destroying him and his abdomen was filled with blood. Internal bleeding. Dying. A sick liver sending ammonia through the blood and to the brain as a byproduct of its dysfunction, causing him personality disorders. I'm not a doctor. I don't know the exact details. I just know what I saw in Morris's case. An internet search later confirmed this basic assumption of the ammonia/alcoholic/liver disease connection. Alcoholic insanity. Ammonia insanity.

Was my first sobriety, my second sobriety, in any way different except by degree?

I breathe in now, thinking about Morris and I sigh and look down, bewildered, just as he did time and again before he disappeared from the wilderness slash unreality of the bar. I can only picture him crawling away into some alternate reality to die, an aging Eskimo in ice, dying. Insane, then simply dead.

Then there was my boss, Angie, so drunk and obviously unable to drive that she said I was fired when I refused to give her car keys back to her. And Kevin, murdered in a Philadelphia blackout sex scene gone terribly wrong. And this. And that. And I could go on and on. One ridiculous alcoholic scenario after another, all seeming perfectly normal and plausible and (sigh, I'm sighing here, again)....

People. Places. Things. "Just a job," I thought, until one year later, I found an empty glass in my hand. People. Places. Things. A not so empty glass. And then... fill 'er up. The old insanity returned.

(**Sotto**): *Vatchi, this is so odd. I can hear Jim relating his past and in my mind he is smoking a cigarette as he tells it because I know he did smoke when these things actually happened in his past.*

It's me. I need something to hold onto. He has me outside myself.

(**Vatchi**): *You need something to hold onto, Sotto? That's everybody, Sotto. Whether it be a hope, a hand, a heart, regardless. There is Jim's addiction to alcohol, while he's using and the habit of something to hold onto when he's not.*

A drink can be like a piece of candy in the dish on the table... "Oh, how did that get in my mouth? I don't remember even picking it up." Sweet insanity.

(**Surimi**): *Elizabeth Taylor stipulated in her will that she be late for her own funeral. Well, Jim is or was late for the funeral of his old self. But no real funeral could ever be held because his old self lies forever dormant within him. His sweet insanity calmly embedded in his brain, patiently waits for him to pick up. No matter how long his new self moves forward in sobriety, it waits.*

I don't think "normies" can ever appreciate the enormousness of what is in an alcoholic's brain, drinking or not, sober or not, sweetly insane or not.

An exact date and time could be given for when I had my last, last drink. But the changes from that sudden change are gradual and grand, subtle and simple, fast and slow. A fear that could paralyze me drunk might more simply motivate my sober self. Change is risky, but it could not be safe to stay the same. "The drunk I was will drink again." Change or die.

EVENING MEDITATION

Denial, fear, pain, ignorance, surrender. Neither hero nor anti-hero, an alcoholic falling on his sword is really just surviving the powerlessness that is surely his downfall.

"Take rest; a field that has rested gives a bountiful crop."
— Ovid

QUESTION FOR TODAY

With what will you replace addiction's myths? Another insanity? A chemical-free insanity? Will you do this? Have you done this? Can you conjugate this? Can you replace this?

81. EMPTY BOTTLES AND REFILLABLE PAIN

"A positive attitude may not solve all your problems, but it will annoy enough people to make it worth the effort."
– Herm Albright

MORNING MEDITATION
Face it. Pass through it. Let go. Move on.

Bad discovery: the day I discovered that when drinking made me puke, drinking more would stop the puking. A few small sips and then more puking. A few more small sips and then still more puking. More sips. More puking. Eventually the puking stops. But the drinking doesn't stop. The drinking does not, will not stop. Fighting against the drink, against the will to drink and to not drink, wanting the puking to stop. Then surrender and drinking to oblivion. I chased the drink until the drink chased me. The porcelain goddess. Kneel to the porcelain goddess. Kneel.
"Would you like a chaser with that?"

(**Sotto**): *He's like a dog chasing his tail. Around and around. No center. No substance. A whole lotta drinking going on. And nothing else.*

Looking back now to my drinking days (daze), I can now see that I was always worse off than I thought I was at the time. I continued downhill. There was always something or someone else to blame and the alcohol would always help, I thought. It could not hurt. Sober now, I can see how others must have seen me then. I don't know if this is like the separation of Siamese Twins or not. Did I have one heart, but two brains? One brain, but two hearts? Are the past and future conjoined in this now, like some sideshow freak show formaldehyde bodies in a jar? Ammoniated brains on my gravy train. Come one, come all! From near! From far! See this freak in a fucking jar!

This will never be easy. The status quo will take me where I don't want to go. That is insane, my friends, that is insane. The status quo will take me back to empty bottles and refillable pain.

This is no ordinary restoration. It will not be. Don't rebuild. Build anew. Christ. No wonder I need help. Ninth Wonder of My Alcoholic World, I am the freak in this fucking jar!

(**Vatchi**): *A dog chasing his tail. Going nowhere fast. That's why people in early sobriety need to be reminded to slow down. Learn patience.*

Crash and burn insanity. Caramelized sugar insanity. The newly sober asks his Sponsor, "What do I have to change?" And his Sponsor replies, "Everything." And the reason is? Because alcoholism is total insanity.

Understanding sober how insane it was when I was drunk is no easy task. Alcoholic insanity defies all reason. Drinking despite negative consequences seems to define alcoholism and yet now sober I cannot want to define myself that way. It will take some time to not be looked at by others as I was. It can be discouraging how others' perceptions of you do not change as quickly as the feelings you feel changing inside.

"Don't rebuild. Build anew." That must be what they mean when they say "Change everything."

(**Surimi**): *Vicious cycles. Vicious circles. No vicious virtue. You're right, Vatchi. Slow down, Jim. Impatience. If there's one character defect I've seen in most, if not every, addict and alcoholic, it's impatience. Always waiting for and wanting the next hit, the next drink. The waiting and wanting have become character traits that have not yet stopped, even after the drinking and drugging stops. The waiting and wanting continue. It takes time to decelerate.*

The child I was before I began drinking, to a certain extent, is the child who must start rebuilding, building anew. The building blocks of recovery. No wonder I need help in my learning how to live. In A.A. you hear repeatedly that "It's a 'we' program," and that is so true to my experience.

At my second two-week Rehab at the Institute for Human Development (now John Brooks), high on Librium as we detoxify on alcohol and other drugs, one guy gave five or six of us a new haircut, one after the other. That was the symbolic start of the emergence of a new and sober self for me. An aboriginal ritual. "Today you are a man. Free of alcohol and drugs. Go forth. Build a new life." None of that was said aloud, of course, and the symbol of the haircut and the reality of the haircut were quite different things. Am I splitting hairs? Yes, but wisely (Har-de-har-har hair).

EVENING MEDITATION

The drink got in the way of safety, time and time again. Time and again I got lucky. Very lucky. And luck is for losers and boozers who survive. In my sobriety, nothing can get in the way of my sobriety, not even a drink. And that is that is that.

> *"Selfishness is not living as one wishes to live. It is asking other people to live as one wishes to live."*
> – Oscar Wilde

QUESTION FOR TODAY

What poetry can be found in dead-drunk dreams? Why are you even looking for poetry? What is rhyme without reason? What dreams have you abandoned? What dreams have abandoned you?

82. YOU CAN'T HANDLE THE PROOF

"He who has a Why to live for can bear almost any How."
– Frederick Nietzsche

MORNING MEDITATION
Isolation and apathy are my recovery's time-bomb, my recipe for relapse.

Loving to drink. Living to drink. Dying to drink. Dying from drinking. This is the progression of alcoholism. Wanting to live. Learning to live. Loving to live. Living with love. This is the progression of recovery. Alcoholism, a progressive disease, requires a progressive solution, a program of recovery (like a 12-step program or anything, really, anything that works).

I have been motivated, inspired, filled with gratitude. This is affirmation arisen from despair. Recovery seems to be broadcloth made from these interwoven threads of motivation and inspiration, a fine tapestry. I want to wear it like a loose-fitting garment. Most of the time meditation and prayer only seem possible in stillness and in silence, but sometimes they seem to linger with me as I move and speak. This is part of the reason why it can be said that gratitude is an action word. It is not only something you reflect upon, but something you carry with you, a fire from within that is to be shared.

(**Sotto**): *So, what do you think, Vatchi? Does Jim have brain damage or did his thirty-minute layover at Newark Airport (turned into thirty years) have no permanent side effects?*

A life awash in alcohol and drugs, I sometimes have to simply stop and take a look around me and reaffirm myself, my conclusions, my reality. It

252

seems that when I drank, for all those decades, I merely plowed forward, drink in hand, stuck in the drink and not knowing it. I did not know surrender. How could I win a battle I didn't even know I was in? My battle with the bottle was internal and silent. I had no power or control over the bottle. The bottle always won.

Who could I have become were I not an alcoholic? There is no answer to be found at the end of that cul-de-sac. The better question is who can I become now that I have put the bottle down? All I know for sure is that the people, places and things I was surrounded by in my very first year of sobriety were not conducive to my continuing sobriety. How naïve was I to think and believe that I could remain sober tending bar that very first year? Today, I know that I need to live sober in order to remain sober. And I have learned that for me, this, I cannot do this alone. Maybe someday. But not this day. Not today. So long as I stay on my current path of recovery, my life will continue to be good. I know this and I believe this, if I, indeed, believe anything at all. Living in the here and now, instead of in the next drink, I am not so hurried or anxious. Anxiety: the anxiety of living drunk is the anxiety of knowing that this drink in my hand is not the solution, but the next one... maybe the next one.

(**Vatchi**): *Alcohol was, once, Jim's servant. It served him well. Until his addiction kicked in and the tables were turned and black was white and what once was heaven became his hell.*

It is a different kind of happiness, now that I am not drinking. It has taken years for me "to know a new freedom and a new happiness." The freedom from that desire to pick up a drink has led me down a better pathway.

I'm over sixty years old and still just now learning how to make friends. Not having to prove to myself and to others that I can handle my alcohol is one big plus of sobriety. Three decades of 100 proof. Unable to handle the proof.

"You can't handle the proof." I can't. And that's the truth.

(**Surimi**): *Jim's sense of humor seems to be improving. So long as it doesn't improve faster than his common sense, I think he has a shot at a continuing sobriety. There is no instant integrity. Or instant humility. Or a lot of other "instants." Like instant gratification. That one has been, and may continue to be an instant trigger for Jim. There is no rush to recovery. The patients must have patience.*

Jim "can't handle the proof." I'll give him that one.

"You can't handle the proof."

The Court of Public Opinion will convict me. "You can't handle the proof." The Masquerade of Time will dispel recovery's urgency. "You can't handle the proof." I'm addicted to self, a lifetime of self. "You can't handle the proof." My disease trails me like a slug praying to catch up. "You can't handle the proof." What is my disease and what do I have left? "You can't handle the proof." Sobriety is my long-last act of love.

I can almost handle the truth.

EVENING MEDITATION

Two-thirds cup of doubt in an empty cup. That was my kind of luck. No leap of faith would fill my drunken cup or keep me sober. My trust in my own recovery is not yet complete, has never been, and may never be. I have to be here fully, or close to full, belly up to my own Recovery Bar. I am my own Trojan horse - a full cup hidden inside an empty one.

> *"Nowadays most people die of a sort of creeping common sense,*
> *and discover when it is too late that the only things*
> *one never regrets are one's mistakes."*
> – Oscar Wilde

QUESTION FOR TODAY

Where is the sound that will take you to the silence within the sound? Where is the blood so red that it journeys into white? Where is the riverbed through which your life flows? When will now begin? Is this what sobriety is? Is?

83. CATCH THE BEAT, DANCE YOUR FEET

"The best way to cheer yourself is to cheer somebody else up."
– Mark Twain

MORNING MEDITATION
Sponsorship (one alcoholic guiding another through the steps of recovery in A.A. or N.A.), that two-way street, will cure complacency.

Dance your feet
Down the street
Come by bike or car
Catch a train
Sun or rain
Even if you fly by plane
Catch the beat
Dance your feet
To where the sprinkles are:
Dunkin' Donut Sprinkles

"What was that?" you ask. It simply is a broken fragment from the last drunken jingle I wrote, yet never had published, for Dunkin' Donuts. I call it "Drunken Donuts." Good as I still envision this jingle to be, in its entirety, there is a melancholy in my mind's ear. It was written after my first relapse, before my second sobriety. Maybe one day....

(**Sotto**): *It's so sad, Vatchi, that even when he produced this fairly well put together piece, he was broken inside. That "art produced in concentration camps" routine. This is the illusion of the creative process for the addicted* *person. The trick was thinking you could only produce because of the addiction, not in spite of it. Living a sad, sad illusion.*

I remember thinking something like "without alcohol, I am nothing." Back then my sense of self-identity was so tied up in the drink. I did not think of alcohol as my crutch, but rather, as my inspiration. I had bought wholesale, retail and at half price, the belief that alcohol was the taproot from which my creative processes grew. To suffer for my art - that was the grand illusion, my biggest excuse. The "holes in time," as Matt, an A.A. buddy, calls it. All the lies, truths, half-truths, everything that has happened to me, have brought me here and I can be happy now. Free of alcohol I have access to my spirit. "Catch the beat. Dance your feet." Go figure.

(**Vatchi**): *Chemical regret. That's what it boils down to. Add alcohol and everything changes. Take alcohol away and everything changes again. Some changes are reversible. Others are not. Chemical regret.*

I bring myself back to the present. I cannot cling to the past. Or onto the present, for that matter. Loving life is a lot like letting go. So this. This right here. I must finish this. I must be done with this. Passing through this. Through this moment. Letting go. The drink has not evaporated me. There is still this.

(**Surimi**): *The insane optimism of attributing any artistic merit to the results of drugs and alcohol. Such a delusion, illusion, insanity. A cultural myth, an addiction myth. The chemical mistress dominates. Song of the Siren.*
Persevere the "pink cloud." The insane optimisms of the newly sober eventually level out, even out, balance out. Cultivate a realistic optimism, Jim. He can do this, Sotto. Without regret, Vatchi.

Catch the beat, dance my feet to where sobriety is (on my way to a meeting). Catch the beat, dance my feet... sober in my mind. I never could have guessed this. Catch the beat. Dance your feet. To here. To now.

EVENING MEDITATION

Memories of my past and future fears obscure the sunlight of my present. When I just let go, life just seems to flow in and fill me up.

"The natural flights of the human mind are not from pleasure
to pleasure, but from hope to hope."
– Samuel Johnson

QUESTION FOR TODAY

Hospital whites, hospital blacks, hospital grays: How can I use these to help someone else so that we may both find another sober day? How can you? How will we? Help me answer all of our questions. Can you? Will you? Won't you?

84. ALL DRINKING ASIDE

*"Human beings are perhaps never more frightening than when
they are convinced beyond doubt that they are right."*
– Laurens Van der Post

MORNING MEDITATION

Compulsively focusing on others can really be used as a form of procrastination, of
denying my own problems, of working on my own steps towards recovery...

Gripped with fear, my anxiety attacks return. My fears have been spelled
out in the nightmares others are living. My drunk dreams explain me. I feel
separated. Night sweats, drunk dreams. Like a wild locomotive with no
breaks. Noise - white noise, black noise - Adrenaline. A drunken grip my
drunk dreams hold on me. The nightmare reality of what reality was like.
Insane drunkenness. The abyss of drunkenness. Anxiety unbound.

Drunk dreams – there just is no poetry there, just a personal, perennial
drunken hell. This is fucked up.

(**Sotto**): *Blind Man's Bluff. Pin the tail on the donkey. Tag. Hide-and-seek.
All those childhood games. I see them everywhere. In the living world. But
this? This is Dodge ball. Dodging the next drink as the excuse for being too
busy to do something, anything. Vatchi, I hope Jim can stay sober. Do you
think he will?*

Turn around, forward, slowly I spin, one foot on the floor, how well I
remember it. Turn around, I would drink. Driving drunk. Driving dizzy.
"Close one eye," I would say to myself out loud, dizzy and drunk and
driving. I could drive drunk with one eye closed because cross-eyed, two-

eyed wouldn't work drunk. In bed, finally, one foot on the floor would stop all the spinning. One eye shut I could drive. One half of me drunk, one half of me senseless. Drive with one eye. Sleep with one foot on the floor. This is normal. That was normal.

(**Vatchi**): *Drunk dreams, driving drunk, driving me crazy, Sotto. Jim seems to be growing, changing, living sober, then gets stuck in his past. Is he okay here? He seems to be losing it here.*
Release. Let go. This is a fishing expedition. All the fish are remembered, are hooked. And all of them, finally, must be released and let go. His past will erode his potential for recovery. That's why he seeks the help of other alcoholics but rarely admits it except out loud. He is speaking recovery yet not listening to himself. I hate to say it, Sotto, but I think Jim needs help here. He's losing it here.

Drunk is a dream. Drunk dreams are drunk. Dream is a drink. Drank is a drunk. Drunk is a dream. Drunk dreams are drunk. Dream is a drink. Drank is a drunk.
"It's only a dream," my Mother used to say to me, this child.
But drunk is not a dream. Never, ever again. There is no running to catch up to, to where I should have been by now. I yam what I yam is Jesus and Popeye and sweet potatoes. Sobriety can erode. Proceed with caution. Keep an even keel. Glide forward. No more annihilation of feelings. Alcohol kills me. Sobriety heals.
The dream was drunk, but I am sober.
This even keel.

(**Surimi**): *One-eyed Jim, driving, one eye closed. Blind drunk, literally blind drunk. Figuratively blind.*
One eye sober, time takes time. Annihilation of feelings. Feelings reborn. Trudge. Trudge. Ping. Virtuous cycles continuing.

Drunk is a dream. Drunk dreams are drunk. Dream is a drink. Drank is a drunk. There is no way to be where I might have been by now. That child was never born. That child could not control the drink. That child was deserted. That child's death is no coincidence. That child could not make it stop. Because I don't remember, perhaps it was not real. I do not know what he feels.
All drinking aside, I did not drink today.

EVENING MEDITATION
There's no room for anger in a barrel full of monkeys. There's no room for rigid

thinkers as we alcoholics are sometimes perceived. There's no need for pain devoid of context. There's no room for blame. We are no longer victims.

> *"The truth is balance, but the opposite of truth, which*
> *is unbalance, may not be a lie."*
> – Susan Sontag

QUESTION FOR TODAY

Can freedom fight fear? What chance for survival do I have? Can I learn to walk again? Can people be my medicine, my prescription to get well? Yes. Yes. Yes. Yes. Yes.

85. THE WORLD BETWEEN

"Serenity is not freedom from the storm, but peace during a storm."
– Anonymous

MORNING MEDITATION
Alcoholism: Forever craving more. Recovery: Forever becoming more.

My Grandmother sits counting her rosary beads. I am ten years old. She whispers a prayer in Latin as each bead slowly moves on. She appears calm in my memory. The light appears to pour out of her as easily as it falls upon her. Her breath is quiet. Her voice is low and calm. There is a unison of sensations going on. Sight is sound is smell is touch. The pause between her inhaling and exhaling lies in some state of eternal evaporation.

Watching her calms me. She could not translate into English a single sound of Latin that she had memorized. The sounds took her out of herself.

(**Sotto**): *The world between dreaming and sleeping, waking and calm. There seem to be no borders between one state of mind and the next. The peace that Jim seems to have found is more than just the absence of chaos, isn't it, Vatchi? A peace that is not an absence, but the thing itself.*

Gold. She spun gold. My Grandmother. Her faith, from the outside, from my ten year old being, seemed based on what? Not knowing? Not not knowing? I would shrug my shoulders. It was the sounds she had memorized but did not know the meaning of, a Latin chant that transported her and gave her a certain faith. A certainty based on the experience of sounds she knew, but did not know the meaning of.

Snowflakes, cut from folded paper in a child's hands. I did not know how each cut would fill and unfill this octagon of paper after being cut and upon being unfolded. I spun gold snowflakes through her prayers. Fool's Gold, spinning gold, playing god spinning more gold.

Driving one eye shut, spinning one foot on the floor. Spinning gold. Fool's Gold. Fool's God. The God of alcohol is spinning me around.

Right now. Period. Done. Fuck.

(**Vatchi**): *This peace you speak of, Sotto. Jim was following it, remembering it, then chasing it until it got away from him. Alcoholism intrudes upon serenity. Alcohol will rear its ugly head like the monsters Sigourney Weaver confronted in the movie "Aliens." Ugly thing, that, any, intrusion upon peace. Carry it forward. Carry it forward. And then, sometime.... This. Peace without words, beyond words.*

I cannot chase (must not) this dream, this sobriety. To chase sobriety is to chase (do not chase) the next drink. Doing push-ups for the next drink. This is not a chase. It is an embodiment. I must enfold it as it enfolds me. Gently. Sobriety – 'this loose-fitting garment' – fits me. This I must have, and the word 'must' destroys it and the word 'have' destroys it.

Like a snowflake, sobriety melts upon my tongue. The hundred states of water. And life. The vessel that contains it. And movement, the silence that describes it. And colors that reflect it. I did not drink today.

Serenity. This silence of letting go.

(**Surimi**): *"Serenity. This silence of letting go." That sounds nice, doesn't it, Sotto? And there are times when it is felt. But it is fragile, this serenity, isn't it Vatchi? It can melt on the nose of a snowy dog. "Let it snow, let it snow..." Let it go.*

This next drink (the one in my brain, my remaining brain) is doing pushups for me. In a collapsible glass. A collapsible life. A foldaway bed. Pack up and run. No!

Serenity. The silence of letting go.

I did not, would not, could not drink today.

Turn it over. I did not _____ today. Peace without words, beyond words. There are no arguments left to demolish. There is only....

EVENING MEDITATION

The seven billionth person on this earth will have been born. I'm struggling to simultaneously be aware of some atomic clock clattering away the current millisecond and to be aware of the infinite now of Zen moments devoid of gradations to the billionth of a second. Our population is still exploding, the universe is still expanding and I am still my sober self in whatever now this is.

> *"When we remember we are all mad, the mysteries*
> *disappear and life stands explained."*
> – Mark Twain

QUESTION FOR TODAY

Could it have been that bad? Am I ready for the side-effects of sobriety? Which wounds have healed and which still need tending? Which should be left alone for now? What are the rules? Will I find a virtuous cycle or will it find me? When?

86. MEMORY-GO-ROUNDS

"The best way to destroy an enemy is to make him a friend."
– Abraham Lincoln

MORNING MEDITATION
The choice is mine: One Day at a Time or One Nightmare All the Time.

I'm on "Antiques Roadshow." Waiting to be authenticated. I'm not in my original package, so I'm sure to be worth less, if not worthless.

"Hell is other people," as the existential philosophers love to say. And then, there's safety in numbers for those like me, with this addiction to alcohol. The wolf of my disease wants to separate me from the crowd. "Divide and conquer," my disease says.

"Shut up, Jim," I say to myself. I'm off to my 8:00 a.m. 12-step meeting.

(**Sotto**): *He seems to be approaching some border, some shore, once far, now near, yet unsure. He seems so unsure. Unsure, and unsure of himself. What will happen to us, Vatchi, if and when he leaves? Will we still be friends, or will everything just end?*

The drinking used to work. To be fun. A two hour escape from the world. Slowly, over the years, it went from three or four times a week and three or four drinks at a time to every day and seven or ten or more and drinking sprees and blackouts and hospitals. Hitting bottom and periods of sobriety and relapses and more bottoms and hospitals and vicious cycles.

I don't know how much brain I've lost to alcohol and how much depth I have achieved from my merry-go-round (and memory-go-round) of relapse and recovery, but I know I cannot drink today.

Humble. Thankful. Grateful. Alive.

(**Vatchi**): *Jim has turned a corner, whereas the light at the end of the tunnel used to be the fear of an oncoming train. His light now is just the simple hope that all will be well so long as he doesn't drink. No matter what, it will turn out better for him without the drink. Helping others does help him. Of course, he might be a tad bashful to admit it. And, Sotto, we were friends before Jim found recovery. We'll find the next bridge, the next open door, the next window on the world.*

Sitting in a bar, I could feel my self-anxiety coupled with the anxiety of waiting for the next drink. That drink. The drink over there. That next drink. I knew it would help. I knew it could squelch, squelch this anxiety. In here. In the pit of my stomach. In the center of my heart. That drink there. This hurt here. Bartender? Bartender? I did not know for a long, long time that the anxiety of waiting for the next drink was the broken tool that could not fix the treadmill I was on. The days when I could savor a drink, turn the brandy snifter in my hand, admiring the dance of light upon it and throughout it, the aroma of its rich vapors, the shades of color, the tinkling of glasses held in a toast, hushed, background chatter of a cheerful crowd, the quieting of a hurried day, revelers lost in the ritual of happy hour... those days have been savagely destroyed in medicinal hospital whites, hospital blacks, hospital grays.

That drink is dead. Long live this drunk.

(**Surimi**): *Neither profound, nor subtle, and barely amusing. And still, and yet, Jim still stands a chance of remaining sober. So long as Ego doesn't block his way. A thousand triggers. A thousand meetings. Balance. I hope for him that he can find some balance in his life. Extreme highs. Extreme lows. That is alcohol. Extreme balance. Let that be his sobriety... Balance.*

I seem to be approaching the present moment at times, like an airplane coming in for a landing. The present moment has always been here, but my alcoholic auto-pilot just never knew that, saw that, felt that. Getting sober takes time. Time takes time.

Humble. Thankful. Grateful. Alive. That drink is dead. Long live this drunk.

EVENING MEDITATION

The fox runs after his dinner, the rabbit runs for his life. I was the dog seen chasing his tail. That's addiction. That was my life.

"The years teach us much, which the days never knew."
— Ralph Waldo Emerson

QUESTION FOR TODAY

How will I rise to the surface of myself? Is it there that all arguments will be demolished? Will I rise to the surface of myself? Will I rise?

87. FIGHT FEAR WITH FLIGHT

"The meaning of your life is to help others find the meaning of theirs."
– Viktor Frankl

MORNING MEDITATION
I can have drunk dreams sober, but I can't have sober dreams drunk.

Wired Weird: The brilliant deduction of some of the world's best scientific minds, simplified. I'm wired weird. We're wired weird, we what-cha-ma-call-its. You're wired weird, if you're one of us. He, she, it are wired weird. They? What about them? Not them. They're not wired weird. They can think when they drink.

(**Sotto**): *Do you think he can make it, Vatchi? Sometimes he seems like a child trying to take his first few steps, looking outward to find confirmations that his answer lies in looking inward. I know that that is convoluted, like the convolutions of the ear and of the seashell when listening keenly for the sound of waves. "He will be free," I want to hear that shell answer back. An echo will not make it so. I wish that he could hear us. The sound of waves.*

Give up this fight. It's futile. Don't fight it. Fight fear with flight. Gimme a light. Fuck. Fear this fight. Don't think it. Drink it. Give up this fight. Fuck it. Don't think it. Drink it. Fight pain with pain. Fuck it. Drink it. Don't think it. Fight pain with pain. Fuck it. Fuck. Fuck. Fuck. Fuck. Fuck it....

(**Vatchi**): *Sotto, moments of doubt, steps backwards, progress, then regression. These are all of our lives. It's just that for alcoholics and* *addicts, people like Jim, one wrong step can have deadly consequences. Daily vigilance is the flipside of the daily reprieve coin. Action and gratitude. Jim still has sick moments that are like little relapses minus the alcohol.*

Who's helping whom becomes a moot point in recovery. People are medicine. The melting pot of recovery is a witch's cauldron. Voodoo. Whack-a-mole. Common prayer. A few kind words. Finally, there is only the knowledge that recovery is possible. Everyone seems to find their own way, sometimes after a string of seeming failures, of near deaths.

Jim's life is coming to an end. Jim's life has barely begun. The tide comes in. The tide goes out.

I did not drink today.

A few moments helping others kept my addictions at bay. Just knowing that all the crap I've been through in my disease could be a tool in helping others find their day of sobriety gives back to me the same in kind, and sometimes more. This is the 'more' of recovery that trumps the 'more' of alcohol.

The hair of the dog that bit me. I must now give him back. Do you see him? He's about to bite you, bite you, bite you.

(Surimi): *All Jim's tools lay broken at the bottom of his hill. What got him there will not lift him up. His old tools are broken. His old tools are no longer even tools. His brain is being rewired. Caution: Life Under Construction. New people, places and things. Daily vigilance. Daily reprieve. Breathe in. Breathe out.*

Recovery. It is what it is.

Drunk dreams sober versus drunken dreams drunk. What different worlds these are. Sober now, my drunk dreams are nearly always nightmares. When I was drunk and drinking and drowning in liquor, my dreams were oh-so different, because my life was different. My life was alcohol then. My life is sobriety, now. Living soberly, now. But the Sirens of Alcohol still call on me from a distant shore. If I stay connected, I will not fall apart. Connections with other alcoholics seems always to work. I am, at last, not some lab rat in a horrible experiment gone wrong.

To remain sober, I have to remain human and to be human is to be connected. Daily vigilance/Daily reprieve. Today, that is enough. Will have to be enough. Is enough.

EVENING MEDITATION

Alcoholism itself is a defect of sorts. I can turn this liability into an asset when I help another recovering alcoholic. Helping someone else get sober helps keep me sober. Oh, but how these words are easier than these deeds.

> *"Nothing matters more than that we remain sober because*
> *when we remain sober everything matters more."*
> – Jim Anders

QUESTION FOR TODAY

Will these questions ever end? Could they, should they, must they? Will someone help me please help someone else? Am I that someone? Are you? Are you?

88. THE NECESSITY OF DOUBT

*"Looking through the lens of gratitude brings us
into the immediate moment."*
– Hazelden (05/24/08)

MORNING MEDITATION

Surrender to my disease when already drinking took me downward in one single direction. Surrender to my disease when sober carries me forward in any direction I choose.

Could it have really been that bad? Sometimes I have my serious doubts. This is the conversation I sometimes have with myself. This is my necessity to doubt. My necessity for doubt. The necessity of doubt. To understand that I cannot know it all.

The sanity in my insanity is doubt.

I doubt that I can ever say that I will never drink again. The sanity in my insanity is my helping another alcoholic and allowing another alcoholic to help me. The sanity of my insanity is doubt.

(**Sotto**): *I want to scream, "You can do this, man. You're already doing it, Jim. You are sober," but he can't hear us. Vatchi, I don't think he knows well enough, going through all that he has, that staying sober has its side-effects, intended or not. There's no hope without help, and no help without hope.*

"You can do this, Jim." Finally, I'm cheering for him. Really.

Helping others helps me to stay sober. And when they fail and relapse or go to jail, I harden where I bleed. Old wounds open and heal. Stealing another day sober is how I feel when they fail. Old wounds open, harden and heal.

I ain't no saint. Just a sober slob. I like most the days when I can say, "This sure beats drinkin'."

(**Vatchi**): *The intended and the unintended consequences of everything. The seen and the unforeseen. Consequence and coincidence. Nothing is new. Everything is new. Sotto, your hope for Jim reflects your hope for others and for yourself.*

My survivor's guilt doesn't last very long when another suffering alcoholic crashes and burns. "But for the grace of God, there go I." That sentiment or something close to that is how I feel. I don't particularly like learning from others' mistakes in their dreadful present moments. I'd rather learn from those long dead and long distant from me. Truth is, in this regard, I can no longer afford to learn from my own mistakes, from my mistakes only.

No more relapse for me. I cannot (never could) afford that. What the fuck and tweet, tweet, trudge. Move me forward. Please.

(**Surimi**): *The more you accept who you are, the more you'll become, the more you'll grow as a person by essentially doing nothing more than simply accepting. Not more 'self' or more 'ego.' More living life itself. The more you connect to the life around you, the bigger you'll become, the more your life will be fulfilled.*

Accept. Connect. Onward. Upward. Outward. Done. This is the virtuous cycle of recovery. If you could hear me, Jim, I would say, "Do not trivialize this one day sober, Jim." One day is the entirety of now. Today is today.

Tweet, tweet.

Sobriety is like that. There are no rules in recovery. Or the rules change as your sobriety changes and grows. There are different ways to live sober, to thrive in recovery. The road to hitting bottom narrows as it becomes more and more about the bottle and the road of recovery widens as life becomes less about the bottle (despite the fact that it will always be about not picking up that first fatal drink).

I can see past myself today. I could not see past the bottle when I boozed. It's all good in the neighborhood today. Today I found another day without a drink.

EVENING MEDITATION

The young, teenage girl, physically malformed, suffering from a severe brain disorder, stood outside the port-cochere at Trump Plaza. Somehow left alone for a few moments as I happened to walk by, she had the composure and the demeanor of someone exquisitely rich, from the upper stratospheres of class, a Kennedy or Vanderbilt, perhaps. Her wealth, inherited, could not be hidden behind her obvious physical and mental deformities.

I have survived this day and my alcohol addiction and wish only to quietly pass by her, rich in my disease, my deformity. I succeed, finally, to pass by her equally noticed and not noticed, equally proud, free and not free.

> *"It is because Humanity has never known where it was going*
> *that it has been able to find its way."*
> — Oscar Wilde

QUESTION FOR TODAY

Did you know that you would get this far? Did it turn out like you thought? What do you control and what controls you? Are you finally tiring of questions asked? Is letting go the ultimate control? Have you helped another alcoholic today?

89. A TALL, DARK STRANGER

"No act of kindness, no matter how small, is ever wasted."
– Aesop

MORNING MEDITATION

Virtue is its own reward, addiction its own punishment. Breathe deep. Breathe in. It costs too much to do nothing. Breathe out. You cannot live your life in these trenches. Breathe deep. Breathe in. Breathe in, then slowly out. You did not drink today.

Fear can be good. A solid part of survival of the fittest. My life has shown me that. But many, many fears that I have had have been unhealthy fears. "A fear faced is a fear erased," as the saying goes, but it may not sound that overtly simple when translated into Spanish or French. I am talking about the meaning behind the words. "A fear faced is a fear erased" for me can sometimes also mean "Turn it over, Rover. Don't let Jimmy take over!"

My name is Jim and I'm an alcoholic.

Carrying the weight of a drink around my neck made me sink, pulled to the bottom, the bottom of the sea. Without that weight, without that drink, I rise to the surface, the surface of myself.

(**Sotto**): *Most all the world can drink safely. But there seems to be safety in numbers for Jim and those like him. Drowning in a sea of alcohol or swimming in a sea of recovery.*

Without the weight of the drink, the structure and function of my sober life are enough for me. For today. I cannot drink today.

(**Vatchi**): *Six billion people in this world. Six billion other worlds. Six billion stars. The infinitely fascinating and the boringly mundane. Ebb and flow. Sometimes that seems enough. Jim has a chance to stay sober. Six billion chances.*
All is one, Sotto, and I am on the brink of "Good night."

My name is Jim and I am an alcoholic. My name is Jim and I can be Jim today. What is, is. And I did not drink today. Jim is Jim and I am him and that is that.

(**Surimi**): *"You will meet a tall, dark stranger," the Gypsy fortune-teller told him. And then he did. But correlation is not causation. Coincidence is in this and any story. And this is Jim's story and in Jim's story, the tall, dark stranger is a beaker full of alcohol. Change the people, places and things in your world and your world will change, too. Yet, a tall, dark stranger is deep within Jim's brain. Don't drink today. Reach inward for self. Reach outward for help. Outward to help. Connect.*
Do not drink today.

I am Sotto, Vatchi, Surimi. I am you and we are all of us. And still, I did not, we did not, we did not drink today. You have helped me, you will help me, should we meet. Someone, someone, one. "One alcoholic helping another." Someone has, will, is helping, helped, has helped me, us.
Sometimes the right things for the right reasons.
We can do this. Not Sotto, Vatchi, Surimi and me. We can do this. You. You and me.

EVENING MEDITATION
This continuous punishment from alcohol has been a bitter gift. But it did not feel like a gift at all when I first got sober. It felt like a punishment, a bitter punishment. Destined, somehow, to remain sober, be miserable and then die. So I thought because so I felt. Eventually the pains of my addiction and my "Why me?" turned some inexplicable corner called Gratitude where simply being alive seemed somehow better than wishing I were dead. Condemned to live a better life as a condition of remaining sober. An irony that I could finally live with. This is where I stop gushing and start blushing.

> *"Real generosity towards the future lies in giving all to the present."*
> – Albert Camus

QUESTION FOR TODAY
Has your crazy stopped or at least slowed down? Can you now hear the music of the spheres? Has clarity increased and your self-pity waned?

Waking up sober is a triumph. How many bubbles are in life's champagne? Are you sober today?

90. PERPETUAL RECONSTRUCTION

"Don't limit a child to your own learning, for he was born in another time."
– Anonymous

MORNING MEDITATION

When I meditate, I follow my breathing, and when a thought intrudes I gently let it go. For me, meditation is the practice of letting go.

Getting as drunk as possible as soon as possible so that I would pass out as soon as possible so that I could get as much sleep as possible so that I could be as sober as possible.... That used to be my Sunday goal for Monday morning. And whenever Monday came (and it would), it never, never, never turned out as I had planned. My disease heard a different drummer, then. And Insanity ensued... How rude!

(**Sotto**): *Most all of us grow old before we grow up. If the only wisdom is that there is hope, Vatchi, I do give thanks for that.*

I do not know the meaning of life, but I know today that life can have no meaning when I'm drunk.

(**Vatchi**): *Whether it is the wind in the willows or a leopard about to pounce, a guarded optimistic caution is most advisable. Let gratitude enter until life's end. The end is always open because the cycle is never complete.*

I once feared and fell for the unreality of my disease, the possibility that it could never be that bad again. But with each passing relapse it always did, eventually, then quickly, get worse. Now I am not afraid of the unreality of

my disease. I need to not go back there.
I did not drink today. So far, so good.

(**Surimi**): *Jim's story is being written. I hope he reads this.*

We are what we are. Life is not a sad guitar.
Because.
We did not drink today.

EVENING MEDITATION

I don't know how helpful I can be to anyone in recovery, really. No false modesty intended. My advice seems mostly to be in the form of "don't do what I did" and "don't become what I became (which is nothing)." Buying a cell phone for someone was a mistake. I learned. But I can't say, "don't do that, either" because every case is different.

About the best I seem able to do is harm reduction. As you can see, it's really me who still needs help. One dysfunction feeds another. One alcoholic helps another. On a good day.

"How beautiful it is to do nothing, and then rest afterward."
– Spanish Proverb

QUESTION FOR TODAY

Fear is not holding you. You are holding fear. Can you not let go? You do not have to let addiction have the last word. Can you find the help you need to regain responsibility?

Addiction wants you to play the victim card. Won't you please, for me, for us, learn some different game?

Can you find playfulness? Can you find an empty glass and a full life?

Yes, we can.

NOTES:

Thank You, Gentle Reader

You have gone this far. You have come this far. You have withstood me. You have endured me.

The favor that I here now ask is for you to pass on this book to someone who needs to know that there is always hope and that recovery is possible.

I would not have been able to get sober alone, indeed, I have learned that in order to remain sober, I must live it.

Thank you for letting me express myself to you. To express yourself in kind, I welcome your best thoughts in review of "All Drinking Aside" on Amazon's website or write to me at janderspub@gmail.com.

Sincerely,

Jim Anders

ABOUT THE AUTHOR

Jim Anders is a former advertising copywriter and graduate of Moravian College in Bethlehem, Pennsylvania. This is Jim's first full-length published work. His drinking career ended nearly a decade before this autobiographical fiction. He currently resides in Atlantic City, New Jersey and is diligently at work on his second book.

Jacket design and illustration: www.dodinet.net
Contact: janderspub@gmail.com

Made in the USA
San Bernardino, CA
23 November 2013